Osteoporosis
Unmasking A Silent Thief

Your Step-by-Step Guide to Understanding,
Diagnosing, Preventing, and Treating One of
the Worst Dangers of Aging

Raymond E. Cole, DO, CCD

*The only "how-to" book you'll ever need to prevent
and treat osteoporosis.*

Wellpower
Publications

Osteoporosis: Unmasking a Silent Thief is written under the auspices of the
Osteoporosis Testing Center of Michigan, whose goals are as follows:

* to increase awareness of the dangers of osteoporosis
* to provide preventive education and recommendations for at-risk populations
* to provide detection at an early age
* to discuss and recommend treatment options for patients with osteoporosis
* to monitor the therapy of patients

For more information, call 1-517-592-WELL (9355) or visit our website
at www.osteotestcenter.com

WellPower Publications
107 Chicago Street
Brooklyn, Michigan 49230

Library of Congress Catalog Number   99 097703

ISBN 0-917073-03-7

First Edition

This book is supported in part by educational grants from Merck & Co. and Procter & Gamble
Pharmaceuticals, Inc.

Great care has been taken to provide accurate and authoritative information in regard to the
subject matter covered. This book is solely educational and informational and not intended as
medical advice. It is sold with the understanding that neither the author or publisher is engaged
in rendering medical or other professional services to you and that without personal examination
and consultation the author and publisher does not render judgment or advice to you for a
medical condition. Please consult your medical or health professional for medical advice. Discuss
the information in this book with your physician before using any of it to determine if it is
right for you. The author and publisher assumes no medical or legal responsibility for having the
contents herein considered as a prescription or for any consequences arising from the use of the
information contained herein. You, or the medical or health professional who treats you, assume
full responsibility for the use of the information in this book. Please pay particular attention
to the precautions and warnings. While every attempt has been made to provide accurate and
up-to-date information, the author/publisher makes no representation, express or implied, with
regard to the accuracy of the information contained in this book, and legal responsibility or
liability cannot be accepted by the author or the publisher for any errors or omissions that may
be made or for any loss, damage, injury, or problems suffered in any way arising from the use
of information in this book.

Acknowledgments

Special thanks to my wife Francine Cole, D.O., and our son and daughter, Chris and Kim Cole, for their love, patience and support over the year and a half it took to write this book. Thanks also to BT for his help and unique sense of humor.

I deeply appreciate the excellent editing, encouragement, and suggestions by Donna Kehoe and the cover, very fine graphics, and superb layout design by Ken Arbogast-Wilson and Tiff Crutchfield.

Special thanks to Scott Fisher, Registered Physical Therapist from Gary Gray's Irish Hills Physical Therapy, and Kris Beyer, Certified Personal Trainer and owner of Kris' Physical Evidence in Brooklyn, Michigan, for their suggestions in Chapter 6 on exercise.

I also appreciate the help provided by Cheyney Bailey, M.P.H., Anand Gupte, Brent DeLaBarre, Lee Albrecht, Jenna Richards, Ron Marine, and Tonya Rosely from Merck & Co.; Ann Barriere B.S.N., R.N., Peter Vincich, and Jennifer Daugherty from Procter & Gamble, Kathy Kinder from Hoechst; Joe Garcia, Dan Leslie and John Sauvé from Novartis, Larry Hildebrand and Patrick Tolstyka from Wyeth-Ayerst, Kathy Smith from Roche, Kym Jaros from Rhone-Poulenc, Sharon Sequite, and Baryona Billington from Lilly, Tracy Mackin from Ortho-McNeil, Marcia Butterfield for her photographs, Kathy Sada for her wonderful typing, Mary Ann Richter for her suggestions, and John Allen, D.O., Gene Kielhorn, D.O., Elizabeth Consengco, M.D., Madhu Arora, M.D., Michelle Gardner, M.D., James Taylor, D.O., and Marc Keys, D.P.M., for their help.

I also appreciate the assistance of Harriet Shapiro, R.N., M.A., Director of Patient and Professional Education of the National Osteoporosis Foundation and Heather Price, Managing Editor, J.B.M.R., the American Society for Bone and Mineral Research.

I also deeply appreciate the assistance at my office of Marci Burke, Sally Melendez, R.T.R., C.D.T., and Aleta Johns, R.T.R., C.D.T., and Denise Phelps, Julie Mattis, C.M.A., Pat Kwiatkowski, Tanya Vandenburg, and Debbie Smith.

Dedication

As one new patient—confined to a wheelchair with severe osteoporosis from years of steroid therapy—said to me when asked if I could take his picture to put into an osteoporosis book, "Please let people know...I'll give you a picture. Don't let what happened to me happen to anyone else...My mind is sharp, but my bones are rotted away. I don't blame the doctors in the past who treated me...Years ago, they didn't know how to treat osteoporosis...But today, no one should have to end up like me, stuck in a wheelchair."

Speaking deeply from my heart, I have been able to better the lives of several thousand individuals at the Osteoporosis Testing Center, and I know that through this work several lives will be saved. It's mind-boggling to consider that curently, one out of six women and 6% of men will experience a hip fracture in their lifetime, resulting in approximately 50,000 needless deaths in the U.S. each year. These are premature deaths of which most could have been prevented if, years ago, doctors (myself included) and patients had the knowledge about osteoporosis we have today. Over the past twenty-five years of medical practice, I personally have seen too many individuals die this way.

If you could take an action that would save one life, wouldn't you be obligated to do so? With this in the back of my mind, the book seems to have written me rather than my writing it. I know that the publication of this book can make a difference in the lives of many thousands of individuals. I have a moral, ethical, and professional obligation to do so.

This book is dedicated to each of the individuals in whose lives I wish I could have made a difference in the past, but from whose pains, suffering, and sometimes death, I have learned about osteoporosis. Thank you. I will do all in my power not just to inform, but to convince and motivate individuals and physicians to take action to prevent and treat osteoporosis.

Table of Contents

Part 3 The Prevention and Treatment of Osteoporosis

Universal Recommendations

Pharmacological Recommendations

Chapter 7: Making an Informed Decision About Estrogen **163**

Chapter 8: Medications Used to Treat Osteoporosis **189**

Appendices, Bibliography, and Index   201

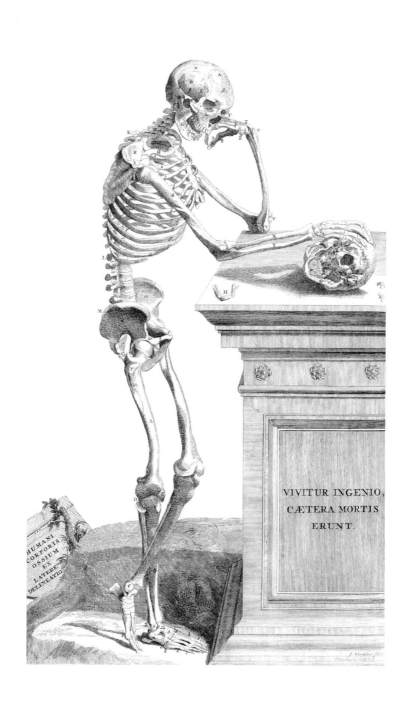

VIVITUR INGENIO,
CÆTERA MORTIS
ERUNT.

What Is Osteoporosis?

Osteoporosis ("brittle bone") is the most common human metabolic bone disease. It affects our whole skeletal system and is characterized by low bone mass and a thinning of bone tissue, which leads to bone fragility and an increased risk of bone fractures.

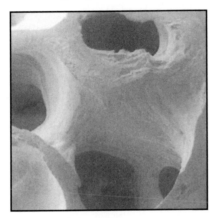 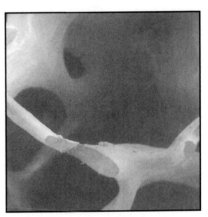

Normal Healthy Bone
is structured and well-connected.

Weak Osteoporotic Bone
is fractured, brittle, and porous.

J. Bone Miner Res 1986; 1: 15–21 Dempster, et al.

The Scope of the Problem

Osteoporosis plagues 10 million Americans, and osteopoenia ("thin bones") plagues 19 million more, placing them at risk for osteoporosis. Brittle, thin bones fracture easily, particularly in the spine, hip, and wrist, although fractures of the ribs, humerus, and pelvis are common as well.

Unfortunately, many men and women are not being educated about the risks of this disease, and people at risk, especially post menopausal women, are not receiving preventive information or treatment. Estimates suggest that less than 30% of women with osteoporosis are diagnosed, and less than 15% of those diagnosed receive treatment. Time and time again individuals are surprised when they discover they have osteoporosis. In response to a diagnosis, people frequently exclaim, "Why don't I have any symptoms?"

Osteoporosis is a progressive disease that often doesn't present symptoms until a fracture occurs—this is why it is often called "a silent thief." The purpose of this book is to unmask this thief and give you the information you need to prevent, diagnose, and treat osteoporosis.

Why Is Osteoporosis Important to You?

Osteoporosis extracts a huge physical, psychological, and economic toll on millions of Americans. You or someone you love is at risk.

Osteoporosis is so serious a health condition that there are now over 1.5 million osteoporotic related fractures per year, including 700,000+ vertebral fractures, 300,000+ hip fractures, 250,000+ fractures of the wrist, and 300,000+ others.

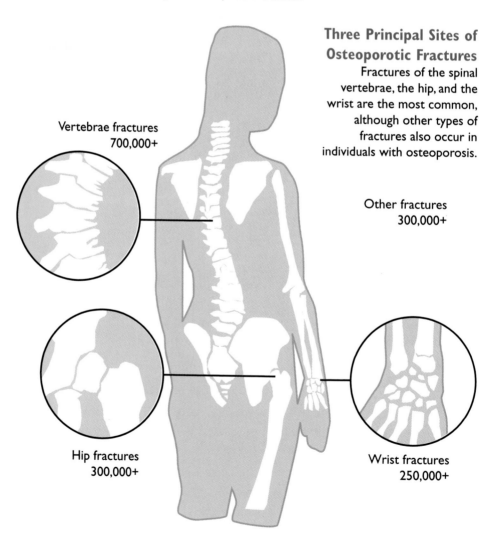

Three Principal Sites of Osteoporotic Fractures
Fractures of the spinal vertebrae, the hip, and the wrist are the most common, although other types of fractures also occur in individuals with osteoporosis.

Vertebrae fractures
700,000+

Other fractures
300,000+

Hip fractures
300,000+

Wrist fractures
250,000+

Not only is the fracture rate high, but the direct/indirect medical cost of osteoporosis is astronomical. Over 14 billion dollars is spent annually in the United States on medical and hospital care, nursing home care, and lost productivity from osteoporotic fractures.

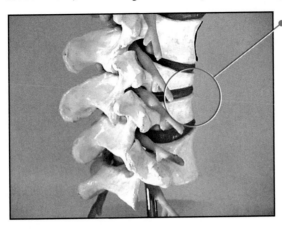

Anterior Wedge Fracture Above and Below A Crush Fracture in the lumbar spine (low back)

Above and below are normal vertebra

One in three women (34%) over fifty years old will experience a vertebrae fracture in her lifetime

■ **Each year osteoporotic fractures affect more women than heart attacks, strokes, breast cancer, and uterine, ovarian, and cervical cancer combined.**

Persons Affected Each Year

1,500,000 Osteoporotic Fractures

500,000 Heart Attacks

225,000 Strokes

184,000 Cases of Breast Cancer

76,000 Cases of Uterine, Ovarian, and Cervical Cancer

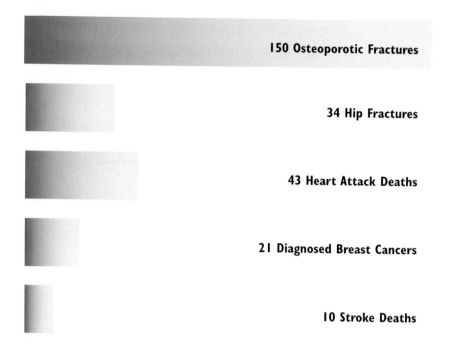

150 Osteoporotic Fractures

34 Hip Fractures

43 Heart Attack Deaths

21 Diagnosed Breast Cancers

10 Stroke Deaths

Research demonstrates that about 40% of all women will experience one or more of either a hip fracture, wrist fracture, or clinically diagnosed vertebral fracture in their remaining lifetime.[1] This risk includes a 17.5% risk of hip fracture, 16% chance of wrist fracture, and a 15.6% chance of clinically diagnosed vertebral fracture.

The Lifetime Fracture Risk of a Woman at Age 50

A 50 year old woman has a 40% risk of developing an osteoporotic fracture during the remainder of her life.

Site of Fracture	Percent Risk
Hip/Proximal femur	17.5%
Wrist/Distal forearm	16.0%
Spinal vertebrae	15.6%
Any of the above areas	39.7%

Further research has discovered that if asymptomatic vertebral fractures are considered as well, then a 50-year-old Caucasian woman has a 54% chance of developing an osteoporotic fracture during her remaining lifetime, including a 34% chance of vertebral fracture (includes both symptomatic and asymptomatic vertebral fractures).[2]

Percentage of Caucasian Women in the U.S. with Osteoporosis*		
Age (years)	Any Site (%)	Hip Alone (%)
50–59	14.8	3.9
60–69	21.6	8.0
70–79	38.5	24.5
80+	70.0	47.5
>50	30.3	16.2

* With a Bone Mineral Density (BMD) greater than 2.5 below the young normal mean.

■ **Seventy-four percent of women ages 45 to 75 have never spoken with their physicians about osteoporosis.**

This lack of awareness in both the medical community and patient population is alarming. A 50-year-old post-menopausal woman who goes to her physician for a yearly physical expects to have her blood pressure taken, her cholesterol measured, and a mammogram performed—that is good medical practice. Likewise, she should expect consideration for bone mineral density (BMD) testing to measure her risk for developing osteoporosis—that, too, is only good medical practice.

Hip Fracture Correlation with High Blood Pressure and Elevated Cholesterol	
1 standard deviation decrease in hip bone mineral density	➡ 2 to 3 fold increase in hip fracture
1 standard deviation increase in systolic blood pressure	➡ 1.5 fold increase in stroke deaths
1 standard deviation increase in serum cholesterol	➡ 1.5 fold increase in deaths from heart attack (coronary heart disease)

■ **Research suggests that low bone mass density is a better predictor of fracture risk than even increased cholesterol is of having a heart attack and high blood pressure is of having a stroke.**[1]

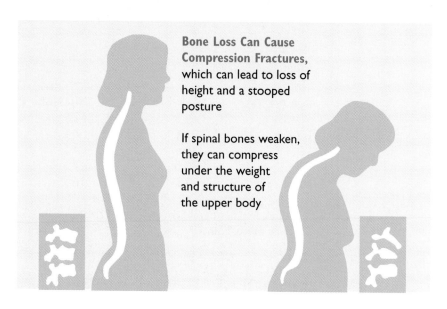

Bone Loss Can Cause Compression Fractures, which can lead to loss of height and a stooped posture

If spinal bones weaken, they can compress under the weight and structure of the upper body

Vertebral Fractures

One in three women (34%) over 50 years old will experience a vertebral fracture in her lifetime. Vertebral fractures often result in acute and chronic pain from nerve impingement, gastrointestinal and respiratory difficulties, increased risk of falling, and subsequent increased risk of a potentially fatal hip fracture or more vertebral and other skeletal fractures. The permanent emotional toll is devastating in terms of loss of self-esteem, depression, and loss of independence that comes with the inability to perform the activities of daily living.

The Progression of Osteoporosis

Osteoporosis patient

Osteoporosis patient requiring cane

Osteoporosis patient requiring walker

Bone loss can cause compression fractures, which can lead to loss of height and a stooped posture. If spinal bones weaken, they can compress under the weight and structure of the upper body.

■ **Women often lose almost half of the bone density of their spine in their lifetime.**

The impact of this loss is often permanent disfigurement, such as thoracic kyphosis (stooped posture or dowager's hump), and loss of height, which sometimes causes the ribs to lie near the level of the hips.

Hip Fractures

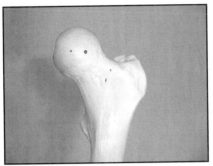 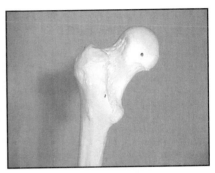

Normal Hip (femur), Anterior View   Normal Hip (femur), Back View

The hip fracture is the most serious osteoporotic fracture. Seventeen percent of Caucasian women over the age of 50 will develop a hip fracture in their lifetime. These 300,000 osteoporotic hip fractures annually result in approximately 65,000 deaths. If you mention the disease of cancer, you have everyone's attention, and there is immediate concern. Yet, if you mention osteoporotic hip fracture, there is not much of a response. However, if you consider the fact that more women die each year from complications from an osteoporotic hip fracture than from breast cancer and uterine cancer combined, there is much cause for concern. One-third of Caucasian women who live to the age of 80 will experience a hip fracture.

> ### Outcomes of Osteoporotic Hip Fractures
>
> **Approximately 20 to 24% of individuals experiencing a hip fracture will die within the first year** from complications such as pneumonia, pulmonary embolism, heart failure, etc. This is a tremendously high mortality rate. Most of these deaths occur within the first 3 to 4 months of the fracture.
>
> **Nearly 50% of patients with hip fractures never fully recover** the mobility or independence they once had.
>
> **Approximately 20 to 25% require a long-term nursing facility, or in-home care.**

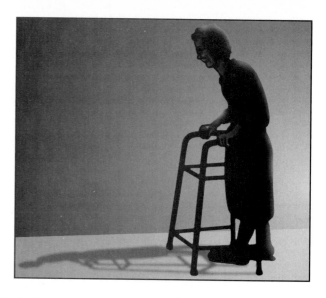

Fracture Fear
Fear of ending their days incapacitated in a nursing home due to a catastrophic event such as a hip fracture is a greater fear for most of the elderly than dying. Many view going into a nursing home as the "kiss of death" and fear they will never come out again.

Only one-third of individuals who suffer a hip fracture fully recover. The other two-thirds experience serious disease and possible death. After undergoing difficult surgery for a complex hip fracture, an elderly individual's intellectual functioning and mental state frequently deteriorate, often never returning to their previous level. A hip fracture is a life-altering event for the family members as well, since they often become full-time caregivers.

As disturbing as all of these statistics are, the reduced quality of life that accompanies osteoporosis cannot be measured. Often the worst results of osteoporosis are lowered self-esteem, loss of mobility, decreased independence, and accompanying anxiety, depression, and loss of social and physical activities.

The Good News

There is good news, however. In the last few years, extensive research and treatment into osteoporosis has caused the medical community to reject the view that the deterioration of bones and subsequent osteoporosis are inevitable aspects of aging. The risk factors predisposing a person to osteoporosis are well documented, and if you can eliminate the controllable risks, you can effectively lower your chances of getting this disease. Accurate diagnosis testing is now available to detect this disease early, and effective treatment plans have made osteoporosis a treatable metabolic disease that can be eliminated.

We now know how to reverse bone loss and increase bone density. We can now increase bones' strength and prevent the disability (morbidity) and fatality (mortality) from osteoporotic fragility fractures. Today, osteoporosis can be diagnosed early and treated before it progresses and a broken bone occurs. It can be treated before the telltale signs of the dowager's hump, the stooped posture, the loss of two to three inches of height, or the painful crack of a fragility fracture.

With increased public and medical community awareness, osteoporosis can someday be a disease of the past, such as vitamin D deficiency and rickets, polio, or the bubonic plague.

The Importance Of Healthy Bones

What is Bone?

Our entire skeleton is made up of two types of bone tissue, either trabecular bone or cortical bone.

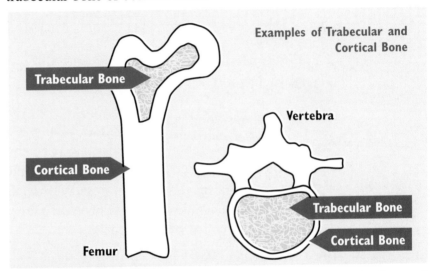

Examples of Trabecular and Cortical Bone

Trabecular bone comprises the interior of the vertebral bodies and is located also in smaller amounts in the ends of long bones. It is a system of struts and arches with a honeycomb appearance. Sometimes it is called spongy or cancellous bone because of its porous, sponge-like, and lattice-like structure. The sponge-like trabecular bones are filled with bone marrow. About 20% of the total bones in our body are trabecular bones. They have a high metabolic rate.

Cortical bone surrounds trabecular bone and makes up the remaining 80% of our bones. Sometimes it is called compact bone because of its densely packed structure. Cortical bone is very solid and strong. It gives long bones like the leg, hip, and forearm bones their strength. Cortical bone, as a general rule, forms the outer layer of the long bones and is very hard. It has a slower metabolic rate than trabecular bone, so it is broken down and replaced (remodeled)

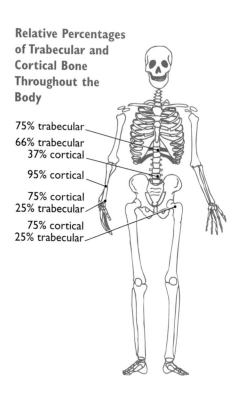

Relative Percentages of Trabecular and Cortical Bone Throughout the Body

75% trabecular

66% trabecular
37% cortical

95% cortical

75% cortical
25% trabecular

75% cortical
25% trabecular

at a much slower rate than trabecular bone.

The percentages of cortical bone (harder, compact bone) and trabecular bone (porous or sponge-like bone filled with bone marrow) vary throughout the body.

For practical purposes, references to trabecular bone are to the vertebrae, which are comprised of 66% trabecular bone versus 34% cortical bone. References to cortical bone are to the hip (femoral neck), which is comprised of 75% cortical bone and only 25% trabecular bone, and other long bones.

How Do We Lose Bone Mass?

Bone is a dynamic, living tissue just like our skin, muscles, and blood cells. All tissue cells are constantly undergoing a process in which old cells are broken down and replaced by new cells. While you read this, millions of your bone cells are undergoing this dynamic process, called bone remodeling.

Bone remodeling takes place by the action of two types of bone cells. Osteoclasts (bone **c**arvers) break down bone. Osteoblasts (bone **b**uilders) form new bone. The relatively stable state of balance between these two cells determines new bone growth, maintenance, and the replacement of old bone.

Normal Bone Remodeling Process

Bone carving by osteoclasts and bone building by osteoblasts is an ongoing cycle throughout our lifetime. During childhood and adolescence, osteoblasts dominate this cycle, so that more new bone is being built than is being carved out and resorbed by the osteoclasts. As a result, the bones grow in size, weight, strength, and density. From age 20 to 30, the bony skeleton is developed and bone mass development slows somewhat from the rapid growth rate of the teenage years.

Normal Bone Remodeling Process

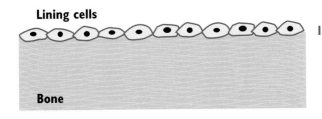

Lining cells

Bone

1. **Resting Phase**
   The bone is covered by a protective layer or lining of cells.

Osteoclasts

Bone

2. **Resorption**
   The osteoclasts invade the bone surface, carve it up, and cut out a cavity by dissolving it.

Cavity made by osteoclasts

Bone

3. **Resorption Complete**
   A complete cavity is created in the surface.

It's like potholes in pavement being formed and repatched.

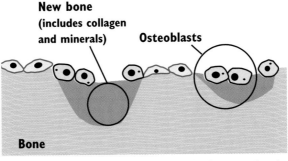

New bone (includes collagen and minerals)   **Osteoblasts**

Bone

4. **Formation–Repair**
   Osteoblasts fill in cavity by building new bone.

The potholes (bone cavities excavated by the osteoclasts) are filled in with new bone (by the osteoblasts).

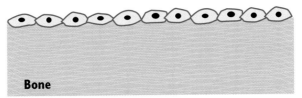

Bone

5. **Repair Complete**
   New bone surface has replaced old bone.

It takes about three weeks for the osteoclasts to dig a pothole (pit in bone) and about three months for the osteoblasts to fill in the pothole with new bone.

Peak bone mass and bone strength are achieved at about the age of 30. As you can see, one of the best osteoporosis preventive measures is achieving optimal peak bone mass during bone building years.

What Causes Osteoporosis?

Bone is remodeled during our entire lifetime. *After age 30, resorption slowly overtakes the formation of bone, and we begin to gradually lose more bone (0.5 to 1% a year) than is being formed.* This loss affects both men and women. At menopause a woman's bone loss greatly accelerates (from 3% to 5%, and sometimes up to 7% a year). Osteoporosis occurs when not enough bone is formed and/or

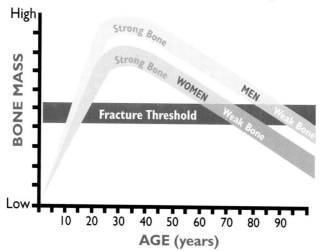

Bone Mass Over Time

Bone mass changes with age in men and women. This chart is characteristic for most people. In general, men usually have greater bone mass than women.

too much bone is being lost.

Bone is made mostly of collagen and calcium phosphate. Collagen is a protein providing a soft framework, and calcium phosphate is a mineral adding strength. They are analogous to the structure of a brick wall, with collagen representing the mortar and calcium representing the bricks, both of which give the wall its strength and density. Together, collagen and calcium phosphate make bone strong, yet flexible.

Bone mass density accounts for approximately 85% of the hardness of bone. Calcium phosphate crystals are laid down over an intricate, dense, microarchitectural trabecular network of collagen. Loss of calcium deposition in this matrix causes a low bone mass density. Along with the effects of decreased calcium, microarchitectural damage is normally caused by the everyday wear and tear to bone, causing a deterioration of the bone's trabecular struts.

This osteoporotic combination of factors weakens bone, increases bone fragility, and makes bone highly susceptible to easy fracturing. This is why the World Health Organization defines osteoporosis as a "systemic skeletal disease characterized by low bone mass and

---

World Health Organization's Definition of Osteoporosis

A systemic skeletal disease characterized by

- **Low bone mass**
- **Enhanced bone fragility**
- **Increased fracture risk**
- **Microarchitectural deterioration of bone**

---

microarchitectural deterioration of bone tissue, with a subsequent increase in bone fragility and susceptibility to fracture."

From the outside, osteoporotic bone is the same size as normal bone and may even look like normal bone, but inside it is thin, weak, and brittle.

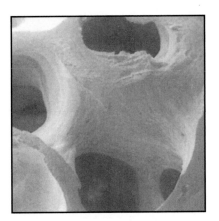

Normal Healthy Bone

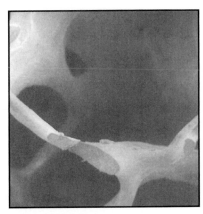

Weak Osteoporotic Bone
is reduced bone strength with increase in possible fracture

There is a high correlation between bone mass and bone strength. *A decrease in bone mass density is strongly correlated with a reduction in bone strength and an increase in possible fracture, which can result from only a small amount of external force.* Even mild stresses like bending to pick up a paper, lifting a vacuum, bumping into a wall, or coughing can cause a fracture in an osteoporotic bone.

The bone remodeling cycle, through which old bone is removed and new bone is built takes place at different rates in different bones. The complete cycle may take four months or up to two or more

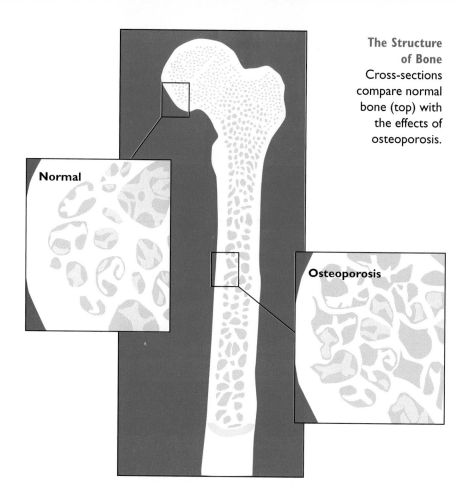

The Structure of Bone Cross-sections compare normal bone (top) with the effects of osteoporosis.

Normal

Osteoporosis

years, depending upon the metabolic rate of the particular bone and other factors influencing it. Trabecular bone has a faster turnover rate than cortical bone because it has a higher metabolic rate. Consequently, improvement with treatment is generally seen in trabecular bone before cortical bone.

Factors Affecting Bone Growth and Breakdown

Various factors influence the bone remodeling process, including estrogen, calcium, vitamin D, testosterone, calcitonin, parathyroid hormone, disease states, medications, and others. The major factors will be discussed in detail in later chapters.

Types of Osteoporosis

Primary osteoporosis occurs because there is a disruption in the bone remodeling cycle, causing a problem within the bone itself.

Primary osteoporosis can be divided into two types: type I, or postmenopausal osteoporosis, and type II, or age-related (senile) osteoporosis.

Type I (postmenopausal) osteoporosis (PMO):
- Affects women only because it is the result of a postmenopausal loss of estrogen from lack of ovarian function.
- Affects primarily trabecular (vertebrae) bone.

Type II (age-related, also known as senile) osteoporosis:
- Affects both men and women and is caused by an imbalance of the bone remodeling cycle.
- Affects both cortical (long bones) and trabecular (vertebrae) bone.

Secondary osteoporosis is caused by medical conditions or medications [see table below] adversely affecting the body's calcium balance and/or the microarchitectural integrity of bone.

Causes of Generalized Secondary Osteoporosis

Endocrine Causes	Nutritional Conditions	Collagen Metabolism Disorders
Hypogonadism	Malabsorption syndromes and malnutrition	Osteogenesis imperfecta
Hyperadrenocorticism	Chronic liver disease	Homocystinuria due to cystathionine deficiency
Thyrotoxicosis	Gastrectomy	Ehlers-Danlos syndrome
Anorexia nervosa	Vitamin D deficiency	Marfan syndrome
Hyperprolactinemia	Calcium deficiency	
Systemic mastocytosis	Alcoholism	**Other**
Porphyria	Intestinal bypass	Rheumatoid arthritis
Hypophosphatasia in adults		Myeloma
Diabetes mellitus, type I	**Medications**	Lymphoma
Thalassemia	Corticosteroid Induced (CIO) i.e. Prednisone	Immobilization
Pregnancy	Dexamethasone, cortisone	Chronic renal failure
Hyperparathyroidism	Dilantin®(phenytonin)	Hypercalciuria
Acromegaly	Phenobarbitol	Various cancers
Turner's syndrome	Methotrexate	Multiple sclerosis
Klinefeltner's syndrome	Excessive thyroid medication	Spinal cord injury
Cushing's syndrome	Lithium	Organ transplantation
Loss of menstrual periods early in life	Mephenytoin	Chronic lung disease
Early surgical menopause (removal of ovaries)	Aluminum antacids	Hemiplesia
Exercise-induced amenorhea	Isoniazid	
Thyroidectomy	GnRH agonists	
	Lasix®, Bumex®	
	Edecrin®	
	Heparin	

Points to Remember

- Osteoporosis is the most common human metabolic bone disease, a disease that affects our whole skeletal system.

- Over 29 million Americans have or are at risk for osteoporosis, a disease characterized by brittle, thin bones that fracture easily.

- Both men and women need to educate themselves about the risks of this disease and take preventive measures to avoid osteoporosis.

- Accurate testing is now available to detect this disease early, and effective treatment plans can help prevent osteoporosis and build healthier, stronger bones that will last a lifetime.

- One of the best osteoporosis preventive measures is achieving optimal peak bone mass during bone building years.

Chapter 1 Bibliography

1   Kanis, K.A., Osteoporosis and Its Consequences. In Kanis, J. (ed.):
    Osteoporosis. Oxford: Blackwell Science, 1994: 1–6.

2   Ross, P.D. et al. Osteoporosis, Frequency, Consequences, and Risk Factors.
    Archives of Internal Medicine 156 (July 1996): 1399–1411.

Natoir invent.   *Avec Privilege du Roy.*   *Vassci sculps.*

Chapter 2

Are You At Risk For Osteoporosis?

Osteoporosis Risk Factors

The National Osteoporosis Foundation (NOF)[1] has identified non-modifiable and modifiable risk factors for primary osteoporosis and diseases and drugs which may be associated with increased risk of secondary osteoporosis in adults.

Risk Factors for Osteoporotic Fracture

Nonmodifiable:
Personal history of fracture as an adult
History of fracture in first-degree relative
Caucasian race
Advanced age
Female sex
Dementia
Poor health/frailty

Potentially modifiable:
Current cigarette smoking
Low body weight (< 127 pounds)
Estrogen deficiency
    Early menopause (< age 45) or bilateral ovariectomy
    Prolonged premenopausal amenorrhea (> 1 year)
Low calcium intake (lifelong)
Alcoholism
Impaired eyesight despite adequate correction
Recurrent falls
Inadequate physical activity
Poor health/frailty

Reprinted with permission from The Physicians Guide to Prevention and Treatment of Osteoporosis 1998, p. 8, National Osteoporosis Foundation, Washington, D.C. 20037

These guidelines were developed because the NOF firmly recognizes the seriousness of osteoporosis diagnosis. As Dr. Robert Lindsay, past president of the NOF, said upon release of the guidelines:

> *Prevention, detection and treatment of osteoporosis should be a mandate of primary care and a routine part of physicals. Bone density tests are now widely available and should be offered to these high risk women to detect low bone density before their bones weaken and fractures occur…. now we have the data and have written a guide that specifically addresses the interpretation of bone density tests, how to apply the results in clinical practice, and when to use these tests which can detect the disease in its earliest stages, before osteoporosis develops. If detected early, therapies can be started to prevent the disease.*

Identifying the person at risk for osteoporosis and eliminating as many of the controllable risks as possible are the keys to the prevention of osteoporosis.

Osteoporosis: A Silent Thief

Since osteoporosis is a disease characterized by low bone mass density leading to increased risk for bone fragility and resulting fractures, anything that helps contribute to the lowering of bone mass density is a risk factor for developing this disease. There are, however, certain risk factors which make it more probable that you may have or may develop osteoporosis. Having some of these risk factors does not necessarily identify you as having osteoporosis, but it does indicate that you are more likely to acquire it.

Nonmodifiable Risk Factors

Personal History of Fracture as an Adult

Fractures beget fractures. An existing fragility fracture is a strong indicator of the possibility of developing a fragility fracture again. One vertebral fracture at baseline gives a five-fold increase of development of another vertebral fracture. If an individual has two

Vertebrae, Back View

or more vertebral fractures, there is a twelve-fold increase in a third vertebral fracture. One symptomatic vertebral fracture gives a two-fold increase in the possibility of development of a hip fracture.

Research into the risk of vertebral fractures found that a 1 standard deviation (SD) decrease in baseline lumbar spine BMD was comparable to the effect of a 17-year increase in age. A 2 standard deviation decrease in lumbar spine BMD gives a four to six-fold increase in the risk of development of a new vertebral fracture.[2]

Vertebral Fractures and Risk of Subsequent Fractures		
1 Vertebral Fracture at Baseline	→	5-Fold Increase in Vertebral Fracture
1 Symptomatic Vertebral Fracture	→	2-Fold Increase in Hip Fracture
2 or More Vertebral Fractures at Baseline	→	12-Fold Increase in Vertebral Fractures

While low bone mass is the most consistent parameter found in the development of subsequent repeat fractures, other factors may play a role as well, such as abnormalities of vertebral stress distribution secondary to the crush injury of one of the vertebrae in the spine. It is also possible that individuals with one fracture may tend to fall and develop subsequent fractures at a greater rate than individuals with no history of fractures.

History of Fracture in a First-Degree Relative

A family history of an osteoporotic fracture is a powerful indicator that genetic factors may play a role in the development of osteoporosis. Osteoporosis often tends to run in families from mother to daughter. In studies of daughters of women with osteoporosis, identical twins were found to have an average of 3% to 7% lower bone mass density than would be normally predicted for their age, suggesting that there may be an inherited genetic component to the development of osteoporosis. There may also be an inherited tendency for the offspring of women with osteoporosis to have lower peak bone mass than normal.

Technically, a history of fracture in a first-degree relative and a family history of osteoporosis are two distinct entities. One's mother may have osteoporosis, yet the mother may not have a fragility fracture. The mother may, however, pass an inherited tendency for osteoporosis to her daughters and sons. In discussing risk factors for osteoporosis, the distinction between having osteoporosis and having an osteoporotic fracture becomes blurred, and many physicians tend to talk about the two as one. Nevertheless, family history is an important risk factor in assessing one's risk of possible osteoporosis and subsequent fracture.

Caucasian Race

Being Caucasian is a major risk factor for osteoporosis. Caucasians tend to have the lowest bone mass density; Afro-Americans tend to have the highest. Not only do Afro-American women tend to develop more bone mass density than Caucasians, but also they lose bone less rapidly as they age than their Caucasian counterparts. Asian Americans and Hispanics fall in between these two. Individuals with Northern European, Japanese, or Chinese ancestry tend to have a greater tendency for the development of osteoporosis as well.

Advanced Age

Increasing age is an independent risk factor for developing osteoporosis. Approximately 30% of women over the age of 50 have osteoporosis, and 50% of women over the age of 80 have osteoporosis.

A woman's risk of developing osteoporosis doubles every 5 years after menopause (age 50). Approximately 1 in 6 women over the age of 50 will experience an osteoporotic hip fracture in her lifetime, and that fracture risk dramatically increases with age.

A number of factors play a role in increasing fracture risk with increasing age. The obvious one, of course, is that *we tend to lose bone mass density at 0.5% to 1% per year after the age of 30.* This risk dramatically increases after the age of 50 in women due to menopause. This risk increases even more dramatically with each

Bone Mass By Age

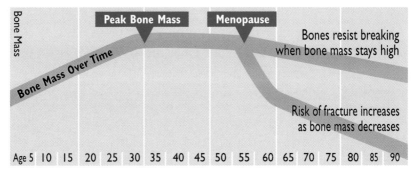

Bone mass increases rapidly during the growth years

Menopause leads to increased bone loss due to a lack of estrogen

decade of increasing age. The elderly also have an increased tendency for falls; one-third of individuals over 65 years of age will fall at least once a year. About 6% of falls for individuals over age 75 result in a fracture.

The elderly also have increasing medical illnesses, which may accelerate the tendency to develop osteoporosis. The need for medications increases the possibility of calcium and vitamin D deficiency from decreased intestinal absorption. With age often comes a decrease in exercise/physical activity and activities of daily living, and this decreased mobility predisposes one to osteoporosis. A decrease in osteoblastic formation of bone may accompany aging, also.

Female

If you are female, you are at risk for developing osteoporosis.

■ Of the 29 million Americans who have osteoporosis (10 million) and osteopoenia (19 million), 80% are women.

In the United States, over 8 million postmenopausal women have osteoporosis, and 15 million have low bone mass (osteopoenia). Four out of five (80%) of all osteoporotic fractures occur in women, and almost all of these occur in women over the age of 50.

Most women, as a general rule, tend to have lower bone mass density than their male counterparts and tend to develop a lower peak bone mass density as well by the age of 30.

For practical purposes, 50 is the age at which menopause is considered likely to occur, and menopause is the major factor contributing to the development of osteoporosis in most women. At menopause, the estrogen inhibitory influence on the osteoclastic carving of bone is removed, and bone is broken down at a faster rate.

■ **During the first five years postmenopausal, there is a rapid increase in bone loss from an average of 1% per year to 3% to 5% per year.**

Sometimes the loss is even as much as 7% per year. Because of this, it is not unusual for a postmenopausal woman to lose 15% to 25% of bone the first five years after menopause without estrogen replacement, and she may possibly lose up to 35% of her total bone mass during this time. As you can see, a woman can lose one-third of her lifetime bone mass in her first five postmenopausal years. At approximately the age of 60 to 65 years, a woman's bone loss begins to slow down and equate that of a man.

Premature menopause, that is menopause before the age of 45 or secondary to bilateral ovariectomy, places a woman at an even greater risk for development of osteoporosis because she may have a greater bone loss with a longer estrogen-deficient life span.

The most critical time for a woman to be making a decision about osteoporosis prevention and treatment should be at age 50 before bone loss has occurred. All too often, the decision isn't made until the age of 60, 65, or 70. By then, significant bone loss has occurred. It is much easier to prevent bone loss than it is to try and rebuild structurally damaged bone. One of the best gifts a woman at age 50 could get would be a birthday card from her family physician with an osteoporosis risk assessment checklist.

Dementia

Dementia tends to predispose an individual to osteoporosis. The slow, progressive deterioration seen in an individual as he or she progresses through the stages of Alzheimer's brings a decrease in nutrition, decrease in activity, and an increased risk of falls, which predisposes the dementia patient to an increased risk of osteoporotic fracture.

Poor Health/Frailty

Many serious medical illnesses are causes of secondary osteoporosis. Frail health disposes an individual to inactivity, polypharmacy, and the use of osteo (bone) toxic drugs. Poor health is associated often with multiple other risk factors such as Alzheimer's dementia, advanced age, and a vast array of associated medical conditions which may systematically predispose a person to osteoporosis.

■ Poor health and frailty may be a nonmodifiable risk factor for some individuals, and for others, it may be a modifiable risk factor.

Potentially Modifiable Risk Factors

Current Cigarette Smoking

How smoking cigarettes decreases bone mass density has not yet been determined conclusively (see Chapter 4—*First Steps to Preserving Bone Health*). However, tobacco smoking has been found to cause a reduction in bone mass density. Some studies have found lower estrogen levels in individuals who smoke cigarettes, and it is postulated that smoking may increase the liver's breakdown of estrogen. Smoking has been linked to an early menopause, which also gives an increase propensity for osteoporosis. One study found that women who smoke half a pack of cigarettes per day or more experienced menopause almost two years earlier than those who did not smoke. Cigarette smokers also tend to be thinner than their non-smoking counterparts, which may play a role as well.

Low Body Weight

Thin, small-framed individuals weighing less than 127 pounds tend to have a lower peak bone mass density than their heavier counterparts. With increasing weight comes increasing stress on one's bones, which causes a subsequent increase in bone mass density. Low body weight, with its consequential decrease in bone mass density and increased fracture risk, affects both men and women equally. Individuals with anorexia nervosa are particularly prone to the development of osteoporosis.

What is considered ideal weight? Weight tables can give you a general idea of where you should be in weight. There are many factors that play a part (body frame, overall health, and at what weight you feel your best).

Another factor contributing to lower-weight individuals developing osteoporosis is that slender individuals have less fat stores. In fatty tissue, androgens (male hormones) can be converted into estrogen (Estrone E_1); thus, with increasing fat, there is an increased amount of androgen bio-chemically converted to bone-protecting estrogen (see Chapter 7—*Making an Informed Decision About Estrogen*), giving individuals who are overweight a lower propensity for the development of osteoporosis. At menopause, the ovaries cease the

production of estrogen and progesterone (only small amounts are
produced thereafter), but approximately the same quantity of androgens is produced by the ovaries and adrenal glands after menopause
as were made prior to menopause.

Estrogen Deficiency

Normal menopause (see Chaper 7—*Making an Informed Decision
About Estrogen*) occurs at about the age of 50 in women. At this
time, the abrupt withdrawal of estrogen dramatically increases the
rate of bone loss.

In premature menopause, that is, menopause below the age of 45 or
menopause precipitated by the removal of the ovaries, the protective
effects of estrogen are also removed. Bone loss accelerates, and frequently osteoporosis develops more rapidly unless estrogen replacement or other therapeutic intervention is begun.

Some young female athletes exercise so much that they actually
have an absence of menstrual periods (premenopausal amennorhea).
When this is the case, estrogen levels are much lower, accelerating

osteoporosis even though the individual may be a very young woman. Highly competitive athletes who have an absence of menstrual periods for greater than one year frequently experience stress fractures, and birth control pills are sometimes recommended for this. If the level of exercise is so intense that a woman does begin to experience menstrual irregularities or amennorhea, then a decrease in the intensity of the training program is recommended.

Correspondingly, birth control pills seem to improve bone mass density. Even low-dose oral contraceptives appear to exert a bone-protective effect.

Low Lifelong Calcium Intake

If there is a decreased blood calcium level, our parathyroid hormones stimulate bone to release its stores of calcium, and this can cause osteoporosis.

■ **The average person takes in 450 to 650 mg of calcium per day, but the recommended intake ranges from 1000 to 1500 mg/day for adults**

The greater the calcium intake in the childhood and adolescent years, the greater the peak bone mass (see Chapter 5, Those All Important Vitamins and Minerals). With low lifelong calcium intake, the peak bone mass density that can potentially be achieved is not. When there is a subsequent loss with normal aging or at menopause, this makes the bone even more susceptible to fracture.

Excessive Alcohol Intake

Alcoholism is associated with a higher rate of osteoporotic fractures (see Chapter 4—*First Steps to Preserving Bone Health*). It is not known for sure whether this is from poor nutrition, a direct effect on the osteoblasts, secondary liver disease, poor absorption of nutrients, possible decrease in the absorption of calcium, or other factors. It is known, however, that alcohol abuse is correlated with a lower bone mass density. The effect of occasional alcohol use is not conclusively known but is generally thought not to cause osteoporosis.

Impaired Eyesight Despite Adequate Correction

Age-related macular degeneration, cataracts, glaucoma, near-sightedness, far-sightedness, astigmatism, arteriosclerotic retinal vein occlusion, retinal detachment, and diabetic retinopathy all contribute to impaired eyesight and secondary falling in the elderly. Despite the finest opthalmologic treatment, many of these eye diseases of the elderly are not correctable.

Recurrent Falls

Many individuals have low bone mass density but do not experience an osteoporotic fracture. However, individuals with low bone mass density who experience frequent falls have an increased rate of fractures (see Chapter 4—*First Steps to Preserving Bone Health*). Falls produce a blunt force which, when coupled with low bone mass density and brittle bones, can cause a bone to break easily. An 80-year-old individual has a 50% possibility that he or she will fall at least once in a year, and the resulting effects of a fall contribute to 40% of nursing home admissions.

Inadequate Physical Activity

Like all living tissue, bones need to be exercised to remain strong (see Chapter 6—*If You Do Nothing Else—Exercise*). If you exercise a muscle, it will become stronger. If you exercise a bone, it will become stronger as well. Physically stressing bone causes an increase in bone formation and subsequent increase in bone mass density and strength. While physical activity strengthens bone, the reverse is also true: the lack of physical activity weakens bones. Immobilization or prolonged inactivity, for example after a surgery where there may be prolonged bed rest, results in weaker bones.

Most parents encourage children to become active in sports activities. A benefit of this is increased bone mass and subsequent bone strength and prevention of osteoporosis. However, activity at any age results in stronger bones. Applied to the topic at hand, the axiom becomes as follows: Use bone or lose bone!

Other Risk Factors for Osteoporosis

Decreased Vitamin D Intake

It is well documented that elderly individuals who have experienced osteoporotic fractures often are found to have low vitamin D levels. Vitamin D is necessary for the absorption of calcium from the intestines and for the maintenance of a homeostatic equilibrium via renal excretion (see Chapter 5—*Those All Important Vitamins and Minerals*). Many elderly individuals do not take vitamins, have poor nutritional intake of vitamin D, and do not go outside in the sunshine where sunlight activates vitamin D in the skin. As a result, vitamin D deficiency is much more common than previously thought.

Excessive Caffeine

Caffeine intake greater than 400 mgs. per day is associated with low bone mass density due to subsequent loss of calcium in the urine (see Chapter 4—*First Steps to Preserving Bone Health: Caffeine*).

Excessive Phosphate

Excessive phosphate intake, such as that precipitated by excessive consumption of cola beverages, may be related to low bone mass density; however, this has not been proven. It may be that excessive consumption of colas in the teenage years and the decrease in milk consumption results in a decrease in calcium intake leading to low overall bone mass density in teenagers. Or it may be that some other mechanisms may interplay as well. For example phosphate intake may have an effect on parathyroid hormone or another mechanism. Phosphorus is also found widely in bread, cereal, potatoes, red meat, and various food additives.

Excessive Protein

Excessive protein results in calcium loss in the urine. A minimum amount of protein is necessary for the integrity of bones. The average woman requires 45 to 50 grams of protein per day; however, the average American woman consumes about 70 grams per day. The RDA is 44 g/per day for a woman and 56 g/day for a man.

Salt Excess

Excessive sodium chloride causes a loss of calcium in the urine. A sodium intake of less than 2400 mg/day is recommended.

Late Menstruation

Women who had the onset of menarche (first menstrual period) after the age of fifteen have an increased incidence of osteoporosis.

Glucocorticoids (corticosteroids)

Oral corticosteroids (i.e. Prednisone) inhibit the osteoblastic formation of bone matrix. Glucocorticoids also cause bone loss by decreasing calcium absorption from food and increasing the loss of calcium in the urine. In one published study of active rheumatoid arthritis patients receiving 10 mg/day of Prednisone, there was an 8.2% loss of bone mass density in the first twenty weeks of therapy.[2]

Additional Risk Factors Associated With Secondary Osteoporosis

For a more complete list of diseases or metabolic causes, nutritional conditions, drugs, collagen metabolism disorders, and other factors associated with secondary osteoporosis, see the table in Chapter 1, page 15.

Relative Risk—Some Factors Are More Important Than Others

The NOF has found that some risk factors are key factors in the development of hip fractures in women over the age of 65 and carry more risk (importance) than others.[3]

Four Risk Factors are Key Determinants for a Hip Fracture, Regardless of Bone Mineral Density

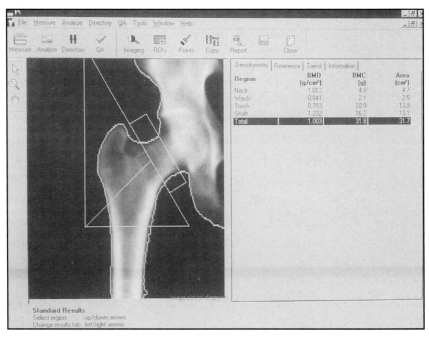

Of all of the above risk factors, the NOF recognizes the following four as *key determinants* for risk of a hip fracture, independent of bone mineral density:

- Personal history of fracture
- Family history of fracture
- Smoking
- Low body weight

The relative risks can we weighted (assigned importance) if one's age is known or if the BMD and age are known.

For Men Only

One in every 8 men over the age of 50 will experience an osteoporotic fracture during his lifetime. On the average, men tend to have a 10% to 15% greater peak bone mass density than women due to the effects of testosterone; therefore, their bones are stronger, and more bone loss must occur before their bones become brittle and break easily. The gradual decline in testosterone as a man ages is associated with a gradual decline in bone mass density and corresponding decline in bone strength.

Man with **Osteoporosis** who is confined to a wheelchair for the rest of his life due to fifteen years of corticosteroid use.

Two million men over age 50 have osteoporosis, and approximately 3 million have osteopoenia (thin bone) and are at risk for fracture. In general, most of the multifactorial risk factors and disease states that are associated with the development of osteoporosis in women apply to men as well. However some, like decreased gonadal (testicular) function and use of Lupron® (a synthetic gonadotrophin releasing hormone [GnRH] used to treat prostate cancer) are gender specific.

Approximately 55% of young or middle-aged men who have osteoporosis are found to have a secondary cause for it. Common secondary causes of osteoporosis in men are alcohol abuse, smoking, chronic obstructive pulmonary disease, chronic kidney or gastrointestinal disease, decreased calcium intake, vitamin D deficiency, corticosteroid-induced (CIO), inactivity, and decreased gonadal function.

About 10% to 20% of young or middle-aged men with osteoporosis are found to have low plasma testosterone levels from partial or complete hypogonadism (decreased functioning of the testicles). Testosterone deficiency is a risk factor, and up to 30% of men with osteoporosis may have long-standing testosterone deficiency. This may be suspected by a decrease in libido (desire for sex) or impotence (decreased sexual function or inability to maintain an erection). If this is suspected as a secondary cause of osteoporosis, it is recommended that the individual have blood tests, a serum testosterone level, DHEA (dehydorepiandrosterone-a precursor to testosterone) and LH (luteal hormone stimulates the testicles to make testosterone) levels checked.

The lifetime risk of a man developing a hip fracture is 6%. The complications, disease rate, and death rate from hip fractures are just as serious for men as for women. During this year alone, approximately 80,000 men will experience a hip fracture.

Treatment of Osteoporosis in Men

Calcium	1,000 mg daily
Vitamin D	800 IU daily
Antiresorptive agents	
Fosamax® (alendronate)	10 mg daily (orally)
Miacalcin® (calcitonin)	200 IU daily (intranasal)
Actonel® (risedronate)	5 mg daily (orally)
Testosterone	
(in hypogonadal men only)	Enathate or cypionate 200 mg every two weeks intramuscular Transdermal patch daily

---

Bone formation tends to decline with aging, and age-related bone loss probably accounts for the greater preponderance of fractures in males. A low trauma fracture of any bone in a man should raise one's index of suspicion for thin or brittle bone.

Treatment of osteoporosis in men is similar to that of women: calcium and vitamin D supplementation, removal of secondary causes of osteoporosis, and pharmacological treatment with a bisphosphonate (i.e. Fosamax, Actonel, or Miacalcin). The use of androgens (testosterone) in older men without frank hypogonadism (decreased testicular function) is highly controversial. Bone mass increases, but there are potentially serious concerns due to a possible increase in adverse cardiac events (heart attacks), lowering of HDL cholesterol (the good cholesterol), and possible increase in rates of acceleration of prostatic cancer.

Points to Remember

- Identifying the person at risk for osteoporosis and eliminating as many of the controllable risks as possible are the keys to the prevention of osteoporosis.

- Anything that helps contribute to the lowering of bone mass density is a risk factor for developing osteoporosis.

- The National Osteoporosis Foundation recognizes the following four risk factors as key determinants for risk of a hip fracture independent of bone mineral density: personal history of fracture, family history of fracture, smoking, and low body weight.

Chapter 2 Bibliography

1   National Osteoporosis Foundation. *Physician's Guide to Prevention and Treatment of Osteoporosis* [Belle Mead, NJ: Exerpta Medica, Inc., 1998]

2   Melton III, L. J., E. J. Atkinson, and W. M. O'Fallon, et al. *Long-term Fracture Prediction by Bone Mineral Assessed at Different Skeletal Sites. Journal of Bone Mineral Research* 8(1993): 1227–1233.

3   *Osteoporosis: Review of the evidence for prevention, diagnosis, and treatment and cost-effective analysis. Osteoporosis International* 1998; 8:S1–S88

4   Ross, P. D., et al., *Annals of Internal Medicine* 114, 1991.

5   Kanis, K.A., *Osteoporosis and Its Consequences.* In Kanis, J. (ed.): *Osteoporosis.* Oxford: Blackwell Science, 1994: 8.

6   RFJM Laan, et al. *Annals of Internal Medicine* 1993 119:963–968.

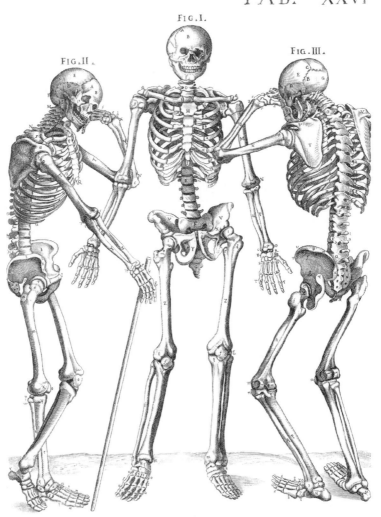

TAB. XXVI

FIG. I.

FIG. II.

FIG. III.

How to Find Out If You Have Osteoporosis

Bone Mineral Density

Bone Mineral Density (BMD) is a measurement of the amount of mineral in a given volume of bone. It is a ratio of bone mass to bone volume and measures how solid bone is. The higher the bone density measurement, the more dense (compact) the bone is. The lower the bone density measurement, the less dense the bone is. It is measured in grams/cm^2. For example, a bone that has 18.0 grams of mineral in 15.0 square centimeters of volume would have a BMD of $18.0 \div 15.0 = 1.2$ g/cm^2. Technically, bone mineral density and bone mass (which measures the quantity of mineral in a bone) are two different things; however, in referring to bone testing, they are used interchangeably as one.

Low bone mass is associated with an increased risk for fracture at some point in the future. Bone mass accounts for 85% of the hardness of bone. By measuring bone mass density, one has an extremely strong indicator of the actual strength the bone has and its resistance to fracture.

■ **Low bone mass is the most important objective predictor of fracture risk.**

The greater the bone mass, the stronger the bone and the greater the force necessary to cause a fracture. The lower the bone mass, the weaker the bone and the less force necessary to cause a fracture.

Bone Mineral Density Tests

What Do They Mean?

A bone mineral density test measures your bone mineral density and compares it to the normal population to give two scores:

1. The T-Score gives comparison to a normal 30-year-old; and
2. The Z-Score gives comparison to an age-matched standard.

The Z-score is a good comparison to others of your age and sex; however, since it is not used for diagnosing osteoporosis, we will not discuss it further in this context, except to say that the Z-score is most helpful when used as a guideline for men and for younger women.

The T-score, a comparison of your bone mineral density to that of a normal, healthy 30-year-old, is used for osteoporosis diagnosis. In 1994, the World Health Organization (WHO) defined specific criteria based on bone mineral density for the diagnosis of osteoporosis in Caucasian women (because they had a large reference population of thousands of Caucasian women).

World Health Organization Diagnostic Criteria for Osteoporosis

Diagnosis	Bone Mineral Density (BMD) (number of Standard Deviations below Healthy Young Mean*)
Normal	Less than 1
Osteopenia	Between 1 and 2.5
Osteoporosis	2.5 or more
Severe Osteoporosis	2.5 or more with fragility fractures

T-score = units of Standard Deviation (SD) that a patient's BMD is above or below the mean peak bone mass of a young, normal, healthy 30-year-old adult Caucasian woman.

WHO Technical Report Services 843, Geneva, 1994

These WHO criteria have been universally accepted as the standards for osteoporosis diagnosis and are as follows:

1 Normal: Within 1 standard deviation (SD) above or below the average (+1 SD to −1 SD).

2   Osteopoenia (low bone mass): Greater than 1 SD but less than 2.5 SD below the average (between -1 and -2.5). Also expressed as (-1.10 to –2.49).

3   Osteoporosis (brittle bones): 2.5 SD or more below the average (≥ -2.5).

4   Severe osteoporosis (brittle bones with fragility fracture[s]: 2.5 SD or more below the average with a fragility fracture[s]).

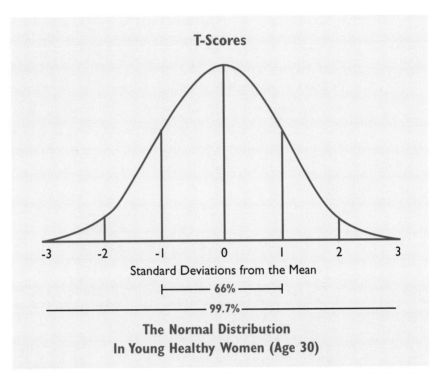

The Normal Distribution
In Young Healthy Women (Age 30)

One SD equals a 10% to 12% difference in bone mineral density. Thus a -1 SD T-score is equivalent to a loss of 10% to 12% of your bones' mineral density as compared to a normal, healthy 30-year-old. A -2 SD would equal a 20% to 24% loss of bone mineral density, and so on. A -2.5 SD would equate to a 25% to 31% loss of bone mineral density.

The WHO designed the T-scores so that in the young (age 30), healthy population, approximately 15% of women will have a T-score giving a diagnosis of osteopoenia, and .5% a diagnosis of osteoporosis. Using these 1994 WHO guidelines, approximately 30% of all postmenopausal women would be diagnosed as having osteoporosis at either the spine, hip or forearm.

The guidelines are designed so that 30% of post menopausal women in the United States have osteoporosis, and 54% have osteopoenia and are at increased risk for osteoporosis. These statistics reflect BMD measured at the hip, spine, or wrist.[1]

This places the number of postmenopausal women at risk for or with osteoporosis as follows:

- Over 8 million women have osteoporosis (brittle bones)
- Over 15 million women have osteopoenia (thin bones) and are therefore at risk for the development of osteoporosis

As your bone mineral density progresses downward from normal to osteopoenic (thin bone) to osteoporosis (brittle bone), your fracture risk also progresses from normal to greater than 10% to greater than 25%. The lower the bone mineral density, the greater the risk of developing an osteoporotic fracture in your lifetime.

Note: Information from bone mineral density testing should be used along with knowledge of your personal medical history to determine the best course of osteoporosis prevention and treatment for you. The WHO definitions categorize the degree of osteoporosis but are not intended to require or restrict therapy on the basis of BMD testing result alone.

Talk to Your Doctor
Consult your personal physician after you have a BMD test. He or she has complete knowledge of your medical history and can help you design an optimal osteoporosis prevention or treatment program that is best for you.

Fracture Risk

Bone mineral density values are particularly important because they can be used to predict fracture risk. There is a quantified increase in risk of fracture per standard deviation decline in bone mass density.

■ **Measuring your bone mineral density (BMD) is the best means of diagnosing low bone mass and predicting fractures.**

To help predict future fractures, global fracture risk and site-specific fracture risk are usually the most common fracture risk data calculated; however, sometimes other calculations are made, such as remaining lifetime fracture risk or lifetime risk of fracture.

Global fracture risk takes a measurement of bone mineral density of a bone and, using the T-score, gives an overall relative risk of fractures for the individual. These fractures are not necessarily at the site measured; for example, you might measure the spine, but the global fracture risk would not be specific for that site. Rather, it would be a prediction of your total risk for developing a fracture anywhere in the skeleton.

Site-specific fracture risk takes a measurement of bone mineral density of a bone and gives a prediction of increased fracture risk depending upon your T-score at that site. Site-specific fracture risk predicts risk of fracture at a specific site; i.e., hip, spine or forearm, but site-specific fracture risk by definition does not mean that the measurement is necessarily performed at that site.

While a BMD measurement helps to predict fracture risk, it can not predict fracture certainty. This depends upon many other variables such as amount of force, falling, and other factors.

For obvious reasons, the best means of predicting the fracture risk of a bone is to measure the bone mineral density of that bone and compare it to the large study populations of fractures and bone mineral density at that specific site. This would correlate the actual measurement of bone mineral density at that site to fracture risk and be most accurate.

Since hip fractures are by far the most serious fractures encountered in individuals and represent a significant increase in mortality and morbidity, these are the fractures one would most likely want to predict. Ninety percent of all hip fractures in elderly women are attributable to osteoporosis.[2]

■ **The most accurate way to predict the fracture risk of the hip is to measure the bone density at the hip.**

Measurement of other sites may give a fairly good indication of fracture risk, but if you really want to know what's going on with the hip, you have to measure the hip. Likewise if you really want to know what is going on with the vertebrae, you should measure the vertebrae.

BMD Measurement Techniques

Conventional X-rays are not used to detect osteoporosis because they are not sensitive to minor losses of bone or early bone loss.

They cannot detect bone demineralization (loss) until 40% of bone mineral loss has occurred. They can, however, be used to detect an osteoporotic fracture such as a crush (compression) fracture of a vertebrae.

Single photon absorptiometry (SPA), single energy X-ray absorptiometry (SXA), and radiographic absorptiometry (RA) are no longer commonly used to measure bone mineral density. They have been replaced by dual energy X-ray absorptiometry (DEXA).

The current scanners used to test bone mineral density are divided into two groups:

Peripheral Testing
1   P-DEXA (Peripheral-Dual Energy X-ray Absorptiometry)
2   Ultrasound

Central/Axial Testing
1   DEXA (Dual Energy X-ray Absorptiometry)
2   QCT (Quantitative Computed Tomography)

Peripheral Testing

Peripheral techniques are screening tests for osteoporosis that measure various extremity sites such as the forearm, fingers (phalanges), and heel. There are different types of scanners used for peripheral testing such as the P-DEXA and the ultrasound.

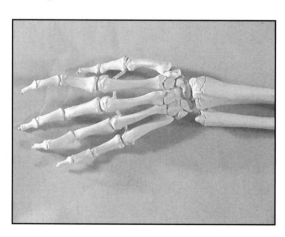

Wrist
P-DEXA can screen for a low BMD at the distal forearm or finger

These scanners are considerably less expensive than the DEXA or QCT units. If you have an abnormal screen on one of these peripheral tests, it is generally recommended that a central DEXA test be performed for more complete diagnosis and confirmation.

There are many peripheral testing machines on the market because these peripheral machines are inexpensive, take only two to five minutes per test, and do not need trained personnel for operation. Portable units can be taken to health fairs or to nursing homes, whereas the central units are generally fixed in place unless there is a large mobile van conversion set up for this purpose.

The cost to the patient for one of these peripheral screening tests is a relatively low $40 to $45 (some health fairs do them for $15 or less); in comparison, the cost of a central DEXA test ranges from $140 to $200.

Peripheral testing machines do serve a purpose in that they can be placed easily in many primary care physicians' offices. They can help to promote an awareness of osteoporosis because when doing the test, the technician and/or primary care physician should also be giving information about osteoporosis prevention and treatment and discussing it with the patient.

Central/Axial Testing

DEXA (Dual Energy X-ray Absorptiometry) is the most widely used central testing machine and *is considered the "gold standard" of BMD measurement technology.*

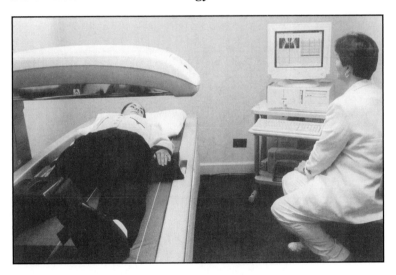

Performing a DEXA Bone Mineral Density Test

The DEXA scanner uses dual X-ray beams consisting of a high energy beam and a low energy beam, which give bone measurement separate from the various soft tissues such as fat, muscle, organs, and blood vessels. Radiation exposure is typically only 1/20th that of a chest X-ray. DEXA can measure central (hip and spine) and peripheral sites (forearm), and the results are highly accurate and reproducible. The testing unit we use at the Osteoporosis Testing Center of Michigan can even perform a total body scan and measure the BMD of all of the bones in the body. The time involved to perform a DEXA test is relatively short, from 15 to 20 minutes, and the test is non-invasive and painless. (See Appendix B—*Frequently Asked Questions About Bone Densitometry*).

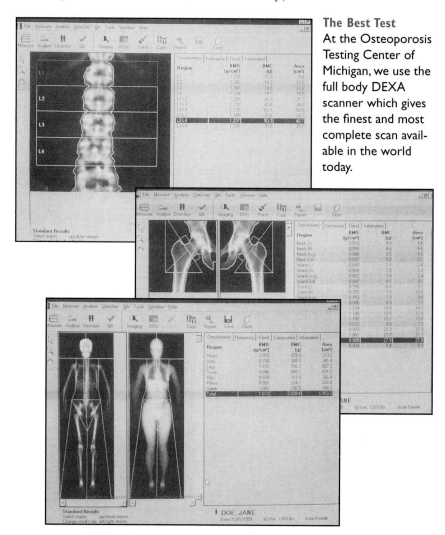

The Best Test

At the Osteoporosis Testing Center of Michigan, we use the full body DEXA scanner which gives the finest and most complete scan available in the world today.

QCT (Quantitative Computer Tomography)

QCT (Quantitative Computer Tomography) is another means for measuring central bone mass density of the spine. QCT utilizes a reference standard (phantom) which is scanned simultaneously with the patient. Using special software and this calibration phantom, QCT compares the density of the vertebrae to that of the phantom and then uses a computer to calculate the density of the trabecular bone of the spine. Because QCT can measure vertebral bone, which is almost fully trabecular (little cortical bone), it is an accurate way to determine trabecular bone loss in the spine. Its value in measuring the hip, however, is limited. Consequently, it is not commonly used for this measurement. QCT provides three-dimensional volumetric measurements (bone mineral content, with results reported in milligrams/cc). The radiation dose from a QCT scan is more than that from a DEXA scan and less or equal to that of a standard chest X-ray.

Multiple Measurement Sites

As we have discussed, the strongest predictor of a fracture at a particular site is an accurate bone mineral density measurement at that specific site. Statistical correlation is sometimes made with a bone mineral density value at a particular site and your risk of overall fracture, or fracture at other sites. Each bone mass measurement has great value, but it also has limitations. Different sites measure different bone composition. For example, in the performance of DEXA testing of the spine and hip, the composition of bone is considered as follows:

The more sites measured, the higher the likelihood that a diagnosis of osteoporosis will be made. Of course, the reverse is also true: if only one site such as a peripheral site is measured, there is a much higher probability of missing true osteoporosis. The peripheral measurement devices are quick and easy to use and particularly useful for screening large populations of individuals, but as a general rule, they are not used to measure response to therapy. However, this may change in the near future.

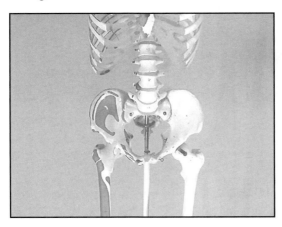

Standing Vertebrae and Hip

For the spine:
• 2/3 trabecular bone
• 1/3 cortical bone.

For the hip:
• 1/4 trabecular bone
• 3/4 cortical bone

The International Society for Clinical Densitometry (ISCD)[3] suggests that testing of BMD may be central (spine/hip i.e. DEXA, QCT) or peripheral (wrist, heel or finger). It recommends that the spine be used to detect changes in trabecular bone in early menopause because of the high metabolic activity of trabecular bone, thus giving an early indication of bone loss. The hip, wrist, heel or finger may be more diagnostic in the elderly.

The ISCD suggests measurement of at least two sites if possible and recommends that diagnosis be based on the lowest T-score. It suggests using the L2-L4 average measurement rather than a single vertebra if possible. [Note: Sometimes this is not possible due to artifactual interference from such things as osteophytes from degenerative osteoarthritis or compression fractures.] In measurements of the hip, either the total hip or the femoral hip measurement is used, whichever is the lowest standard deviation. The ISCD suggests the lowest T-score of these measurements in the hip be used for the diagnosis of osteoporosis at the hip.

Repeat BMD Measurements

• If Initial BMD Test is Normal

There are no universal recommendations for how often a person who is at risk for osteoporosis but has an initial BMD that is normal should have a BMD measurement. Generally, if the BMD is clinically indicated because of increased risk factors for osteoporosis and the initial BMD measurement is normal, it would be satisfactory to repeat the BMD scan in two years to see if there has been a change indicating accelerated bone loss.

• If Initial Test Shows Osteoporosis or Osteopoenia

As a general guideline, if the initial BMD measurement is abnormal, indicating either osteoporosis or osteopoenia, treatment should begin and the bone mass measurement repeated in one year to determine treatment effectiveness and adequacy.

Improvement in BMD is very gradual, taking place slowly over a long period. Many individuals think that taking calcium for two to three months will bring their bone mineral density back to normal, at which point they can stop taking calcium and be fine. This is not the case. The American Association of Clinical Endocrinologists (AACE) in its *1996 Clinical Practice Guidelines* indicated that a change in bone mass of 5% (measured by DEXA) is considered clinically significant and usually not observed in less than two years.

Margins of error for most bone measurement devices are 1% to 2%. With treatment, a person can expect a 1.5% to 3% improvement per year in BMD, so changes on serial measurements usually are not dramatic. Interestingly, however, even with slow improvements in bone mineral density, fracture rates often decrease considerably. This is thought to be due to improved bone quality.

Bone Mineral Density Testing Guidelines

Who Should Have a BMD Test for Osteoporosis?

On November 5, 1998, the National Osteoporosis Foundation issued *The Physician's Guide to Prevention and Treatment of Osteoporosis.* (Their recommendations represented ten multidisciplinary medical organizations including the National Osteoporosis Foundation, the American Academy of Orthopedic Surgeons, The American Academy of Physical Medicine and Rehabilitation, The American Association of Clinical Endocrinologists, The American College of Obstetricians and Gynecologists, The American College of Radiology, The American College of Rheumatology, The American Geriatrics Society, The American Society for Bone and Mineral Research, and The Endocrine Society.) The recommendations were limited to Caucasian postmenopausal women and not subpopulations because the data from which they derived their recommendations came from this population group. This group was particularly studied because 80% of individuals who have osteoporosis are women, and for reasons discussed in previous chapters, most of those who experience osteoporotic fractures are postmenopausal women experiencing Primary Osteoporosis Type 1 (also known as Postmenopausal Osteoporosis) and/or Primary Osteoporosis Type 2 (also known as Age-

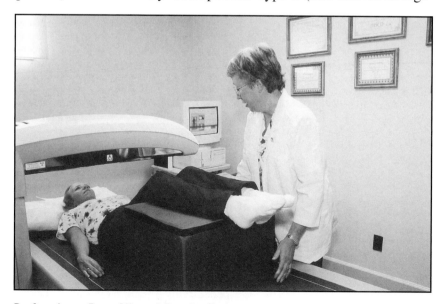

Performing a Bone Mineral Density Test

related Osteoporosis). The NOF recommendations are based upon measurements of bone mineral density at the hip and on the basis that testing could influence a treatment decision.

The NOF BMD Testing Guidelines for Postmenopausal Women

1. All postmenopausal women under age 65 who have one or more additional risk factors for osteoporotic fracture (besides menopause).
2. All women aged 65 and older regardless of additional risk factors.
3. Postmenopausal women who present with fractures (to confirm diagnosis and determine disease severity).
4. Women who are considering therapy for osteoporosis, if BMD testing would facilitate the decision.
5. Women who have been on hormone replacement therapy for prolonged periods.

Reprinted with permission from The Physicians Guide to Prevention and Treatment of Osteoporosis 1998, pp. 12–13, National Osteoporosis Foundation, Washington, D.C. 20037

If more than one risk factor is present other than menopause at age 50, then bone mineral density testing for osteoporosis should be undertaken. If you stop and think about it, almost all postmenopausal women have one or more risk factors (see Chapter 2—*Are You at Risk for Osteoporosis?*) and should contemplate therapy for osteoporosis. The average woman has low calcium intake (only 450 to 650 mg. calcium per day), the majority of American women are Caucasian, and the majority of women over age 50 do not exercise regularly.

Sometimes a postmenopausal woman considering estrogen replacement is not sure she wants to commit to estrogen therapy. She may not be sure if it is right for her and questions if the benefits of estrogen replacement are equal to or greater than her risks. For her, a BMD test would be of great benefit and should be performed to help her make a decision.

BMD Testing Guidelines for Premenopausal Women

The NOF Testing Guidelines are somewhat limited in scope as they address only Caucasian postmenopausal women; however, this does not mean that premenopausal women, other races, or men do not develop osteoporosis.

If risk factors are present in premenopausal women which suggest the possibility of secondary osteoporosis, then bone mineral density testing is clinically indicated and further testing for secondary causes of osteoporosis should be explored. Such risk factors are amenorrhea (especially associated with extensive exercise), anorexia or bulimia, malignancy, steroid or other bone-robbing medication use, endocrine disorders, renal disease, gastrointestinal disease, and others (see Chapter 1).

BMD testing should be considered also in all premenopausal women who have a fragility fracture (a fracture precipitated with apparently little external force) or who have a maternal family history of osteoporotic fracture. As discussed, this is a powerful indicator of possible development of osteoporosis in the offspring, and sibling osteoporotic fracture (fracture by a sister or brother) is also a strong indicator.

BMD Testing Guidelines for Men

There are no definitive published guidelines as to which men should be tested for osteoporosis except for Medicare beneficiaries. The Bone Mass Measurement Act[4] provides coverage for a BMD Test if a man has vertebral abnormalities demonstrating demineralization (suggests osteopoenia or osteoporosis) on a standard X-ray, a vertebral fracture, primary hyperparathyroidism, or is on corticosteroids. Coverage is provided also if a man is being monitored to assess his response to or the efficacy of a Food and Drug Administration (FDA) approved medication for osteoporosis.

In addition to male gender-specific risk factors such as testosterone deficiency, the same risk factors for women apply to men (see Chapter 1) such as being Caucasian, having a personal history of fracture as an adult, advanced age, dementia, poor health/frailty, cigarette smoking, excessive alcohol use, low lifelong calcium intake, low body weight, and various diseases and medications like oral prednisone for asthma or rheumatoid arthritis. Men with multiple risk factors should be considered for BMD testing.

Medicare and Insurance Coverage

Medicare Coverage of BMD Tests

The Bone Mass Measurement Act[4] provides a national coverage policy for BMD testing reimbursement in qualified Medicare beneficiaries at clinical risk for having osteoporosis, as determined by the following:

1. A woman who has been determined by the physician (or a qualified non-physician practitioner) to be estrogen deficient (generally a woman who is postmenopausal or had her ovaries removed before menopause) and at clinical risk for osteoporosis, based on her medical history or other findings.
2. An individual with vertebral abnormalities, as demonstrated by an X-ray, to be indicative of osteoporosis or osteopoenia, or vertebral fracture.
3. An individual receiving or expecting to receive glucocorticoid (steroid) therapy equivalent to 7.5 mg of prednisone or greater per day for more than three months.
4. An individual with primary hyperparathyroidism.
5. An individual being monitored to assess the response to or efficacy of an FDA- approved osteoporosis drug therapy.

Please note that number 1 refers only to women who are estrogen deficient (i.e., postmenopausal) whereas numbers 2 through 5 refer to both men and women.

Under the BMMA act, coverage for follow-up bone mass measurements is limited to only one measurement every two years (twenty-three months must have elapsed since the patient's last BMD) for beneficiaries who receive coverage of bone mass measurements. Follow-up bone mass measurements performed more frequently than once every two years may be covered when medically necessary if qualified under a special exception.

The Medicare special exceptions to providing BMD payment for medically necessary tests more frequently than every 23 months are:

1. Monitoring beneficiaries on long term glucocorticoid (steroid-equivalent to 7.5 mg. prednisone or greater therapy for longer than three months).
2. If the initial test was performed with a technique that is different from the proposed monitoring method, a Medicare exception allows for a confirmatory baseline bone mass measurement to permit monitoring the benefit of treatment in the future. Most often this means that a central spine and hip confirmatory test can be performed for confirmation of osteoporosis if a peripheral screening test is abnormal. For example, if a peripheral screening test (i.e., P-DEXA) of the finger or heel or forearm is done at a local health screening fair or family practitioner's office, the

patient might be referred for a more complete confirmatory central hip and spine test.

3. Individuals undergoing bone marker testing for bone turnover.

Will All Insurances Pay for BMD Testing?

The National Osteoporosis Foundation and Bone Mass Measurement Act have set standards of indications for bone mass measurement for the entire country. However, each insurance company differs in reimbursement and/or follow-up. Most all insurances now pay for BMD testing; however, some of the HMOs and PPOs require precertification. This simply means that the ordering physician (usually a nurse who handles these matters in the physician's office) must call and give the indications for performing the test and obtain approval. In my experience, insurance companies almost always approve the test once the risk factors are given (i.e., 63-year-old postmenopausal Caucasian female, lifelong history of calcium intake deficiency, smokes cigarettes, and has diabetes.)

Other Medical Testing

Often osteoporosis is multifactorial in origin. If a secondary cause of osteoporosis is suspected, then other testing might be necessary, such as blood or urine testing (i.e., comprehensive medical profile, thyroid profile, calcium, phosphorous, parathyroid hormone, serum protein electrophoresis, vitamin D level [serum 25-hydroxy-vitamin D (25-{OH}D)], 24-hour urinary calcium, 24-hour urinary cortisol, estradiol, FSH [follicle stimulating hormone], testosterone, DHEA [dehydroepiandrosterone], LH [luteinizing hormone]), or serum osteocalcin, or others as dictated by your medical history and physical examination by your physician or professional health care provider.

Sometimes, biochemical bone marker testing to assess bone formation or bone resorption might be needed to assess bone turnover. Markers may be helpful along with BMD for clinical assessment. For example, a higher rate of bone turnover may indicate a higher risk for hip fracture.

Bone Turnover Markers

Formation Markers
- Serum total alkaline phosphatase (ALP)
- Serum bone specific alkaline phosphatase (BSAP)
- Serum osteocalcin (OC)

- Serum procollagen I carboxy terminal propeptide (PICP)
- Serum procollagen type I N-terminal polypeptide (PINP)

Resorption Markers
- Urinary hydroxyproline (Hyp)
- Urinary total pyridinoline (Pyr)
- Urinary total deoxypyridinoline (dPyr)
- Urinary free pyridinoline (f-Pyr)
- Urinary free deoxypyridinoline (f-dPyr)
- Urinary collagen type I cross-linked N-telopeptide (NTx)
- Urinary collagen type I cross-linked C-telopeptide (CTx, also referred to as crosslaps)
- Serum carboxyterminal telopeptide of type I collagen (ITCP)

Points to Remember

- **Information from BMD testing should be used along with your personal medical history to determine the best course of osteoporosis prevention and treatment.**

- **DEXA is the most widely used central testing machine and is considered the gold standard of BMD measurement technology.**

- **If more than one risk factor is present other than menopause at age 50, then BMD testing for osteoporosis should be undertaken.**

- **Most insurance companies pay for BMD testing; however, some HMOs and PPOs require precertification.**

Chapter 3 Bibliography

1   *Osteoporosis: Review of the Evidence for Prevention, Diagnosis, and Treatment and Cost-Effective Analysis. Osteoporosis International 1998, 8:S1–S88).*

2   *Melton III, L. J., M. Thamer, N. F. Ray, et al. Fractures Attributable to Osteoporosis: Report from the National Osteoporosis Foundation. Journal of Bone and Mineral Research 12 (1997): 16–23.*

3   *International Society for Clinical Densitometry Physician Certification Course-Version 1.2-2/98 original compilation Paul D. Miller M.D.*

4   *The BMMA Act—Federal Register, Volume 63, Number 121 (HCFA-3004-IFC), 1998.*

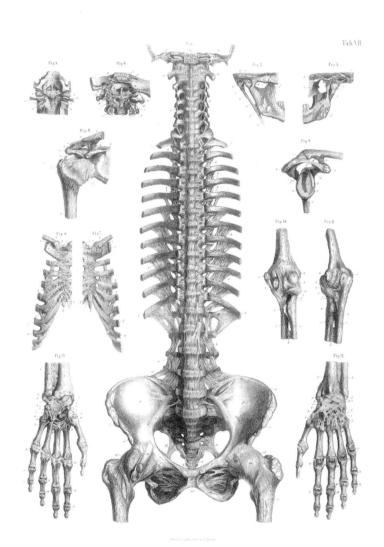

Tab.VII

First Steps To Preserving Bone Health

Chapter 4

Building Better Bone

The ultimate goal of osteoporosis prevention and treatment is to prevent fractures. The aim of a prevention and treatment strategy is to reverse bone loss and build better bone mass. With effective preventive and treatment methods, weak, brittle bones can become strong, hard bones. With stronger bones, there is less likelihood of fracture and subsequent disability, disease, and fatality.

Eliminating the Risks

An elderly 75-year-old woman with multiple chronic medical disabilities said to me, *"If I'd known I was going to live so long, I'd have take better care of myself when I was younger!"*

It's never too late to prevent and treat osteoporosis. Some of the risk factors for osteoporosis (see Chapter 2) are those over which you have no control—age, sex, and race, for example. Other factors such as tobacco use, alcohol and caffeine intake, and steroid use can be lessened or eliminated by taking control of your life and making wise decisions regarding your health.

Eliminating Tobacco Use

Cigarette smokers break down estrogen in the liver more rapidly into non-active 2-hydroxy-estrone, which is excreted in the urine. Because cigarette smoking increases the metabolism of estrogen in the liver, the overall levels of the three major estrogens are lower among smokers. In women who smoke, as compared to non-smokers, ovaries may have decreased estrogen production. These women tend to have accelerated bone mineral density loss with a resulting increase in osteoporotic fractures. They are also generally thinner and may experience an earlier natural menopause.

All individuals at risk for osteoporosis should stop smoking immediately as a preventive measure for the development of osteoporosis. Likewise, all individuals with osteoporosis should immediately stop smoking as a treatment measure for their osteoporosis.

A Step-by Step How to Quit Program

"It's easy to quit smoking," Mark Twain is supposed to have said. "I've done it hundreds of times." Apparently, his was not a unique experience. Like diet books and diet programs, books and courses on how to stop smoking are more popular than ever. But are these programs and techniques effective? Yes, for the most part—provided the smoker makes a commitment to quit. In truth, all aids, from a medication which decreases your desire to smoke (i.e., Zyban®), or nicotine patches (i.e., Habitrol®, Nicoderm®, Nicotrol®, Prostep®), or nicotine chewing gum (i.e., Nicorette®), or nicotine inhalers (i.e., Nicotrol® Inhaler) and filters can work as tools. Some people find that buying a set of filters, to gradually decrease nicotine content works. Others chew on chewing gum or suck candy or cinnamon sticks. Some use hypnosis to focus their attention and interest and motivate them. Some go "cold turkey." However, these tools only work for the person who has made a decision once and for all to stop smoking.

A pattern of smoking was developed over many years, and unlearning that pattern can be very frustrating and difficult. There are many ways to stop smoking, but ultimately it all comes down to the smoker as an individual and his or her self-discipline. Any way will work if the person really wants it to work. The key that unlocks the door to smoke-free living is the motivation to stop smoking.

Often people will quit for a short while, expecting their health to change overnight. When it doesn't, they go back to smoking. But it takes six months to see real changes in the lungs once a person quits smoking. Even after someone quits, he or she may continue to have a hacking cough, chronic sinus congestion, and hoarseness for several weeks. On a lung test, the smoker's airways may continue to show obstruction. Some people report an increase in sinus infections shortly after they quit. This is the result of the sinuses attempting to purge themselves of toxins built up over the years from smoking. These symptoms are a positive sign!

Most people who stop smoking will decide to do so using only determination. These people will want to cut down gradually and soon stop smoking completely.

If you are a smoker, the following section is for you!

Step One: Preparing to Stop

Many of you may find it best to see a physician and obtain a prescription for Zyban (bupropion hydrochloride, Wellbutrin SR®). After taking Zyban for ten to fourteen days, most individuals lose their desire to smoke and find it easier to stop smoking. One of the advantages of taking Zyban (bupropion) is that it also has antidepressant properties. (Bupropion is also marketed as an antidepressant under the name of Wellbutrin SR®). Because of this, individuals who take Zyban tend to feel better, and they also have been found not to overeat or gain weight while taking it. Overeating to satisfy the oral stimulation urge is often a problem for people after they stop smoking.

Some of you may not be able to take Zyban or may find it easier to use nicotine patches which decrease in strength over a few weeks; i.e., usually from 21 mgs to 14 mgs to 7 mgs. Some of you may find it preferable to use a nicotine nasal spray or a nicotine inhaler. Some may use a combination of Zyban with nicotine patches or another method a personal physician or qualified professional health care provider may recommend. Whatever the case, the basic pattern of behavior modification to stop smoking is the same.

It generally makes sense to cut down the number of cigarettes smoked before quitting for good. There are several reasons for this. First, by cutting down, your body's need for nicotine is gradually being reduced. This will cause fewer acute withdrawal symptoms. Secondly, cutting down will give you an opportunity to successfully test your willpower. If you can cut down from one pack to half a pack a day, you are demonstrating that you can stop smoking!

Another way to prepare to quit smoking is to announce to others your intention, particularly to people who have wanted you to quit. They will reinforce this agreement with yourself; they will be your *witnesses*. Ask them to support you by calling you periodically during your first weeks as a nonsmoker. They will be glad to help you through this difficult time, and they will keep you honest.

Visualization is an effective way to program your mind to get the outcome you desire. But it is easier to picture yourself thinner, let's say, than it is to picture yourself a nonsmoker. What does nonsmoking look like? To think of not smoking, you must necessarily picture smoking, and that may reinforce your habit. One way around this is to picture yourself going through the activities of the day without smoking. You can also replay the most enjoyable times in your life before you became a smoker. This will enable you to see and feel that you can enjoy yourself without smoking. Make a list of your greatest pleasures (not including smoking!). Plan how you will do one or more of these pleasures each day as a reward for not smoking.

Step Two: Stopping

The first action is to cut your smoking in half. For example, if you smoke one pack per day, then smoke no more than a half-pack a day. To do so, analyze your smoking habits. When are you most susceptible to smoking one cigarette after another? Make cigarettes harder to get during these times. Eliminate those cigarettes which you are smoking out of habit and not for enjoyment. Try doing nothing else while you are smoking and experience the cigarette fully. Postpone your morning cigarette by fifteen minutes. After a meal, see if you can do away with smoking entirely.

Take a good look at how badly you really need cigarettes. Rate each cigarette you smoke on a need scale of one to ten, one meaning that you don't really need it, and ten that you absolutely must have it. You might find it effective to carry a 3"x 5" card with you and record each cigarette that you have, the time you have it, what you were doing at the time, and your need from one to ten. This will enable you to make smoking a conscious effort rather than an automatic reflex.

Cigarette Need Scale

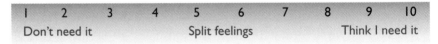

Change the brand of cigarettes you smoke to a low-tar, low-nicotine brand, and use a filter so that you can gradually reduce physiological dependence while still smoking the same amount. Buy cigarettes a pack at a time rather than by the carton. This means you will have to make a decision—and a trip—each time you want a pack of cigarettes.

Make it difficult to have access to your cigarettes. Put them in an out-of-the-way place or in an unfamiliar pocket. Make yourself walk to find an ashtray. Use your opposite hand to smoke a cigarette.

These things will help you break previously established patterns and smoking reflexes. Buy low calorie foods such as celery, carrots, or sugarless gum if you have the need to put something in your mouth, or put a toothpick in your mouth!

After two weeks, cut the number of cigarettes you are smoking in half again. For example, if you now smoke one-half pack a day, them decrease it to one-fourth pack a day. After two weeks at one-fourth pack a day (five cigarettes), decide on a day when you are going to stop smoking. On the night before that day, throw a party with your family and close friends, gather up all the cigarettes in your home, and destroy them—every one of them! This includes the reserve or emergency pack you may be keeping in the glove compartment of your car or under your bed. Throw out the ashtrays, too. Then do something you like as a reward.

Go to bed with a strong, positive feeling, and use creative visualization to see yourself as a strong, powerful, confident person who has conquered a habit that once controlled you. Visualize yourself as a vibrant, happy, energetic person, free forever of the smoking habit. See yourself regaining your keen sense of smell, tasting foods again, and having clean breath. See yourself as never having a cigarette again in your life because you know there is no such thing as a harmless cigarette. See your bones as stronger and your lungs as healthier. See your ability to breathe improving, and the oxygen flowing into and out of your small, medium and large airways to freely oxygenate your blood, thus giving you more energy. See yourself waking up in the morning breathing in more energy and becoming healthier each day.

Step Three: After You Stop Smoking

Once you stop smoking, it is essential that you fill your life with rewarding activities and pleasures which will enhance rather than ruin your health. You are probably familiar with the old saying, "If something feels good, it's either immoral, illegal, or fattening." Forget that nonsense! There are many things which feel good and are life-enhancing. Make a list of ten activities you love which are not harmful to your health. These might include going to a movie, playing music, listening to a favorite record, attending a lecture or workshop, taking a class, chopping wood, skiing, sitting in a hot tub, doing volunteer work, or taking a drive in the country. You may find it helpful to take up new hobbies such as sewing, knitting, stained glass, or woodcarving. You may find it helpful also to write letters or email to friends, to socialize, surf the web, or talk on the telephone more. Keep yourself active so as to distract yourself from old smoking habits.

You may also want to increase your physical activities. For example, you might exercise at your local fitness center; play tennis, golf, or racquetball; try country or line dancing, aerobic dancing, or bowling. You may find it helpful to do slow, relaxed abdominal breathing exercises, progressive relaxation exercises, or meditation to release tension. All of these pleasurable activities—done without smoking—will increase your enjoyment of life.

Warming Up on an Exercise Bike
You may want to enhance your enjoyment of life by exercising at your local fitness center

Rather than identifying yourself as a nonsmoker, take on a positive identity as a life enjoyer! Many studies have been done recently on the healing power of laughter. During the difficult transition from smoker to nonsmoker, make sure there's plenty of laughter in your life. Get together with other friends to quit smoking, and make your weekly meeting fun. Have each person tell a joke. Watch videotapes or listen to records of comedians, see a funny movie, or go hear local comedians. It is impossible to laugh and feel miserable at the same time.

Be particularly careful not to overeat. There is a natural tendency for this when you stop smoking, since food in the stomach provides immediate satisfaction and gratification. If you need to eat, do not buy junk food but rather low-calorie, low-fat foods such as fresh fruits and vegetables.

Use visualization daily to reinforce your new self-image. Go to bed each night with a positive feeling and see yourself thoroughly enjoying the next day's activities—without a cigarette. Visualize yourself as vibrant, healthy and happy with no need to renew the smoking habit. Imagine regaining your keen sense of smell. Imagine tasting foods more fully than you have in years and smelling the sweet smells you have missed. Feel how fresh your nonsmoker's breath is.

Picture your bones stronger, your lungs pink and soft and healthy, your breathing easier and fuller. Feel that increased energy!

The first few weeks after you stop smoking are the most critical. Avoid situations where you may be tempted to light up a cigarette. If you find yourself wanting to light up after eating, then get up immediately after your meal and keep busy. Distract yourself by focusing your attention on other things. People who drink alcohol often smoke. So if necessary, avoid these types of parties or activities. If the high pressures of your work are conducive to smoking, then substitute other means of stress release (i.e., slow relaxed abdominal breathing, relaxation techniques, exercise, recreation, chewing gum, or eating low calorie foods). Ask yourself. "Do I really need this cigarette? What's causing me to desire it? What would I really get out of the cigarette if I smoked it? What can I substitute in its place?" If you find yourself craving a cigarette, wait five minutes. Most intense cravings last only from three to five minutes, during which time you can analyze what in your situation may be causing the desire to smoke (i.e., stress, sitting in front of the television, being around smokers, depression, frustration, or boredom) and take steps to correct it. If you eliminate the source of the problem, the problem will correct itself. And, lastly, continue to see and visualize yourself as more energetic, more mentally alert, more emotionally satisfied, and physically healthier.

Eliminating Alcohol Abuse

Years of alcohol abuse takes its toll on bones. Individuals who abuse alcohol tend to have lower bone mineral density. The mechanism is thought to be a direct adverse effect on the osteoblasts (bone building cells). *Alcohol damages osteoblasts, making it difficult for these cells to build new bone.* There may be other indirect ways alcohol adversely affects bone growth through the poor nutritional habits that many alcohol abusers have, such as secondary liver disease, or inability to absorb calcium, vitamin D, and nutrients (i. e. magnesium, vitamin K, and other vitamins and minerals required for bone building).

Alcohol abuse is also associated with an increased risk of falls and secondary fractures. These risks are seen with individuals who drink more than two glasses of alcohol per day. Researchers are still studying the effects of moderate alcohol use and its relationship to bone mass density and increased fracture risk. Since there is such a strong correlation between alcohol abuse and osteoporosis, we will look at various kinds of abuse and identify steps to eliminating this risk factor.

Types of Alcohol Abuse

One of the most tragic things about alcohol abuse is that the chronic abuser is least likely to admit that he/she has a problem. Therefore, it is useful to identify the characteristics of each stage of alcohol abuse. If you see yourself in here, admit that you have a problem and take the steps necessary to deal with it.

Stage I

1. The social drinker drinks occasionally at social gatherings, holidays, celebrations, or other events. This drinker occasionally becomes intoxicated—up to four times per year.

2. The habitual excessive drinker becomes inebriated or partly inebriated more than four times per year and looks forward to these social situations to escape from problems. He or she is a heavy social drinker.

Stage II

The problem drinker begins to drink more heavily and regularly with increased tolerance to alcohol. He becomes inebriated or partly inebriated frequently, often drinking more and eating less as problems increase. He may stop drinking for a while, but eventually returns to it. Although this person may deny he has a problem, he also feels guilt. As he begins drinking earlier and earlier in the day, he may lose interest in his activities, work, family, and friends. He may begin to feel resentful, hostile, and easily angered, picking fights easily with family members. He may slur his speech and develop a fine tremor in his hands. He may find himself doing things under the influence of alcohol that he would not ordinarily do, like fighting. He may find himself depressed or boisterous. As his problem becomes more serious, he may experience withdrawal symptoms such as shaking if he does not have alcohol in his system.

Progression from the social drinker to Stage II problem drinker usually occurs over a period of years. The problem drinker is psychologically addicted to alcohol for problem-solving, for happiness, and for satisfaction, often using alcohol as a defense mechanism to help him survive. In the problem drinking stage, a person can still stop his drinking. However, a characteristic of this stage is that often the person does not look at his drinking and himself objectively. Since alcohol interferes with his ability to observe, judge, and evaluate himself realistically, everyone around him can see that he has a problem long before he does. If he does see he has a problem, he often denies it.

Stage III

This person is addicted totally to alcohol. He can't control his drinking and needs alcohol to function. He experiences severe personality changes and becomes socially isolated and depressed. He begins to exhibit physical symptoms such as tremors and severe slurring of speech.

In true alcoholism, a person is psychologically addicted as well as physically addicted to the drug. Physical addiction means he needs the alcohol in his blood in order to function. Psychological addiction means he needs the alcohol in his system to deal with everyday reality. The alcoholic needs to drink more and more as time goes on. His personality suffers severely as he attempts to conceal his drinking.

How to Stop Alcohol Abuse

If you've seen yourself described in the above stages, acknowledge your position and take steps to become healthier, both physically and psychologically.

Treatment of Stage I: The Social Drinker and Excessive Habitual Drinker

Social drinking is the more treatable alcohol problem. You can prepare for a social event by remembering the following:

- Keep in mind that the reason to attend a social event is to socialize, not to become intoxicated.
- Sip your drinks; do not gulp them.
- Drink for enjoyment rather than for the effect it may have on you.
- Add water to your drinks.
- Do not take "one for the road."
- Stop drinking immediately if you begin to experience dizziness, headache, tiredness, nausea, or other symptoms.
- Do not drink out of obligation.
- Alternate an alcoholic beverage with a non-alcoholic beverage.
- Set limits for yourself.
- Drink for quality, not quantity.
- Don't drink socially as a way to avoid or solve your problems.

Treatment of Stage II: The Problem Drinker

The problem in this stage is having enough self-esteem to admit that you have a problem. Having done that, the next step is to develop a desire to do something about your problem and make a commitment to conquering it. Alcohol is a serious problem in Stage II, but you do exert control over it. You can stop drinking and experience only mild withdrawal symptoms.

It is important at this stage to recognize that drinking is most likely a symptom of a more serious deeper problem. You must be open, observe, and seek to understand what that problem may be. Is it unhappiness with your work? A marriage that is not working? A poor self-image? Guilt? Unhappiness about a situation you are in? Inability to accept the responsibilities of family life? Boredom? Dissatisfaction with your life? Do you feel victimized? Do you feel you have no control over your life?

Is alcohol a substitute for the inability to develop or maintain mature relationships with others? Is it a relief of stress or anxiety? Is it used as a narcotic to withdraw inside from an unpleasant environment? Is it used to relax you, to help you deal with your problems? Whatever your answer, you must confront these deeper psychological, physical, emotional, and spiritual problems, or your second stage alcohol problem drinking may cross the thin line into the realm of severe alcoholism and uncontrolled drinking. Remember, in this stage you have control. Let this stage ring a bell in your mind, alarming you to the realization that you must exercise your powers for healthy living and do something about your problem now.

Be aware of the rationalizations you may give yourself to justify what you are doing. You may be saying to yourself, "I only drink three or four beers a day." Be aware that if you are drinking more than ten beers per week or are at times dependent upon it, you are injuring yourself. Or you may tell yourself, "I only drink on weekends; therefore I don't have an alcohol problem." But, if you become intoxicated when you drink, you have a problem. Or, you may be deluding yourself by saying, "I never get drunk when I drink. I can hold my liquor." This may be true, but the reality is that you have built up a tolerance to the alcohol. More alcohol is required to produce an effect equal to a lesser amount of alcohol you may have drunk in the past. You may act sober because you have a tolerance to alcohol, but the increased blood alcohol levels are seriously harming your body. Whatever your justification, you can be sure that excessive alcohol is doing you no good and that you can stop drinking at this stage without severe difficulties.

Once you understand that drinking makes you a victim in life, you have already taken the first step towards a firm commitment to control your life and your drinking, rather than being controlled by it. Many people in Stage II find that they are intrinsically motivated never to drink again. They realize dependence on alcohol is an illness, just as a cold or a urinary tract infection is. Stage II alcoholism is a disease to be dealt with properly and disposed of so as not to interfere with proper functioning in one's daily life.

For many individuals, once the deeper emotional problems underlying the drinking are dealt with, dependence on alcohol decreases. For others, Antabuse® (disufiram) is used on a daily basis. When taking Antabuse, an individual cannot take alcohol in any form or a severe reaction such as nausea, vomiting, flushing of the face, shortness of breath, palpitations, headaches, or weakness, will occur. Occasionally, the mixture can result in death. People taking Antabuse cannot take any cough syrups or use any lotions which contain alcohol. I have found that people in Stage II and taking Antabuse along with undergoing counseling and seeking the help of alcoholic organizations such as Alcoholics Anonymous achieve a high rate of success.

The key is your motivation as an individual. You must begin to visualize yourself as a successful, happy, healthy person in control of your life. You must be able to see yourself as confident and self-assured, and carry this attitude out into the world. In Stage II, many, if not most, people find it best not to drink at all. Some people may continue to drink occasionally but never again to the point of dependence or alcohol abuse.

Treatment of Stage III: Alcoholism

In Stage III, you are totally dependent on alcohol. You have no control over your drinking. It interferes with your physical and mental functioning, your personal life, your work, and your day-to-day environment. You may even be suffering from physical illness, such as cirrhosis and central nervous system tremors, and the cessation of alcohol results in withdrawal symptoms including anxiety, tremor, possibly seizures, abnormal eye movements, wakefulness, nausea, hallucinations, or in severe cases, delirium tremens. Treatment of the severe alcoholic consists of two stages: detoxification and rehabilitation.

Treatment should take place in a hospital or in a detoxification center set up to deal with withdrawal symptoms, which may last up to seven days. All too often, alcoholics hit "rock bottom," so to speak, before they seek help. They may lose their jobs, their families, and their health. Hopefully, you have not hit rock bottom.

If you are considering making a change, you will examine your values in life and decide if drinking is worth it. It may take you a long time to realize you are physically addicted to the drug and can never drink again. It will take an even longer time for you to desire to change, to believe in yourself, and to expect that you will never take that first drink again. Support during this stage includes various alcoholic programs, alcoholic rehabilitation centers, and individual group and family counseling.

Alcoholics Anonymous (AA)

Alcoholics Anonymous is probably the best and most effective treatment and rehabilitation program for people who really want to stop drinking. Alcoholics Anonymous has over one million members, requires no membership dues, and is founded upon a 12-step program based upon support—staying away from that first drink one day at a time, obtaining emotional and psychological supportive help, and developing a sound basis for living and philosophy of life. The commitment is total abstinence from alcohol, and this experience is nurtured by common experiences and struggles with others who have rehabilitated themselves using AA. If you are a Stage III alcoholic or have a serious Stage II alcohol problem, then I recommend that you go to Alcoholics Anonymous, no matter what other treatment modalities you use! To succeed, nothing works better than success. Alcoholics Anonymous was formed and is run by successfully reformed alcoholics who can give you the support you need and show you the tools to use to reform yourself.

If you need help, call their number now: 1-800-266-5584.

Caffeine

Many of us (including myself) drink caffeine in the form of coffee as a "pick me up" in the morning, using it to give us an extra physical and emotional uplift. However, in moderate to large amounts, is caffeine harmful to the health of our bones?

We do know that excessive caffeine promotes calcium loss into the urine via the kidneys, but studies are conflicting about exactly how much caffeine is detrimental to our health. The average person loses 100–250 milligrams of calcium into the urine each day. Researchers have found that the greatest calcium loss in the urine after drinking caffeinated coffee appears to occur within the first three hours after drinking coffee.[1] This calcium loss can be minimized if calcium intake is at least 600 milligrams per day. Greater than 1,000 milligrams per day of caffeine markedly increases calcium loss in the urine.

How Much Is Excessive Caffeine?

A caffeine intake of 100 milligrams per day produces significant bodily effects; caffeine intake greater than 250 milligrams per day may have adverse effects on our health; and *caffeine intake greater than 400 milligrams per day (roughly equivalent to 3 to 4 cups of coffee) is the "critical point" which many pharmacologists say distinguishes safe from potentially dangerous use.* Levels above this will produce serious adverse symptoms and may place you at risk for osteoporosis through urinary calcium loss. This is particularly true if your calcium intake is less than 600 milligrams per day.[2] Have you noticed that too much caffeine puts you in high gear continuously? It is sometimes called the "high idle" syndrome or, more appropriately, caffeinism. I've seen many individuals over the years with this, and they've described themselves as "walking time bombs." They are tense all the time, irritable, anxious, and suffer from insomnia.

Of note is that by some estimates 30% of Americans who drink coffee consume 500–600 milligrams of caffeine per day, and 10% more Americans consume more than 1,000 milligrams per day.

Coffee: Our Primary Source of Dietary Caffeine

Caffeine is primarily obtained in the diet through coffee.

Your intake will vary depending on the size of cup or mug you use. Small, formal dinner cups may hold only 5 ounces, a regular cup may hold 8 ounces, whereas larger mugs may hold 10 to 20 ounces. Just think about it! If you drink only three 10 ounce mugs of drip or percolated coffee in the morning, you have already exceeded your caffeine limit per day and risk causing serious detrimental effects to your bones.

Caffeine Per Eight Ounce Cup of Coffee		
Type of Coffee	Milligrams (average)	Range (depending on brew)
Regular Drip	150	95–285
Percolated	125	65–270
Instant	66	50–190
Decaffeinated	5	3–7
Decaffeinated Instant	3	2–5
	approximate	

Excessive Caffeine: How To Stop

To avoid withdrawal symptoms such as headaches and sluggishness, you may not want to stop drinking coffee cold turkey but rather decrease your coffee intake and taper off over a two or three week period. First, cut your coffee intake in half by deciding which cups of coffee you really need and which you drink out of habit. Then, brew your coffee by mixing half regular coffee and half decaffeinated coffee. Substituting tea or another drink (e.g., juice) instead of coffee is another alternative. Decrease your coffee intake over a two-week period until you have reached the goal you set for yourself. It might be one or two cups a day in the morning, or none at all. You might choose to drink only decaffeinated coffee. If you should desire to discontinue caffeine use totally, you may wish to use herbal tea in place of regular coffee or regular tea, as most herbal teas are caffeine free. Keep in mind, however, that if you have a history of kidney stones, excessive tea may accelerate the formation of calcium oxalate stones.

Another approach to cutting back on caffeine slowly in order to eliminate withdrawal headaches and lethargy is to mix decaffeinated with regular coffee gradually. The following chart can give you direction how to do this:

Cutting Back on Coffee Gradually
Days 1–5............Mix 1/4 cup decaffeinated with 3/4 cup regular
Days 6–9............Mix 1/2 cup decaffeinated with 1/2 cup regular
Days 10–13 ......Mix 3/4 cup decaffeinated with 1/4 cup regular
Days 14+...........Drink only a full cup of decaffeinated

Other Sources of Caffeine

Caffeine is also found in many other beverages, foods, and medicines.

A host of medications contain caffeine, such as Anacin®, Emperin®, Excedrin®, Mydol®, Nodoz®, Vanquish®, Caffergot®, Fiorinal®, Soma® Compound, many diet pills, and other medications.

Summing It Up

In summary, a moderate amount of caffeine is okay, but excessive caffeine may cause calcium loss in the urine and adversely affect your bones' health. For optimal bone and physical health, maintain a limited caffeine intake by decreasing caffeinated coffee to no more than two cups per day or eliminating it, and be aware of the hidden caffeine in colas and various other drinks, foods and medications.

Additional Sources of Caffeine		
Food or Beverage	**Milligrams of Caffeine**	
	Average	**Range**
Soft drinks		
Mountain Dew® (12 oz.)	54	54
Coca-Cola® (12 oz.)	45	45
Pepsi®	38	38
Tea (8 oz. cup)		
Brewed (major U.S. brands)	48	32–145
Brewed, (imported brands)	96	40–175
Instant	48	40–80
Iced	46	44–50
Cocoa beverage (8 oz.)	8	4–30
Chocolate milk (8 oz.)	5	2–10
Milk chocolate (1 oz.)	6	1–15
Dark chocolate, semi sweet (1 oz.)	20	5–35
Baking chocolate	26	26
Chocolate flavored syrup (1 oz.)	4	4

Minimizing the Risk of Falls—A Serious Problem for the Elderly

Bones break when the forces applied to them exceed their strength. Vertebral compression fractures can occur with very minimal force if your bone mineral density is low and your vertebrae subsequently weak. However, wrist fractures frequently occur when you fall on an outstretched arm trying to prevent yourself from landing hard on the floor, and the more serious hip fractures occur from falling as well.

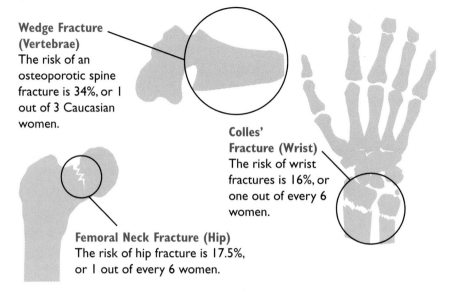

Wedge Fracture (Vertebrae)
The risk of an osteoporotic spine fracture is 34%, or 1 out of 3 Caucasian women.

Colles' Fracture (Wrist)
The risk of wrist fractures is 16%, or one out of every 6 women.

Femoral Neck Fracture (Hip)
The risk of hip fracture is 17.5%, or 1 out of every 6 women.

■ Osteoporotic hip fractures kill 50,000 people a year.

■ 300,000 hip fractures occur annually in the United Staes, and 95% are the result of falls.

■ Twenty-four percent of hip fracture victims die within one year, usually from complications such as pneumonia or blood clots in the lung related to either the fracture or the emergency surgery.

■ Fifty percent of hip fracture victims will be incapacitated (many permanently).

■ Twenty to twenty-five percent will require long-term nursing home care.

■ Only one in three will fully recover.

■ Ninety percent of all hip fractures among elderly women are attributed to low bone mass (osteopoenic) or brittle (osteoporotic) bones.

■ Hip fractures in the elderly occur in approximately 1 to 1.5% of falling incidences. Approximately 59% of the elderly who have a history of falling will fall at least once again per year.[3]

Falls increase with advancing age. Numerous studies have found that approximately 20 to 30% of those over the age of 65 living at home or in their communities fall each year, 30 to 35% over the age of 70 fall each year, and 50% over the age of 80 fall each year.

Accidental death is the sixth leading cause of deaths in the elderly in the U.S., and most of these deaths are caused by falls.[4]

On average, a man loses 20–30% of his total bone mass in his lifetime, and a woman loses 30–40%. Due to age-related bone loss, most women and many men in their seventies are at risk for fractures from falls. While beginning aggressive treatment at this age will help to quantitatively increase bone mass, it can not repair the lifelong qualitative damage to bone consisting of microarchitectural destruction of the supporting struts and arches of bone tissue. Aggressive treatment at this age should be instituted, however, to halt the progression of bone loss and to afford whatever protective benefits can be achieved to prevent hip fractures and subsequent hospitalization, surgery, and possible death. For most individuals in their seventies, a fall sideways from standing height with impact on the hip exceeds their bone's strength fracture threshold and can result in a fracture of the hip. Greater than 90% of hip fractures are the result of falls.

For many, a hip fracture marks the end of an era of independent living, as falls are responsible for 40% of all nursing home admissions. Many of the elderly view entrance into a nursing home as one of their greatest fears. Nursing home residents have an incidence of about 1.5 falls per person a year with an annual rate

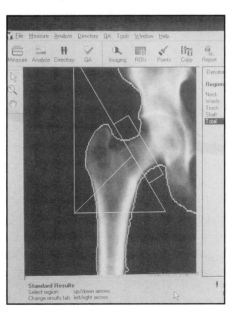

of hip fractures of approximately 5%. Fifty percent of nursing home residents fall each year. Approximately 2 to 5% of these falls will result in a fracture.[5]

Often a hip or painful spine fracture causes a decrease in activities of daily living, social withdrawal, depression, loss of self-esteem, and subsequent further loss in muscle strength and mobility from decreased physical activity. It sometimes sends individuals into a downhill slide of further muscle wasting and weakness, overall deterioration of health, and eventual death.

Risk Factors for Falling and How to Prevent Falls

The strategy to prevent falling is two-fold:

1. Eliminate possible causative factors, and
2. Improve balance mechanisms by increasing muscular strength in the lower extremity legs and upper extremity arms.

To eliminate possible causative factors, identify your potential risk factors for falling from the list below and address each one as best you can. If you need help, call your local health department or center for aging and request it. I work with several home health agencies, and frequently I'll call for elderly individuals and ask for a supervisor to go into the home and assess the patient and his/her environment and make recommendations. Often a physical therapist

Fear of Falling
The fear of falling experienced by many of the elderly is certainly a real and significant threat.

is required to go into the home and work with a frail individual to strengthen his or her leg and arm muscles so the person can remain mobile.

Decreasing fall frequency is a powerful means of decreasing fractures. Not all falls can be prevented, but many can with proper diligence and the initiation of a fall risk prophylaxis plan.

■ **The worse your vision, the greater your risk of falling.**

Have your opthalmologist (eye doctor) correct your vision as best as possible. Cataracts may need to be removed. You need to be aware of any decrease in visual acuity and depth perception and any blind spots or loss of peripheral vision.

- **The risk of falls is much greater if you take four or more medications.**

  Avoid polypharmacy (multiple medications) whenever possible, but never stop or skip medications without first consulting your doctor and having his/her consent.

- **Chronic diseases such as Parkinson's, transient ischemic attacks (TIAs), stroke (CVA—cerebral vascular accident causing hemiparesis [weakness] or hemiplegia [paralysis]), arthritis, Alzheimer's, or seizure disorder increase your risk of falling.**

  If chronic disease such as degenerative osteoarthritis or stroke impairs your ability to walk freely, use a straight cane, small four-pronged walking cane, or walker for stability. Many individuals find it best to use a 4-wheeled walker with rear spring adjusted wheels so that it can glide rather than having to be lifted with each step. Some individuals prefer wheels on the front of the walker and small skids which slide on the rear. Medicare will pay for these with a prescription from your doctor with accompanying appropriate diagnosis indication.

- **Neurologic diseases such as multiple sclerosis, muscular dystrophy or diabetic neuropathy increase your risk of falling.**

  Consider that these may interfere with balance and propriocetion mechanisms.

- **An acute illness increases your risk of falling.**

  Be aware that acute illnesses can make you weak and unstable, and take extra precautions to reduce falling during these times.

- **Carotid stenosis (arteriosclerosis of the carotid arteries) increases your risk of falling.**

  Carotid artery plaques can cause postural dizziness, particularly when first arising from bed in the morning. Upon arising, you may find it necessary to sit up on the side of the bed for a minute or two until the dizziness subsides, and then get up slowly. This can be a very serious hazard if you must get up in the night to go to the bathroom.

- **Heart valve abnormalities, particularly aortic stenosis, aortic regurgitation, and cardiac arrhythmias (irregular heart beat, i.e.: atrial fibrillation, frequent PVC's, dropped beats) can increase your risk of falling.**

Be aware that a combination of carotid plaques with aortic valvular insufficiency or other valve leakage is a very serious problem. Take extra precautions to reduce your risk of falling should you have this.

■ **A previous history of falling increases your risk of falling again.**

As mentioned above, 59% of the elderly who have fallen previously will fall again at least once per year. Take extra precaution to make your environment fall-safe.

■ **Increasing age, particularly greater than 80 years old, increases your risk of falling.**

As mentioned previously, 50% of individuals over the age of 80 fall each year. If you are advancing in age, at risk for falls, or have fallen, I highly recommend that you enlist the aid of an appropriate home health care agency to make a visit, evaluate the risk factors in your environment, and help you take appropriate action to make your home fall-safe.

■ **A history of falling from factors such as a vasovagal reflex (blacking out from action of the vagus nerve on the blood vessels, i.e., fainting at the sight of blood or passing out when standing up after a difficult bowel movement) increases your risk of falling.**

This transient loss of consciousness can result in a serious fall. Evaluate these occasions of falls and take appropriate action to safeguard yourself in each situation.

■ **Improper, slippery, or poorly fitting footwear may increase your risk of falling.**

Wear proper fitting non-skid shoes and slippers (preferably with non-slip rubber soles) which have a back over the heel rather than platform type shoes or those with soles of soft fabric.

■ **Hospitalizations are associated with an increase risk of falling.**

Physicians are aware of the rule of thumb that for each day an elderly person lays in a hospital bed, it takes about two days to get the person up and functioning again. Being hospitalized for a few days with an acute illness or surgery can make the elderly further debilitated and unsteady. Be very careful to have support the first several times you try to get up and around after being bedfast.

- **Postural hypotension and dizziness, also known as orthostatic hypotension (lowering of your blood pressure with a change in posture to the standing position), increases your risk of falling.**

  Almost one in five women over the age of sixty-five admit to some degree of postural dizziness. If you suffer from this, rise slowly and carefully when standing. Seek any potential causes and correct them if possible.

  High blood pressure medications can lower your blood pressure, causing dizziness with changes in posture. Coupled with arteriosclerosis in the elderly, this can lead to so-called "drop attacks."

  Be aware of the risks, and take appropriate precautions. Be careful when making a change in posture.

- **Other medications such as diuretics, nitroglycerin, and peripheral artery dilators may lower your blood pressure and/or otherwise increase your risk of falling.**

- **Balance (vestibular or inner ear) and proprioceptive (awareness of positioning, pressure, or stretching) abnormalities i.e., dizziness, vertigo, and poor coordination, increase your risk of falling.**

  Inner ear problems such as Meniere's or labrynthitis (vestibulitis) can be a recurrent enigma. Antivert® or other such treatment often helps but may not completely eliminate this problem. Poor positioning sense and poor reaction time deficits must be taken into consideration. Poor coordination and balance may be helped by a cane or walker, or you may need to develop a widened stance as a support base and undergo balance training. A physical therapist can help with this.

- **Alcohol intake increases your risk of falling.**

  Sedation, disorientation, and uninhibited actions as a result of alcohol intake increase your risk. Drink only in moderation, and be aware that the adverse effects of alcohol intake change with advancing age.

- **Frequent nocturnal (nighttime) urination or bowel movements, such as from diarrhea or irritable bowel syndrome, may lead to an increase in falls.**

  Tripping over items in the pathway to the bathroom while half-asleep contributes to many falls. Make sure passageways are clear of any impediments that might precipitate a fall, like loose throw rugs, curled carpet, unexpected objects on the floor, or steps or furniture that you may run into.

■ **Intellectual deterioration and confusion associated with brain (cortical) atrophy and slow progressive Alzheimer's deterioration and forgetfulness may lead to falls.**

Caregivers for these persons are responsible to make the environment as fall-safe as possible to reduce the occasion for falls.

■ **Confusion, disorientation, combativeness, resistance, belligerence, and hallucinations increase your risk of falling.**

Each of these altered states of consciousness carries an increased risk. The cause should be addressed and treated as best possible.

■ **Sedation as a side effect from various medications such as antihistamines, narcotics, or "sleeping pill," may predispose you to easy falling by interfering with your balance and coordination.**

Be aware of the risk and make your environment as fall-safe as possible.

■ **Tranquilizers (benzodiazepine hypnotics-anxiolytics), antidepressants, and anti-psychotics may increase your risk of falling.**

Be aware that this medication makes you feel better, so your risk of falling may increase because of the increased physical activity and increased risk-taking behavior.

■ **Weakness of the leg muscles from stroke, inactivity, neurologic diseases, or muscle wasting in a frail individual makes it difficult to get up, and you can fall to the ground getting out of a chair and fracture a hip.**

Osteoarthritis of the hip or knee, or a knee "giving out" frequently leads to a fall. Use walking aids such as a regular cane, four pronged cane, or walker.

■ **Having to use an assistive ambulatory device such as a cane or walker increases your risk of falling.**

Use a cane in the arm opposite your painful knee or hip for increased stability.

■ **Upper extremity musculoskeletal weakness or impaired mobility/ range of motion of the arms increases your risk of falling. This weakness of the arms makes it difficult for you to pull yourself up or hold onto a rail or piece of furniture for support.**

Request aid whenever possible.

 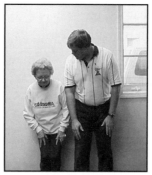

- **Foot problems increase your risk of falling.**

  Maintain the health of your feet, and keep a wide support base for optimal balance.

- **Gait problems increase your risk of falling. A normal individual walks with a pendulum-like motion of the legs. Gait disturbances such as from hemiparesis (weakness on one side of the body) or from severe degenerative knee or hip disease may result in loss of balance and increasing propensity for a subsequent fall. Individuals with a poor tandem gait (one foot in front of the other) are at very high risk for falls.**

  Use extreme precaution when walking, and walk slowly and with walking aids if necessary.

- **Poor hearing increases your risk of falling.**

  Sound helps orient us. If necessary, have a hearing test and buy a hearing aid.

- **The following environmental hazards increase your risk of falling: area or throw rugs, torn or curled carpeting, raised doorsills, slick floors, slippery bathtubs or showers, uneven stairs, electrical cords or loose items on the floor or stairs, poorly lit areas, climbing step-stool or ladder to reach items on high shelves, chairs without armrests, cracked pavement, and icy sidewalks in winter.**

  Environmental hazards cause approximately one-third of all falls. Seventy-five percent of falls in the elderly occur indoors. A large number of falls occur when the elderly trip over an object while walking or slip when getting up from sitting. Environmental safety may require modifications of the bathroom, stairs, kitchen, family room, and bedroom.

  Consider eliminating throw rugs or at least secure their edges with double-sided tape or safety strips. Replace tattered, frayed, or curled-up carpeting. Repair cracked tiles and uneven wood floors. Do not wax floors, and avoid wet floors. Be aware of thresholds and uneven flooring. Install handrails on both sides of the stairs. Curl up and tuck away loose electrical and telephone cords. Consider a portable phone that has no wires to trip over. Install safety bars (sometimes called "grab bars") above the bathtub, in the shower, near the toilet and on walls near the bathtub or shower for stability when stepping into and out of the tub or shower. A handbar can be attached to the tub by pressure bolts if necessary to assist as well. If you are too weak to stand to take a shower or cannot get in and out of the bathtub, install a non-skid chair with arms to use as necessary. Install non-skid strips or a non-skid rubber mat in the tub or shower. All of these required items can be purchased at your local medical supply store.

Remove clutter from the floors and stairs and remove any chairs or furniture that may be a potential obstacle in a commonly used traffic area. Keep clothing off the floors as it might be a potential item to trip over. Keep stairwells well lit. If light bulbs are

 burned out, replace them and keep installed night lights in several strategic locations as guides when you are semi-awake at night and have to go to the bathroom. Keep a flashlight next to your bed for use when necessary

Keep readily used food and other frequented items in easily accessible low shelves, not up high where you may need a step-stool to reach them. Chairs with armrests provide you a stable support for getting into and up from the chair. Repair all cracked or uneven pavement and be especially careful in cold, icy weather. In inclement weather use warm boots with rubber soles for increased traction and use a walker or cane as extra insurance against falling.

■ **Transferring to or from a chair, wheelchair, bed, tub, or toilet increases your risk of falling.**

Transfer with caution and, if necessary, with aid and support.

Minimizing the Risk of Osteoporosis from Secondary Risk Factors

Secondary risk factors should be minimized by adequately controlling or eliminating them. For example, insulin-dependent diabetes mellitus type 1 should be tightly controlled, thyroid replacement therapy should be monitored closely for correct dosage, COPD treatment should be optimized, and aluminum-containing antacids should be discontinued.

The most common cause of secondary osteoporosis is chronic use of corticosteroids, now commonly called glucocorticoid-induced osteoporosis (GIO or GIOP). Whenever possible, the lowest dose of corticosteroid (such as prednisone) should be used for treatment of rheumatoid arthritis, COPD, sarcoidosis, or other diseases. Whenever possible, corticosteroids should be discontinued.

All secondary causes of osteoporosis should be addressed and adequately treated to the fullest extent possible. (See Chapter 1—*Secondary Causes of Osteoporosis.*)

Other risk factors, such as low calcium and vitamin D intake, lack of exercise, and estrogen deficiency are explored in detail in the following chapters.

An Essential Partnership

To identify and achieve optimal prevention of and treatment for osteoporosis, it is critical that you work in partnership with your physician or professional health care provider. Only then can the risks be properly evaluated and a treatment plan put into place that will ensure that your bones' health is maintained and strengthened.

A Partnership with Your Health Professional
A professional health care provider works with an osteoporosis patient to develop an effective treatment plan.

Points to Remember

- With effective preventive and treatment methods, weak, brittle bones can become strong, hard bones.

- It is never too late to prevent and treat osteoporosis.

- All individuals at risk for osteoporosis, and all individuals with osteoporosis, should stop smoking immediately as a treatment measure.

- There is a strong correlation between alcohol abuse and osteoporosis.

- For optimal bone and physical health, maintain a limited caffeine intake.

- Due to age-related bone loss, most women and many men in their seventies are at risk for fractures from falls.

Chapter 4 Bibliography

1   Massey, L.K. and T. A. Berg, The Effect of Dietary Caffeine on the Urinary Excretion of Calcium, Magnesium, Phosphorus, Sodium, and Potassium in Young Healthy Females. Nutrition Research 4 (1984): 43–50.

2   Barger-Lux, M.J., R. P. Heaney, and M.R. Stegman. Effects of Moderate Caffeine Intake of the Calcium Economy of Premenopausal Women. American Journal of Clinical Nutrition 52 (1990): 722–725.

3   Ray, N. F, et al,. Journal of Bone and Mineral Research 12(1), 1997.

    Consensus Development Conference, American Journal of Medicine 94, 1993. Riggs, B.L. and Melton, L.J. III, Bone 17(5), 1995

    U.S. Congress, OTA, Hip Fracture Outcomes..., OTA-BP-H-120, 1994.

    Cummings, S. R., et al., Archives of Internal Medicine 149, 1989.

4   Tinneti, M. E., M. Speechley, and S. F. Ginter. Risk Factors for Falls Among Elderly Persons Living in the Community. New England Journal of Medicine 319 No. 26 (December 1988): 1701–1707.

5   Rubenstein, L. Z., K. R. Josephson, and D. Osterweil. Falls and Fall Prevention in the Nursing Home. Clinical Geriatric Medicine 12, No. 4 (November 1996): 881–902.

6   Graafmans, W. C. et al. Falls in the Elderly: A Prospective Study of Risk Factors and Risk Profiles. American Journal of Epidemiology 143, No. 11 (June 1996): 1129–36.

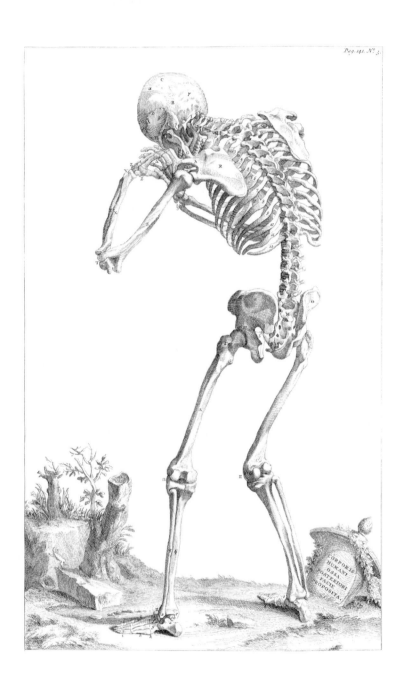

CORPORIS
HUMANI
OSSA
POSTERIORI
FACIEI
PROPOSITA.

Those All-Important Vitamins And Minerals

Calcium

Role of Calcium in the Body

Calcium phosphate crystals deposited in a collagen matrix are the major determinant of a bone's strength (85% of its strength). Bone is made up of a structural framework anchored by a protein called collagen. This collagen matrix (called collagen type 1) provides 35% of the volume of bone. The rest is supplied by bone minerals, of which calcium phosphate crystals are the major component (Others to a lesser degree include trace minerals, fluoride, sodium, potassium, citrate, and others). Calcium phosphate crystals provide strength and hardness to the structural framework just as bricks provide the strength to the wall of a brick home.

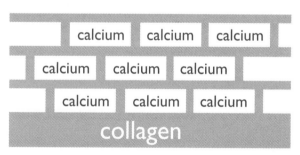

Bricks and Mortar
Calcium gives a bone its strength.

■ **The initial treatment of all osteoporotic individuals must begin with adequate calcium and adequate vitamin D intake, otherwise, bone building cannot take place. All treatments of osteoporosis will not be of optimal benefit unless calcium and vitamin D are sufficient.**

Ninety-five percent of the body's calcium is in your bones (Of the remaining calcium, approximately 4% is in the teeth and 1% in the blood). In addition to providing strength to your bones, adequate calcium is necessary for your muscles to contract, your heart to beat regularly, your nerves and brain to function properly, your kidneys to operate, your teeth to be hard, and your blood to clot.

Because calcium is so vital to life-functioning processes, nature has installed a regulatory mechanism within the body for its supply, demand and balance to vital tissues and bone.

Bone Bank Account

■ **Your bones are like a bank savings account for calcium. If your calcium supply is adequate, savings deposits are made and your calcium bone bank account builds up. If your dietary calcium intake is low, then your body makes withdrawals of calcium from your bones. If you have insufficient calcium funds in your bone bank account, you've "bounced your account," and you may have to pay up with a fracture.**

Calcium tends to be stored in your bones during the day and slowly released during the night. Various factors affect this dynamic, homeostatic equilibrium including parathyroid hormone, blood calcium level, calcitonin hormone, and vitamin D.

The parathyroid hormone maintains an adequate calcium level in the blood. If the blood calcium level falls, then your parathyroid glands (four glands in the neck behind the thyroid gland) secrete parathyroid hormones to stimulate the supply areas of your body to keep the calcium level adequate, supplying life-giving tissues such as your brain and heart. The parathyroid hormone simulates the withdrawal of calcium from the bone to supply the calcium for life-preserving vital functions.

Your body requires adequate daily calcium because it cannot produce calcium. It is entirely dependent on the calcium consumed in the foods you eat. The body does not distinguish if this elemental calcium comes from food sources or is supplied as calcium supplements. Dietary means, however, are generally considered the best method of obtaining calcium.

Calcium-rich food sources include milk, yogurt, cheese, ice cream, tofu (soy bean), dark green leafy vegetables (broccoli, soybeans, collards, kale, turnip greens, bok choy), fish and shellfish (oysters, sardines with bones, salmon with bones, shrimp), almonds, eggs, cornbread, and calcium-fortified foods such as bread, cereals, and orange juice.

Orange juice fortified with calcium is a particularly good source of calcium, especially for individuals who cannot or will not drink

Calcium Content of Foods

Food or Beverage — **Approximate Calcium (milligrams)**

Milk Products
Milk (whole, 3.3%, I cup) 290
Milk (low fat, 1%, I cup) 300
Milk (skim, I cup) 300
Buttermilk (I cup) 285

Cheeses
American (pasteurized process, I cup) 175
Cheddar (I oz.) 205
Cottage (large curd, creamed, 4%, I cup) 135
Cottage (low fat, 2%, I cup) 155
Mozzarella (part skim, low moisture, I oz.) 205
Swiss (I oz.) 270

Yogurt
Plain (low-fat, 8 oz.) 415
Plain (nonfat, 8 oz.) 450

Desserts
Ice milk (vanilla, hardened, 4% fat, I cup) 175
Ice cream (vanilla, hardened, 11% fat, I cup) 175
Sherbet (about 2% fat, I cup) 100

Poultry
Chicken breast (roasted, skinless, 3.5 oz.) 15
Chicken breast (roasted, with skin, 3.5 oz.) 14
Turkey (light meat, roasted, skinless, 3.5 oz.) 19
Turkey (light meat, roasted, with skin, 3.5 oz.) 19

Eggs
One egg (large) 25

Meat
Roast beef (eye round, lean and fat, 3 oz.) 5
Roast beef (eye round, lean only, 2.6 oz.) 3
Ground beef (lean, broiled, 3 oz.) 10
Ground beef (regular, broiled, 3 oz.) 10
Pork chop (loin broiled, lean and fat, 3.1 oz.) 3
Pork chop (loin broiled, lean only, 2.5 oz.) 5
Lamb (leg, lean and fat, 3 oz.) 8
Lamb (leg, lean only, 3 oz.) 6

Fish and Shellfish
Flounder (baked, no added fat, 3 oz.) 15
Salmon (red, baked, 3 oz.) 25
Trout (rainbow, broiled, 3 oz.) 75
Salmon (pink, canned, with liquid and bones, 3 oz.) . 170
Tuna (canned in water, solid white, 3 oz.) 1
Lobster (steamed or boiled, 3 oz.) 50
Shrimp (steamed or boiled, 3 oz.) 35
Sardines (canned with bones, 3 oz.) 170

Calcium Content of Foods (continued)

Food or Beverage	Approximate Calcium (milligrams)
Nuts	
Almonds (whole, 1 oz.)	65
Vegetables	
Broccoli (1/2 cup)	50–60
Collard greens (1/2 cup)	130
Kale (1/2 cup)	85
Spinach (1/2 cup)	85
Carrots (1/2 cup)	25
Okra (1/2 cup)	75
Beans	
Tofu (1/2 cup)	130
Snap beans (1/2 cup)	30
Lima beans (1/2 cup)	30
Black beans (1/2 cup)	30
Lentils (1/2 cup)	25
Pinto beans (1/2 cup)	50
Other	
Macaroni and cheese (1/2 cup)	180
Waffle (homemade)	180
Orange (medium)	50
Calcium-fortified 100% orange juice (8 fl. oz.)	300
Cooked brown rice (1/2 cup)	10
Cooked oats (1/2 cup)	20

milk. Many elderly have an enzyme deficiency (lactose dehydrogenase, also known as lactase, the enzyme required to digest lactose) and cannot tolerate milk. They are known as lactose-intolerant and will get nausea, gas, bloating, intestinal cramps, and diarrhea if they take in milk or milk products. Lactose-intolerance is much more common than previously thought and seems to increase with advancing age.

Many teenagers will not drink milk, so orange juice fortified with calcium is an excellent alternative for providing them with daily calcium and other essential vitamins and minerals as well.

■ **For most individuals, milk and milk products provide most of the calcium in their diets.**

Low-fat foods such as low-fat or skim milk, low-fat cheese, and low-fat yogurt, are preferable for those who need to regulate their daily intake of fat.

Adequate calcium is absolutely essential to the maintenance of bone's strength and the prevention of osteoporosis-related fractures. Osteoporosis is really a nutritional disease that begins in childhood and adolescence; thus, the age at which you should begin aggressively preventing osteoporosis is not during the golden years but rather during the younger years when you are building strong bones. Education regarding prevention should begin in the pediatrician's and family practitioner's office.

Studies have shown that increased calcium in the diet of children and adolescents results in increased bone mineral density, stronger bones and fewer fractures. Eating a diet with adequate calcium or possibly adding a calcium supplement to your routine in the developing years may increase the bone mineral density a few points, which may be crucial in the prevention of a potentially fatal hip fracture later in life.

Since approximately 90% of your peak bone mass is accumulated when you reach the age of 18, and 100% of peak bone mass is reached by the age of 30, preventive measures should begin in the early formative years and continue throughout your lifetime.

■ **Clinicians universally agree that the single most important thing you can do to prevent and treat osteoporosis is to obtain adequate daily calcium and vitamin D.**

Calcium Intake Recommendations

Daily calcium recommendations are based on total requirements including dietary sources and supplementation. The percentage of minimum daily requirement, which is used for comparison on labels of foods and vitamins in the United States, is based on a daily requirement of 1000 mg/day. The U.S. RDA is an abbreviation for the United States Recommended Daily Allowance that used to be found on labels of packaged foods. This was based on a U.S. RDA for calcium of 1,000 mg. This means that if a packaged food said it contained 25% of the recommended U.S. RDA, it contained 250 milligrams of elemental calcium. This did not mean that amount was adequate for everyone. It was a reference point only.

% Daily Value* has replaced the U.S. RDA on the Nutrition Facts labels of packaged foods as of 1994. This is the recommended amount required daily based upon a 2,000 calorie diet. Your particular needs may be higher or lower. At the bottom of the label is the value of nutrients for a 2,500 calorie diet as well.

Nutrition Facts

All packaged foods now must have a label indicating the "Nutrition Facts." By comparing the labels, you can make informed choices and can choose foods highest in calcium. To calculate how much calcium the food contains, simply add a "0" onto the % Daily Value* calcium percentage. (Example, 30%=300 mg of calcium; 25% =250 mg.)

Nutrition Facts	
Serving Size 8 fl. oz. (240 mL)	
Servings per container about 4	
Amount per serving	
Calories 130 Calories from Fat 35	
	% Daily Value*
Total Fat 4g	**6%**
Saturated Fat 0.5g	2%
Cholesterol 0mg	**0%**
Sodium 105mg	**4%**
Potassium 440mg	**15%**
Total Carbohydrate 13g	**4%**
Sugars 7g	
Protein 10g	**20%**
Vitamin A 30% • Calcium 20%	
Iron 10% • Vit D 10% • Vit E 25%	
Thiamin (B1) 10% • Riboflavin (B2) 4%	
Niacin (B3) 4% • Pantothenic Acid (B5) 6%	
Pyridoxine Hydrochloride (B6) 8%	
Folate (B9) 10% • Vitamin B12 50%	
Biotin (Vit H) 4% • Phosphorus 15%	
Magnesium 15% • Zinc 6%	

Not a significant source of dietary fiber, Vitamin C.
* % Daily Values are based on a 2,000 calorie per day diet. Your needs may be higher or lower depending on your calorie needs:

	Calories	2,000	2,500
Total Fat	Less than	65g	80g
Sat Fat	Less than	20g	25g
Cholesterol	Less than	300mg	300mg
Sodium	Less than	2,400mg	2,400mg
Potassium		3,500mg	3,500mg
Total Carbohydrate		300g	375g
Dietary Fiber		25g	30g
Protein		50g	65g

Nutrition Facts

By drinking 8 fluid ounces of this, you are consuming 200 milligrams of calcium.

The National Institute of Health (NIH) consensus development conference [June 1994] developed recommendations for optimal calcium intake from diet and supplements.

Adequate calcium intake is absolutely fundamental for osteoporosis prevention and treatment. Up to 2,000 mg/day supplementation is considered safe; however, 1,500 mg/day in divided doses is generally the maximum advised.

Although the exact amount of calcium required daily for optimal health may vary from person to person, the bottom line is that most Americans do not consume enough calcium in their diets. In fact, over 50% of women and adolescent girls take in less than half the

Age	Amount of Calcium (milligrams per day)
Adult women	
25–50 years (premenopausal)	1,000
50–54 years (postmenopausal taking estrogen)	1,000
50–64 years (postmenopausal not taking estrogen)	1,500
65 years and older	1,500
Pregnant or nursing	1,200–1,500
Adult Men	
25–64 years	1,000
65 years and older	1,500
Adolescents and Young Adults	
11–24 years	1,200–1,500
Children	
1–5 years	800
6–10 years	800–1,200
Infants	
Birth–6 months	400
6 months–1 year	600

National Institute of Health (NIH) recommendations for daily calcium intake

calcium required by their bones.[1] Only 14% of teenage girls obtain the recommended daily amounts of calcium.

For all too many teenagers, consumption of milk and other dairy products has been replaced by cola and other sugar-laden carbonated beverages. Not only are they not getting enough calcium, but this increased intake of cola drinks is often accompanied by an increased intake of processed foods with phosphorous additives and red meat. Foods containing excessive phosphorous tend to decrease bone mineral density. It is postulated that this may be through an increase in urinary calcium excretion, although the exact mechanism is not understood. For this reason, it is best to avoid excessive colas, salt, caffeinated beverages, processed foods with phosphorous additives, and a diet high in protein such as red meats because these cause excessive amounts of calcium to be lost in urine.

As mentioned in Chapter 1, peak bone mass is reached at approximately the age of 30. After that, there is a gradual decline of 1% bone mass per year. It is critical to slow this process of bone loss by maintaining an adequate calcium intake as an adult. If not, less calcium will be absorbed into the blood stream, which will result in an increase in the parathyroid hormone, which results in calcium being removed from the bone. The result will be a decrease in bone mass density. When calcium levels are increased to normal, e.g., by supplementation, the parathyroid hormone will no longer be secreted, and thus calcium will no longer be removed from the bones at an increased rate.

Factors Affecting Calcium Absorption

Age

With age the absorption of calcium in the intestine decreases. Approximately 75% of calcium is absorbed during adolescence, 50% is absorbed as an adult, and 30% is absorbed in the elderly.

Many factors associated with aging, particularly decreased gastric acid production and various disease states, affect absorption. You may be taking in lots of calcium, but that doesn't mean you're absorbing an adequate supply of calcium.

These Two Teenagers absorb about 75% of their dietary calcium.

As Adults they will absorb about 50% of their dietary calcium.

When Elderly, they will absorb about 30% of their dietary calcium.

Certain Medications

Calcium absorption is decreased when taking certain medications. Individuals under treatment with stomach H2 inhibitors (Zantac®, Pepcid®, and Tagamet®) and proton pump inhibitors (Prevacid®, Aciphex®, and Prilosec®) must keep in mind that they may have decreased absorption of calcium. For most of these individuals, the calcium citrate form of calcium supplement such as Citracal® is preferred because the citrated form of calcium is not dependent upon stomach acid for absorption, and it can be taken with or without meals. All forms of calcium should be taken with 6 to 8 ounces of water or other fluids to help to maximally dissolve the calcium tablet in order that it will be absorbed.

Divided Dosage

Calcium is best absorbed if taken in divided doses, preferably no more than 600 mg at a time for maximum absorption. Most calcium is completely absorbed in the small intestine within four hours of taking it. The calcium citrate form of supplement can be taken at any time, with or without meals, and does not need gastric acid for absorption.

Absorption Needs

The calcium carbonate forms of calcium should be taken with meals because they need gastric acid for absorption. Individuals with decreased stomach acid absorb approximately 4% of calcium in the calcium carbonate form but absorb almost 50% of calcium in the calcium citrate form.

Most over-the-counter calcium supplements are in the form of calcium carbonate such as Caltrate®, Os-Cal®, and Tums®. As mentioned above, the calcium citrate form of supplements can be taken at any time, with or without meals, and does not need gastric acid for absorption.

Certain Foods

Some food items contain high amounts of oxalates which can inhibit calcium absorption by binding to calcium in the intestine and forming a non-soluble salt which is passed out with a subsequent bowel movement. Some of these high oxalate foods are rhubarb, spinach, beet greens, and almonds.

Some foods such as wheat bran and legumes (peas, pinto beans, and navy beans) contain high amounts of phytates that can inhibit calcium absorption.

These foods which contain oxalates and phytates should not be eliminated from your diet because they contain other nutrients and vitamins and minerals which your body requires. In moderate amounts they impair calcium absorption, not prevent it.

Vitamin D3

Vitamin D3 is necessary for your intestinal tract's absorption of calcium (see the following section). 400 to 800 IU/day of Vitamin D3 is generally recommended, and most multivitamins, e.g., Centrum®, have 400 IU's. Many forms of calcium are now available in combination with vitamin D3 such as:

- Citracal®+D caplet (calcium 315 mg + vitamin D3 200 IU),
- Caltrate® 600+D tablet (calcium 600 mg + vitamin D3 200 IU)
- Caltrate® 600+D chewable (calcium 600 mg + vitamin D3 200 IU)
- Os-Cal® 250+D tablet (calcium 250 mg + vitamin D3 125 IU)
- Os-Cal® 500+D tablet (calcium 500 mg + vitamin D3 200 IU)
- Viactiv® Soft Calcium Chew (calcium 500 mg + vitamin D3 200 IU)

Problems With Calcium

Many of the very elderly have difficulty swallowing large pills. Fortunately, several delivery forms of calcium are available. For example, Citracal® comes in a pill (calcium 200 mg) or caplet (calcium 315 mg) that must be swallowed, and it is also available as Citracal Liquitab® (calcium citrate 500 mg) which is dissolved in a glass of water. Alternatively, Caltrate® 600 (calcium 600 mg) comes in a tablet that must be swallowed and also is available in a chewable form. Viactiv® (calcium 500 mg + vitamin D3) is a soft calcium chew available in various flavors. Chewable and liquid calcium supplements dissolve easily and are broken down before they enter the stomach.

Calcium must be started at a low dose—no more than 500 to 600 mg/day for one week, and then if it is tolerated, it can be increased gradually to 1000 to 1200 mg/day in divided doses (i.e., 500 mg with breakfast and 500 mg with dinner) for another week or two. If the daily required supplement amount is 1500 mg/day, it can be increased gradually to this amount.

Despite this gradual increase, fluids may have to be increased to prevent side effects such as constipation or intestinal gas. Sometimes the addition of daily juice can help, or eating a high fiber food such as oatmeal or bran can prevent a problem. Sometimes a fiber supplement is required such as Metamucil® or Citrucel®, although Metamucil often tends to cause more gas than Citrucel. If the calcium carbonate form of calcium is giving you gas or causing uncomfortable constipation, then try switching to the calcium citrate form of calcium.

In the past, certain preparations of calcium from dolomite, bone meal, and unrefined oyster shells had significant contamination with lead. Some investigated by the National Resources Defense Council

(NRDC) contained more than the federal limit of lead per 1,000 mg of calcium. Since then, manufacturers have agreed to manufacture calcium supplements containing 0.5 micrograms or less of lead.

More than 2,000 mg per day of calcium is not recommended because it may increase the incidence of kidney stones in individuals prone to developing them. If you have a history of kidney stones, consult your physician before taking large amounts of calcium. If you have had kidney stones, calcium citrate is the preferred form of calcium for you. In individuals with no history of kidney stones, high calcium intake only rarely causes kidney stones.

Calcium can decrease your ability to absorb iron by as much as 50%, so it is best not to take calcium and iron supplements at the same time or within two hours of one another.

Calcium can also interfere with the absorption of certain medications. For example, it decreases absorption of tetracycline. Any medication that needs to be taken on an empty stomach should probably not be taken with a calcium supplement. If in doubt, consult your physician or pharmacist. Aluminum, in large amounts, can be harmful to bone. Some antacids contain calcium with aluminum and should be avoided.

Types of Calcium Supplements

The chemical nature of calcium mandates that it always be "attached" to something else, and when this is the case, it is referred to as a calcium salt (not to be confused with table salt). Our bodies are concerned with the elemental calcium, and references to calcium intake refer to elemental calcium. The type of calcium salt the elemental calcium is attached to, however, may determine the ease with which the calcium is absorbed and the type of side effects that may occur.

Calcium Carbonate

Calcium carbonate is the most common form of calcium available on the market and is included in supplements such as Os-Cal®, Tums®, Caltrate®, and Viactiv®. Since calcium carbonate is a mixture of elemental calcium in a calcium carbonate form of compound, calcium carbonate actually contains only 40% elemental calcium. In other words, 1000 mg of calcium carbonate contains only 400 mg of elemental calcium. Calcium carbonate supplements are usually derived from limestone rock, or oyster shell powder.

As mentioned earlier, *calcium carbonate is best taken with meals because it needs gastric acid for absorption.* Supplementation with calcium carbonate is best absorbed if taken no more than 500 to 600 mg at a time. In other words, if you are going to take a total supplement of 1200 mg per day, it is best taken as 600 in the morning with breakfast and 600 in the afternoon with dinner. This twice a day regiment gives much better absorption than once a day.

Generic calcium supplements are inexpensive and easily available, and most are in the calcium carbonate form. The absorption and bioavailability of these varies; however, they can be tested to see whether or not they will absorb properly. Place a tablet in 6 ounces of white vinegar. Stir it occasionally. The tablet should dissolve within 30 minutes. If it does not, it will not disintegrate and dissolve in your stomach, either. Be sure to check the label on generic calcium to see exactly how much elemental calcium is in each tablet.

Calcium Citrate

Calcium citrate (i.e., Citracal®, Centrum® for Bone Health) does not need gastric acid to be absorbed, and thus it does not matter whether or not it is taken with a meal. This is usually the preferred form of calcium for the very elderly, since many elderly individuals have decreased gastric acid.

Calcium citrate is also the desired form of calcium for an individual to take if he or she has a history of kidney stones because this form of calcium does not precipitate out into the urine. If kidney stones are a concern, your doctor may order a 24-hour urinary calcium level, which checks the calcium in your urine, after one has been taking calcium supplementation for two weeks. Individuals who have a history of calcium oxalate kidney stones may be asked to have a urinary calcium check before calcium treatment begins and after two weeks of supplementation to see if excess calcium is being spilled into their urine with calcium supplementation. If excess calcium is being spilled into the urine, the amount of calcium should be reduced or a diuretic such as hydrochlorthiazide 50 to 100mg/day can be prescribed, which will help to prevent this.

Calcium citrate is 24% elemental calcium. In other words 1000 mg of the calcium citrate salt supplies 240 mg of elemental calcium.

Calcium Phosphate

Tribasic calcium phosphate (i.e. Posture®) and calcium diphosphate (e.g., Shaklee® sells a brand of this, and Dical-D®) are other options available. Calcium attached to phosphate is the naturally occurring type of calcium found in milk and dairy products.

Tribasic calcium phosphate is 39% elemental calcium. In other words, 1,000 mg of the tribasic calcium phosphate salt provides 390 mg of elemental calcium. Dibasic calcium phosphate is 30% elemental calcium. In other words, 1,000 mg of the dibasic calcium phosphate salt provides 300 mg of elemental calcium.

Calcium Lactate

Calcium lactate (i.e., Shaklee's Calcium Complex consisting of ground limestone [calcium carbonate], calcium lactate, and calcium gluconate with minerals [magnesium, zinc, copper, manganese] and sodium) is available but is not a common form of calcium supplementation. Calcium lactate is only 18% elemental calcium. In other words, 1,000 mg of calcium lactate salt supplies only 180 mg of elemental calcium.

Calcium Gluconate

Calcium gluconate (i.e., Shaklee's Calcium Complex consisting of ground limestone [calcium carbonate], calcium lactate, and calcium gluconate with minerals [magnesium, zinc, copper, manganese] and sodium; Calcet®, and Fosfree®) is available but not a common form of calcium supplementation. Calcium gluconate is only 9% elemental calcium. In other words, 1,000 mg of calcium gluconate salt supplies only 90 mg of elemental calcium.

Available Delivery Forms Meet Everyone's Needs

Calcium supplements come in various delivery forms to meet the specific needs of different individuals. They are available as tablets, capsules, caplets, soft-gels, liquitab effervescent (dissolves in water to be taken as a liquid), chewable tablets, and chews (i.e., Nature Made®'s Cal Burst Soft Chews). Some come in assorted flavors such as chocolate, caramel, or mocha (i.e., Viactiv® Chews). Calcium supplements are even available in various fruit flavors.

Calcium Supplements

Calcium supplements are available in combination with many other supplement options as well, particularly various minerals and vitamins associated with bone building such as vitamin D3, vitamin K, magnesium, zinc, manganese, copper, boron, and others. Some supplements of calcium include a combination with soy, and some multivitamins include extra calcium (usually 500 to 600 mg).

Calcium is also found in other products not necessarily used as a calcium supplement. For example, each caplet of Fibercon®, a laxative, contains 625 mg calcium polycarbophil.

Vitamin D

Role in the Body

Sunlight converts the inactivated form of vitamin D stored in your skin into the activated form of vitamin D. Vitamin D is also stored in the liver in a partially activated form (25 hydroxy-vitamin D3). Most of the body's vitamin D is in this form of vitamin D3 so this serum (serum 25-[OH] D level, also expressed as 25 hydroxy-vitamin D level), is the form of vitamin D measured in the blood if your physician should draw a sample of your blood to see if you have a vitamin D deficiency. When necessary, it is removed from the liver, carried through the blood stream to the kidney, and converted into 1,25 dihydroxy-vitamin D3, the activated form of vitamin D. This activated form enables calcium to be absorbed in the intestines and also stimulates your kidneys to reabsorb calcium from the urine and keep it in the blood stream. In this way, vitamin D has an important role in the homeostatic calcium balance mechanism within your body and the maintenance of a homeostatic calcium level in your bloodstream.

Sources of Vitamin D

Vitamin D is supplied to your body through the skin and through dietary intake in foods such as egg yolks, liver and saltwater fish. Plants contain vitamin D2, which is converted into vitamin D3 in your body. Most of the milk you drink is fortified with vitamin D. Your body requires only fifteen minutes of ultraviolet radiation per day in the form of sunlight to manufacture and store all the vitamin D you need.

Vitamin D Intake Recommendations

Researchers recommend you receive *400 to 800 IUs of vitamin D per day either from dietary means or from a supplement.* Studies have shown that if you are exposed to some sunlight, 400 IU vitamin D supplement per day is optimal. However, if you do not obtain adequate exposure to sunlight, 800 IU of vitamin D per day is required. *Most multivitamins contain 400 IUs of vitamin D.* The maximum recommended dose of vitamin D per day as a dietary supplement is 1,000 IUs. Supplementation in extreme excess can cause vitamin D toxicity with associated hypercalcemia and associated symptomatology.

Vitamin D Deficiencies

Individuals particularly at risk are those who reside in areas of the country where daylight hours are shortened in the wintertime, individuals who are hospitalized for extended periods of time, and individuals who may have a vitamin D deficiency in their diet. For these populations, a multivitamin is the best alternative to obtaining adequate vitamin D intake.

Vitamin D levels may also be decreased in individuals who have intestinal malabsorption syndromes and thus cannot absorb the water soluble vitamins A, D, E and K efficiently.

The elderly are particularly at risk, including those in nursing homes who often do not obtain adequate sunlight exposure or adequate nutrition. Vitamin D production also decreases in the elderly. Reduced dietary vitamin D, particularly if compounded with intestinal malabsorption of fats that frequently occurs in the elderly, can lead to serious vitamin D deficiency and calcium imbalance. The absorption of dietary calcium without vitamin D is approximately 15% to 20%; however, with adequate vitamin D, the efficiency of the intestinal absorption of calcium can be increased to as much as 60%.

Vitamin D deficiency in children causes a defect in bone formation called rickets. Vitamin D deficiency in adults can also cause the adult counterpart of rickets, a softening of the bones called osteomalacia.

There is strong evidence that the factors surrounding vitamin D deficiency are important in causing osteoporosis, and vitamin D deficiency is more common than formerly thought. A vitamin D3 level of 25 hydroxy vitamin D less than 20 mg/ml is generally considered low.

Some clinicians have suggested more detailed criteria regarding vitamin D nutritional status to define vitamin D deficiency, insufficiency, and sufficiency.[3]

Deficient: Serum 25-hydroxyvitamin D level of less than 10 ng/ml.

Insufficient: Serum 25-hydroxyvitamin D level of 10–20 ng/ml. Associated with increased serum levels of parathyroid hormone (PTH). (Note: Their high levels of PTH can be suppressed by vitamin D therapy).

Sufficient: Serum 25-hydroxyvitamin D level of greater than 20 ng/ml.

A recent study by LeBoff[2] et. al. found that 50% of postmenopausal women with hip fracture had inadequate vitamin D.

Some clinicians recommend that you take a supplement of 400 IU vitamin D (found in most multivitamins) if the serum vitamin D (25-(OH) D) level is >20 ng/ml. If the blood level is <20 ng/ml, a supplement of 800 IUs should be taken for several months and then a second blood level obtained to evaluate the adequacy of treatment. Some clinicians recommend that a supplement of 600 to 800 IU vitamin D be taken by everyone over 70 years of age. If in doubt, obtain a blood level of vitamin D.

Vitamin D is obtained in the diet through vitamin D fortified dairy products such as milk, egg yolks, saltwater fish, and liver. Most multivitamins contain 400 IUs vitamin D3, and many calcium supplements come in combination with vitamin D.

Other Vitamins and Minerals

Magnesium activates alkaline phosphatase, an enzyme involved in the formation of calcium crystals. It also appears that magnesium is required to convert the inactive form of vitamin D3 into the active form of vitamin D3. Up to 50% of magnesium in your body is found in your bones. Magnesium has also been shown to be of benefit to decrease the death rate from a myocardial infarction (heart attack).

The % DV (Daily Value) recommended of magnesium is based on 400 mg/day. Some nutritionists recommend up to 600 mgs/day. Magnesium deficiency is relatively common in the elderly. Many women in the United States consume low amounts of this mineral, particularly elderly women. Some studies have shown up to a 20% prevalence of hypomagnesemia. There is a high incidence in those with poor nutrition, and an increased incidence in individuals who have a history of alcohol abuse, diabetes, hypertension, asthma, and renal disease. Some calcium supplements contain magnesium. Magnesium is found in high amounts in dark-green, leafy vegetables, legumes, nuts, whole grains, and seafood.

Vitamin K is required for healthy bones and is involved in the syntheses of a bone protein called osteocalcin. Decreases in vitamin K are related to hip fractures. Vitamin K is best found in dark-green, leafy vegetables. In addition to containing about 160 mg of calcium and 400 IUs of vitamin D, most multivitamins contain about 25 mcgs of vitamin K.

Vitamin C (ascorbic acid) is essential in the formation of trabecular collagen. A deficiency in the bones weakens the trabecular cement-like proteins of connective tissue which form the internal supporting structure of bone.

Zinc may be involved in the biochemical action of vitamin D, or it may be involved in the regulation of bone turnover by affecting the production of calcitonin.

Copper may also be a co-factor involved in the formation of strengthening cross-linking collagen strands of bony matrix.

Manganese is necessary for bone mineralization, and as a result it is found in high concentrations in our bones. The optimal intake of manganese is not known but the % DV has been established at 2 mg/day. Manganese is found in high quantities in leafy vegetables, nuts, seeds, whole grains, and meats. Most multivitamins contain manganese.

Boron may play a role in the health of bones by increasing the natural occurring human estrogen 17 Beta-estradiol.

Strontium, which is mostly found in bones and teeth, may exert a beneficial effect by decreasing bone resorption.

Silicon may play a role in the bony matrix by strengthening the trabecula with cross-linking collagen strands and by playing a role in formation of the bones' protein matrix.

Folic acid has been found to improve bone health, particularly in menopause. Folic acid deficiency may occur in as much as 22% of the institutionalized elderly.

Pyridoxine (vitamin B6) may be a co-factor also necessary for the formation of connective tissue collagen strands.

Healthy bones require healthy eating habits. Even though America is the "land of plenty," eating the typical American diet does not ensure you are obtaining all the essential nutrients your body needs. The typical American diet is often deficient in calcium, vitamin D, magnesium, and possibly other vitamins and nutrients that may be necessary in small or trace quantities. This is because food sources such as corn, wheat, potatoes, carrots, and beans are grown in the same soil year after year, depleting the soil of the trace elements, minerals and some vitamins our bodies need.

I recommend that all my patients take a good multivitamin with minerals for the maintenance of healthy bones. Another reason that I typically recommend this is because many of the individuals I see with osteoporosis are elderly individuals who frequently have compromised eating habits and poorer absorption of nutrients from the gastrointestinal system. A multivitamin with minerals may help them to obtain adequate vitamins and trace minerals that may play smaller but important roles in the health of their bones.

Points to Remember

- Clinicians universally agree that the single most important thing an individual can do to prevent or treat osteoporosis is to obtain adequate daily calcium and vitamin D.

- Healthy bones require healthy eating habits.

Chapter 5 Bibliography

1   Abraham, S., et al. Dietary Intake Findings, United States 1971–1974. Hyattsville, MD: National Center for Health Statistics, 1977.

2   LeBoff MS, Hurwitz S., Franklin J., et al. Occult Vitamin D deficiency in Postmenopausal Women with Hip Fracture JAMA 1999;281:105–1511

3   Rao, D.S., Perspective on Assessment of Vitamin D Nutrition, ISCD 1999 Volume 2, Number 4, pp. 457–464

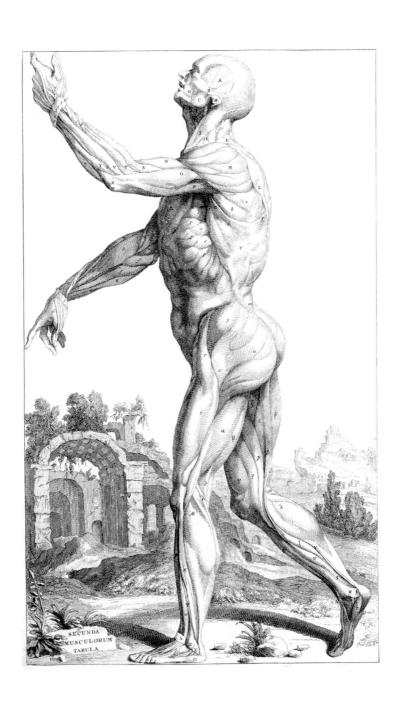

SECUNDA
MUSCULORUM
TABULA

If You Do Nothing Else—Exercise

Why Regular Exercise Is More Important Today Than Ever

Until recently, physical labor was the lot of the vast majority of humanity. Over the past half-century, however, the balance has shifted toward occupations and lifestyles that involve more mental than physical activity. In today's computerized, technological society, much labor is now accomplished by the push of a button. While the dishwasher or gas-burning furnace does the work, we sit in front of the television. The sitting that we do, however, is in part responsible for the tiredness that we complain of, the obesity many exhibit, and even the low back problems many have. It is also the prime cause of deconditioning.

The seductive trap of deconditioning caught most Americans unaware. The first shock came during the Korean War when a surprising number of young men couldn't pass the most elementary fitness test. Ten years later, President John F. Kennedy's Council on Physical Fitness was formed to develop and maintain basic standards of fitness among America's youth. Today there is an even greater awareness of the importance of regular exercise and physical fitness. But the problem is far from solved. According to the American Council on Exercise, only 50% of Americans do any type of exercise at all. While health spas are thriving and the sales of walking shoes, jogging suits, portable CD players and radios are booming, many Americans are still less fit than ever.

How important is exercise? Important enough for the nutritionist Paavo Airola to say that he would rather see a person eat junk food and exercise regularly than eat health food and not exercise! Airola was careful to explain he was not recommending that people eat junk food. He was saying, however, that without exercise, even the best diet can not be metabolized properly.

When the first astronauts went into space, a remarkable phenomenon was observed. Not only did the astronauts' muscle tissue atrophy because of their weightless condition, but their bone mass decreased rapidly as well. In other words, when we work against gravity, we condition and strengthen our bones.

From skeletons discovered in the mid-1700s and early 1800s, researchers have found that modern day pre- as well as postmenopausal women have lower bone densities at the hip than women of these earlier eras. This supports the theory that osteoporosis tends to be a disease of our modern civilization.

Considerations Before Beginning an Exercise Program

Before beginning a regular exercise program, find out if there are any conditions that could limit your activity or any problems that might cause a regular exercise program to be harmful to you. The American Heart Association says that 1% of men under the age of 35 and 10% of those over 35 have hidden heart disease. Although most of these conditions should not rule out exercise, it makes good sense to know as much as possible about your current physical condition. The newly revised American College of Sports Medicine Guidelines recommend a maximal exercise stress test for all seemingly healthy men over age 45 and women over age 55 before beginning an exercise program in which the individual exercises at 60% or more of their maximum capacity.

■ **Before starting an exercise program, consult with your physician or qualified health care provider.**

Consult your physician or professional health care provider and have an assessment of your cardiovascular fitness before beginning an exercise program if you have a family history of heart disease or hypertension, emphysema or chronic obstructive pulmonary disease, asthma, elevated cholesterol or triglycerides, obesity, smoking, diabetes, or any other potential risk factors. Your physician may want to perform a comprehensive history and physical examination, blood pressure check, complete blood count and comprehensive medical profile of tests, lipid (cholesterol and triglycerides) profile, urinalysis, EKG, a chest X-ray, exercise tolerance test, echocardiogram, and possibly other tests, depending upon your medical findings.

If you have any history or symptoms of dizziness or blackouts, you should see your physician for an evaluation and have a carotid ultrasound to check for plaque (arteriosclerosis) in the main arteries of your neck (carotid stenosis). Carotid plaque could decrease the flow of blood to your brain and cause you to experience a lightheaded feeling when you perform exercise movements and cause a possible fall with serious consequences such as a fractured hip, spine, or wrist.

Having a chronic disease such as osteoarthritis, rheumatoid arthritis and chronic obstructive pulmonary disease does not mean you should not exercise. In fact, if you are debilitated with chronic disease, you probably stand to benefit the most from a moderate exercise program.

Individualizing Your Program

An exercise prescription must be individualized to your particular needs. For example, if you are an athletic 5'4", 120 pound, 45-year-old healthy woman who has had a hysterectomy and bilateral ovariectomy, your exercises may be fairly intense with brisk walking and aggressive weight training.

On the other hand, if you are a 5'2", 180 pound, 55-year-old, inactive, postmenopausal woman with secondary degenerative osteoarthritis of your knees and chronic low back pain from degenerative disc disease of your lumbar vertebrae, your exercise program may be much less intense and tailored differently to avoid further damage to your knees and back. For you, an intense walking program may be impossible, only leading to more problems with your knees and back. You may have to forgo actual weight-bearing exercise in favor of a recumbent exercise bike. You may need to perform your weight training upper body muscle exercises while sitting so as not to further hurt your back and knees, and you may find it beneficial to pay more attention to the back flattening exercises to help alleviate your back pain.

Finally, if you are a 5'1", inactive, 100 pound, 72-year-old white female with a prominent dowager's hump, 3" lost height from kyphosis and scoliosis, lumbar compression fracture, are inactive and practically homebound, and have poor balance, and a hip T-score of –3.4, your exercise will be entirely different as well. You have minimal aerobic endurance, minimal muscle strength, and limited muscle mass from muscle wasting. Your exercise prescription will involve more stretching and balance exercises, with an emphasis on maintaining and gradually increasing mobility.

The variability of these three different exercise prescriptions is quite diverse in regards to program type, aerobic intensity, muscle toning and strengthening.

Also keep in mind that when beginning an exercise program your current activity level, health, and age will determine the intensity of your starting workout.

Abdominal Breathing is Essential When Exercising

An essential prerequisite for an optimally successful exercise program is relaxed, abdominal breathing. The yogis have known the value of proper breathing for centuries, and this is why abdominal breathing is the first thing learned in a yoga or meditation class. Musicians who play wind instruments, singers, and long distance runners all know the value of abdominal breathing.

Take a deep breath, then stop and examine your breath. Do you take the air in by expanding your chest or by expanding your diaphragm downward into your abdominal cavity? One way to find out is to look at your stomach. If on the inhale you look as if you are three months pregnant, you are using the abdomen properly. Breathing is not something that takes place solely in the chest but involves the entire abdominal cavity as well. Beginning to breathe through the abdomen may at first seem like trying to write with the left hand (or vice versa if you're left handed), but as you persist, it will come more and more naturally to you.

You might begin by imagining air coming into your lungs and inflating an imaginary balloon in your belly. Or you might actually visualize your diaphragm muscle pulling downward, and, as it does so, actually pulling air into your abdomen.

The main advantage of abdominal breathing is the vastly increased capacity to take in oxygen. The expansion of your rib cage actually accounts for only 10% of your lung's capacity, while the expansion of the abdominal wall (diaphragm muscle) downward accounts for 90%. It takes a lot of energy, relatively speaking, to expand the rib cage since each of the intercostal muscles must be used. The downward movement of the diaphragm, or belly breathing, takes much less energy and provides you with slower, more efficient, and more relaxed breathing. You move oxygen through your lungs and to the blood cells most efficiently when you fully use your diaphragm. If you have never been trained in abdominal breathing and can run one mile, chances are you will be able to run three to four miles after learning and practicing abdominal breathing. This is because abdominal breathing is efficient enough to increase your work capacity by three to four times.

A secondary benefit of abdominal breathing, one that is well known to those of you who practice yoga, is relaxation. People who hyperventilate (have rapid, shallow breathing) tend to use only their upper chest. Not only is this an inefficient way to breathe, but it causes and reinforces tension and anxiety. Among people who are anxious, tense, or nervous, the practice of slow, relaxed, abdominal breathing brings immediate, positive, relaxation results. Notice that as you relax you breathe more slowly. As your breathing slows to six to eight abdominal breaths per minute, your autonomic nervous system naturally places your body into a relaxed mode.

How To Learn Abdominal Breathing

It takes practice to integrate abdominal breathing into your everyday life. In my experience, daily practice for two to four weeks will make abdominal breathing your natural way of breathing, so natural you will no longer have to think about it. Once it is firmly established as a part of your life, however, you will find yourself more efficient in all areas of your life. You will have higher energy levels, feel more relaxed in the face of daily problems, and stress will no longer trigger the inappropriate conditioned bodily responses it once did.

Find a quiet place where you can be undisturbed for ten minutes twice a day. Do not practice within one or two hours after eating, as the alkaline tide will tend to make you too drowsy to practice. Be patient with the process; don't force it.

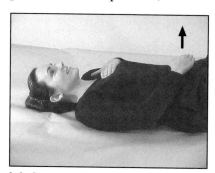

Inhale

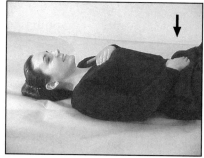

Exhale

Abdominal breathing demonstrated by Marci Burke from The Osteoporosis Testing Center of Michigan

Preferably, lie on your back. You may learn by sitting comfortably in a chair. Place one hand at your navel (belly button), the other on your chest. Take air into your abdomen. In doing so, your diaphragm will expand downward into the abdominal area. I ask patients to imagine as they breathe in that air is coming in through their nose and going into their belly so that it appears as if they are three months pregnant. Sometimes I tell them to imagine the air is going into an imaginary balloon in their belly.

As you inhale and expand the diaphragm downward, the hand on your belly will rise, and the hand on your chest will not move.

If the hand on your chest is rising, then you are using your intercostal rib cage muscles, and you need to practice until you can inhale into your belly without appreciably expanding your chest.

Exhale through the mouth. Let your jaw muscle (masseter muscle) relax and your mouth drop slightly open as it relaxes. It is generally recommended that you inhale through the nose and exhale through the mouth, but this is not essential at this stage. Your main focus at the beginning is in developing a natural rhythm and flow by focusing attention on the relaxed abdominal breathing. I find it helpful to purse my lips slightly, as this creates a backflow of air, slowing my exhalation. I teach my "chronic lungers" this method, and it's particularly beneficial. You may find it helpful to pause for a short moment after inhaling, then exhale slowly and completely, pausing again before the next breath. When you are breathing properly with your abdomen, exhalation, as a general rule, takes twice as long as inhalation. In other words, strive for a two (exhalation) to one (inhalation) rhythm. Get a sense of following your breath rather than focusing your breath into a rigid pattern. Do not force it, but rather let it happen. After a few weeks of steady practice, you will get the feeling you are *being breathed* rather than exerting any effort.

The twenty minutes or so a day you practice abdominal breathing may be one of the most valuable time investments you'll ever make towards better health. For example, if you're running late on your way to work and the light changes to red in front of you, take a few abdominal breaths and practice relaxing. If you are feeling agitated with a family problem or a problem at work, practice three slow, relaxed, abdominal breaths before proceeding. When learning abdominal breathing, you might train yourself to practice three slow, relaxed, abdominal breaths when your phone rings. Take every opportunity to practice. You will find that after two to four weeks you will automatically have incorporated more efficient abdominal breathing into your life.

After a few weeks, most individuals no longer need to practice regularly but instead use the technique automatically. As one patient said to me after learning this powerful breathing technique, "I don't know why God didn't make us breathe properly when he made us, but thank goodness this is something we can learn to do." But in fact, we were created to breathe properly. Notice that babies breathe with their abdomen.

Incorporating abdominal breathing into your life will not only help you have better physical health, it will also help you experience better mental health. In spite of living in modern civilization, our human autonomic nervous system is still set for *fight or flight* as it was millions of years ago. In response to acute stress, our senses heighten, our heart rate quickens, and adrenalin rushes through our bodies to prepare us for every contingency. The fight or flight response is appropriate for life and death situations but inappropriate for most everyday situations. Next time you are late for an appointment and find yourself stuck in a traffic jam, notice what goes on in your body. You probably experience tension at the base of your neck, forehead, and jaw as you slam on the brakes and begin to look for ways to make the traffic move faster. When your efforts fail, your tension and frustration mounts. Your jaw becomes tense, your brow furrows, your neck aches, your upper back (trapezius) muscle tightens, you feel pain in the lower arch of your back, and your stomach may even churn a little. As you become more emotionally upset and agitated, notice that you are experiencing rapid shallow breathing confined to your chest and upper rib cage.

It is only a traffic jam, a very insignificant incident in our lives, yet we are responding to the stressor as if we are facing down a saber-toothed tiger. The tiger is really not there to kill us, but our unchecked autonomic flight or flight response might. Most of us respond to the stresses and frustrations of daily life as if our survival were at stake. Our breathing is that of the fight or flight response because our autonomic nervous system is in a constant state of *red alert* from everyday stresses inherent in our modern, fast-paced everyday life.

Learning abdominal breathing and incorporating it into your everyday life as the normal way you breathe is literally a *breath of life.* Learning it before you begin a serious exercise program is akin to tuning up your car before going on a long trip. Although you do not absolutely have to use abdominal breathing when performing aerobic or muscle strengthening exercises, it makes sense to do so. The breath provides oxygen and thus the energy necessary to condition your body for optimal performance.

Warm Up

Have you ever noticed that your muscles feel stiff when you awaken in the morning or when you've been sitting for long periods of time? They are literally cold. Warming them up involves gradually increasing the blood flow to your muscles and getting them used to movement. This actually does increase the temperature of your muscles. If you exercise when your joints, ligaments, and muscles are cold, abruptly tensing them to their limits may tear some of the fine connective tissue fibers and cause strain, pain, inflammation, and possibly serious injury. This damage that can be seen if the tissue is put under a microscope is analogous to that caused by taking celery and bending it so that some of the fibers break.

None of us would ever get into our car on a cold morning and immediately rev up the engine to its maximum and drive away at high speed. Just like our car engine's moving parts needs to be warmed up when cold, so do the moving parts of our body: our muscles, tendons, and ligaments. Warming up our muscles before exercising greatly reduces the risk of soreness twelve to twenty-four hours after exercising. Even more importantly, it greatly reduces the risk of injury.

Warming your muscles, heart, and respiration may consist of a few minutes of light aerobic exercise such as walking with arm motion or a recumbent exercise bike (preferably with arm motion). Another very fine way to warm up is to go through the motions of your weight exercises without weights. This not only prepares your body physically for exercising but prepares you mentally for doing the exercises with the proper motion.

Stretching

After your warm up, you should proceed with gentle stretching. Stretching improves the flexibility of your muscle fibers. It improves your joints' range-of-motion, loosens them, makes them more pliable, and improves mobility so that when you exercise more vigorously they will not be damaged.

Correct stretching takes your joints, ligaments, and muscles through their full range-of-motion to improve flexibility in a mildly tense yet relaxed way. Stretching should never be jerky but rather slow and gentle, and last just until tissue resistance is met. You should hold the motion of a sustained stretch position for ten to thirty seconds with your attention centered on the muscle(s) being stretched. Move slowly and easily through your range of movement without jerking, bouncing (as in calesthenics), or straining. You want to elongate the muscles and ligaments while still feeling relaxed. Movement should be through but not beyond the range of motion or to the point of pain.

If a ligament, tendon, or muscle is stretched too fast or too far, a stretch reflex causes the muscles to automatically contract to prevent serious injury. Too much force and fine tears of the muscle fiber can occur, causing pain and even scar tissue if the injury is severe or the tissue repeatedly injured. It's analogous to the skin being cut or torn. The skin heals but leaves a fine scar. Correct stretching does not hurt. Your muscles should not be sore afterwards (only more pliable), feeling good and ready to do work.

The following examples are simple yet effective stretching exercises. Hold for 10 to 30 seconds. Do not hold your breath while stretching, but breathe freely with slow, relaxed, abdominal breaths.

1. Arms Overhead Stretch Upward

2. Arms Back Low Extension Stretch

3. Arms Overhead On Elbow Side Body Stretch

4. Total Side Body Stretch

5. Quadriceps Stretch

6. Calf Stretch with Arms on Wall

7. Triceps Stretch

8. Head Tilt Sideways and Arms Extended Back Stretch

Allow your slow, rhythmic, abdominal breathing to relax you. Allow each stretch to be effective yet effortless without strain. Hold each stretched position for 10 to 20 seconds, up to 30 seconds if you desire. Feel your muscles elongate. Then slowly relax with a smooth motion. Take a complete breath, then go on to the next stretch. If you desire, you may repeat a particular stretch. Obtain a complete slow stretch but without strain each time.

Another less common method of stretching includes taking a muscle to its maximum length (without weights) until minimum tissue resistance is met and holding it for 10 to 30 seconds. You might do this for each of the muscles you are going to exercise. For example, for the biceps flex the arm until you feel minimum tissue contraction of the biceps muscle and hold this for 10 to 30 seconds. Then go to the triceps and extend your arm until you feel minimum tissue resistance and until minimum contraction of the triceps muscle, then hold this for 10 to 30 seconds. Of course, you are actually stretching the opposing muscle for each exercise. For example, if you flex your arm for a biceps exercise, you will be stretching your triceps. Correspondingly, if you extend your arm, you would be stretching your biceps. Remember to focus your attention on the muscle(s) being gently stretched. If doing a full body exercise routine, this also imbeds the exercises you will do in your mind.

You may want to tailor your stretching to your type of exercise activity, age, posture, and fitness. For a detailed program, refer to *Stretching* by Bob Anderson (Shelter Publications). I highly recommend that you purchase this book.

Cool Down

A cool down consisting of light intensity aerobic exercise, i.e., slow walking followed by gentle range-of-motion stretching, should be done after moderately intense aerobic or muscle strengthening exercise. This allows your heart and lungs to slowly return to normal and your muscles, ligaments and joints to gradually return to their normal character. A stretching exercise must be included after any strenuous activity because exercise tends to shorten and tighten muscles. For example, running tends to shorten your lower back muscles, reducing their flexibility.

After exercise, higher levels of the hormone norepinephrine are present in your tissues. A cool down helps remove it, reducing soreness and tissue pain you might feel from vigorous exercise. Precipitously stopping exercise leaves blood pooled in your extremities, your heart racing, your blood pressure elevated, your lungs breathing more rapidly, and your body temperature elevated. It also leaves stagnant metabolic waste products including lactic acid in your tissues. (Note: When a muscle is exercised so that oxygen needs cannot keep up with its need for energy, nonoxidative metabolism to produce energy takes place and one of the major metabolic waste products of this is lactic acid, which causes muscle soreness). A slow cool down enables your heartbeat and respiratory rate to gradually slow, your blood pressure and temperature to lower gently, and lactic acid and other aerobic waste products to be removed.

Exercise To Prevent Osteoporosis And Maintain Bone Health

A moderate weight-bearing aerobic exercise (walking) program, in combination with moderate muscle-strengthening, balance, and posture exercises 3 to 5 days a week, should be a universal prescription for the prevention of osteoporosis.

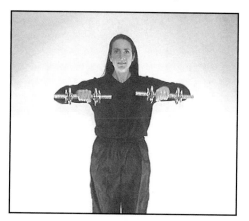

Exercising with dumbell weights

A good exercise program to build and maintain bone health incorporates both aerobic weight-bearing exercise and strength training exercise. Aerobic exercise exerts its most dramatic effect upon cardiovascular health (uses oxygen, improves heart and lungs) but has limited effect on muscle mass, strength, and bone density. Strength training, on the other hand, has a powerful, positive effect on increasing bone mineral density but less of an effect on aerobic cardiovascular fitness.

Better balance reduces fractures. For optimal prevention of fractures, your osteoporotic fracture prevention program should also incorporate balance exercises. How do most people fracture their bones? By falling, of course. Falls cause 90% of all fractures. While some aerobic and many muscle strengthening exercises using light weights improve balance, some exercises work specifically to improve this.

Risk of falling is lessened by improvement in muscular strength and improvement in flexibility, mobility, agility, loss of sway, balance, and neuro-muscular coordination.

Better posture decreases the possibility of deformity from thin or brittle bone. A kyphotic (stooped over, Dowager's hump) posture exerts considerable compressive force on the anterior (front) bodies of the vertebrae and frequently causes compressive deformities and fractures. This force is particularly magnified if you flex (bend forward) your spine. Thoracic vertebral compression fractures cannot only cause chronic pain, loss of height, and severe kyphosis of your spine but can also cause anatomical chest deformities with decreased chest expansion, secondary shortness of breath, and subsequent easy fatigability.

A lordotic (extended backwards) posture in the low back can magnify compressive deformities of the low back and, with little added force to thin or brittle bone, subsequently cause compression fractures of the lumbar vertebrae. This can be a cause of low back pain and lead to progressive immobility and a subsequent cycle of increased bone mineral density loss. Men and women alike who develop a "gut" or "belly" or "middle-age spread" of the abdomen are particularly prone to this. Weak abdominal muscles frequently contribute to the problem in combination with poorly developed lower back extensor muscles.

The optimal osteoporosis fracture prevention program includes the following:

1. Aerobic Weight-Bearing Exercise
2. Muscle Strengthening Exercises
3. Balance Exercises
4. Posture Exercises

Aerobic Weight-Bearing Exercise

Aerobic weight-bearing exercise 3 to 5 times a week not only strengthens your bones but also increases your muscle strength, improves your balance, and improves your mobility. Weight bearing exercises such as those involving various loading stresses on bone seem to work the best—in other words, exercise that forces you to work against gravity such as walking, slow jogging, hiking, stair climbing, and dancing. Non-weight-bearing exercises such as swimming and bicycling, while having excellent aerobic (cardiovascular) benefits, do not seem to give the same bone building benefits.

The reason weight-bearing exercise is emphasized over non-weight-bearing exercise is that it puts considerable mechanical stress on your hip and subsequently has dramatic influence on increasing your BMD at the neck of the femur. Since breaking your hip is the most dangerous of fractures, it makes sense that this would be the most important bone in the body for you to strengthen. While breaking your wrist, ankle, ribs, and vertebrae may be debilitating and painful, these fractures are usually not fatal. Weight-bearing exercise such as walking demonstrates positive increases in BMD in the hip and spine and subsequent decreases in both hip and vertebral fractures.

Moderate exercise stimulates osteogenesis (the formation of bone). When a muscle exerts tension on a bone, the bone formation cells are triggered to stimulate the formation of bony matrix. This builds bone. Sometimes we forget that bone is a living tissue just like the other tissues of our body, such as the muscles, connective tissues, heart, lungs, and others. Just as muscles are strengthened through exercise, bone is strengthened by exercise.

Some individuals are adamant about achieving aerobic target heart rate. Aerobic physiologists have determined that there is a training zone based on heart rate in which there is enough activity to produce aerobic cardiovascular fitness but not so much as to exceed a safe level. This training zone has been determined to be between 70% to 85% of your maximum heart rate. Your approximate training zone can be determined by this formula:

(220 minus age) x 70% = Lowest training heart rate

(220 minus age) x 85% = Highest training heart rate

For example, if you are a 50-year-old woman:

(220 minus 50) x 70% = 119 beats per minute (lowest training heart rate)

(220 minus 50) x 85% = 144 beats per minute (highest training heart rate)

If you are sedentary, not in good physical condition, and beginning an aerobic exercise program, then begin at 60 percent of maximum heart rate for the first few weeks. Again, if you are a 50-year-old woman, that would be:

(220 minus 50) x 60% = 102 beats per minute (beginning training heart rate)

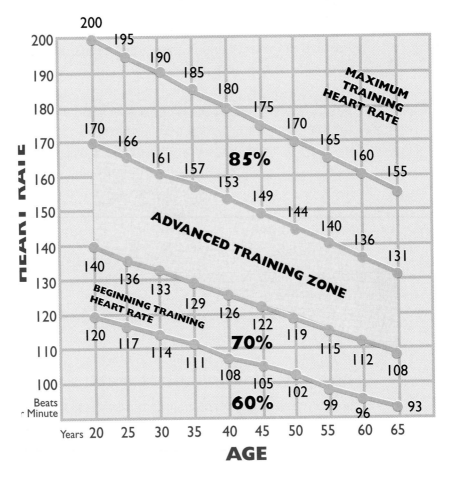

The most common locations for taking your pulse are at your wrist (radial artery) and at your neck (carotid artery). Using your watch, count your pulse for 10 seconds and multiply this by 6. This gives you your heart rate in beats per minute.

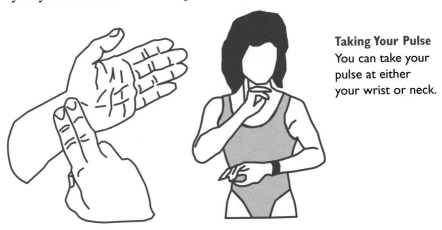

Taking Your Pulse
You can take your pulse at either your wrist or neck.

To take your pulse at your wrist, place your first two fingers just below the base of your thumb inside the wrist and slightly above the tendons running up the top of your wrist. Press lightly and move your fingers around until you feel the pulse of your radial artery.

To take your pulse at your neck, place two fingers on either side of your Adam's apple and move your fingers around until you find the pulse of your carotid artery.

Many of you reading this are, like myself, over the age of 50. I firmly believe that individuals over the age of 50 would probably find it in their best health interest not to take up impact exercises such as jogging, running, rope-skipping, or high-impact aerobics. In fact, it is my opinion that individuals beyond their natural physical peak at approximately age 30 to 35 should think twice before engaging in these activities on a regular basis. The reason—injury!

Impact activities such as running on a regular basis place severe stress on the balls of your feet, ankles, knees, and, of course, the low back. I speak from first-hand experience. I used to run 6 miles every other day and had this activity abruptly halted due to chronic pain in the ball of my foot (anterior metatarsalgia). It developed one winter when our Michigan snows forced me to run inside on an electric treadmill. The treadmill's elevation could be adjusted to increase the intensity of the workout, and as I did so, the pain developed. All my medical knowledge, medications, physical therapy, orthotics, injections, two orthopedic specialists, and a podiatrist specializing in sports injuries could not provide lasting relief. Over the next few years, my foot would feel better and then as soon as I'd start running again, it would flare up with intractable pain. The sports podiatrist summed it up best when he said, "Give up running. As you're getting older, your feet can't take the constant pounding."

Over my 25 years of medical practice, I've seen patient after patient with similar scenarios: knee pain, pain in the forefoot, heel spurs, pain in the medial arch, pain in the ankle, hip pain, and low back pain. In the older individual with a history of impact exercise activity earlier in life, the knee is the most common chronic painful joint I see in the office. The pain is usually located on the medial aspect of the knee in the major weight-bearing area (medial tibial tuberosity), and there is joint space narrowing from wear and tear of the cartilage.

So having been there, and done that over the years, I've developed a broader perspective as regards exercise. I believe that not only must we *Eat Fit for a Lifetime,* but also we must *Exercise Fit for a Lifetime.*

■ Exercise Fit For a Lifetime

In my opinion, the short-term benefits of daily high impact aerobic activities are not worth it when considering the lifetime wear and tear on your body. Rather, you must look for the long-term benefits of moderate exercise activity when exercising for a lifetime. Think of exercising as a long-term investment for your health rather than just a short-term gain for the day.

Walking seems to be the easiest and best aerobic (cardiovascular) weight-bearing exercise for most individuals to incorporate into their daily lives. Walking is one of the most natural exercises we can do. Sixty million Americans walk regularly for recreation and health.

Walking allows you to get your aerobic weight-bearing exercise while holding a conversation with your spouse, significant other, or friend; it enables you to think, take in fresh air, and enjoy the scenery. Walking is inexpensive, requires

Go for A Walk
Aerobic weight-bearing exercise, such as brisk walking for thirty minutes or more, is a great way to increase bone mass density of weight-bearing bones and improve cardiovascular fitness.

no special equipment, can be done almost anywhere, offers little risk of injury (unless you jaywalk or walk on a highway!), can be done any time and almost any place, and can be done without necessarily getting smelly and sweaty. Walking is appropriate for people of all ages, particularly if you are over 35, if you are obese, or if you are thin! And walking can easily be done even if you have been inactive for a long time. Even in inclement weather, you can walk in an enclosed shopping mall or at home on a manual or electric treadmill.

Take Steps to Care for Yourself

Walking can vary in intensity and length of time to fit your needs, from a brisk paced, four m.p.h., one-mile, fifteen minute "quickie" to a leisurely two m.p.h., three-mile stroll. Walking is also a way to relax, burn off stress, and clear your mind. Walking around the house picking up after the kids, or walking at work from your desk to the coffee machine or water cooler, is not considered aerobic exercise since it does not does not offer any measurable aerobic weight-bearing or cardiovascular conditioning benefit.

■ Walking is a step in the right direction for healthier bones

You respect someone who takes steps to take care of themselves. While walking may not necessarily be the best aerobic weight-bearing exercise, it is an exercise which practically everyone can do and is a step in the right direction for healthier bones.

Muscle Strengthening Exercise

Women and men of all ages, even in their nineties, can safely build bone using light weight muscle strengthening exercises. The two basic principles of osteoporosis prevention and treatment are to 1) minimize bone loss, and 2) maximize bone gains. Addressing the risk factors for osteoporosis minimizes bone loss. Light weight strength training exercise is one of the finest means known of building bone and maximizing bone mass and strength.

Muscle Strengthening Exercises build muscle strength, increase bone mass density, and improve balance, flexibility, and posture.

Strength training is a potent stimulator to improve your bone mineral density, muscle mass, and your muscle strength. It also improves your balance, leading to less falls and thereby less potential for fractures. Muscle strengthening improves your mobility, agility, coordination, and posture. Again, moderation must be emphasized. Light weight strength training is for fitness, not for body-building. Leave body-building to the Olympic athletes. For them, the axiom may be true: No pain, no gain. But this does not apply to the rest of us nor to moderate exercising with light weights for fitness. It's okay to feel challenged during muscle strengthening exercises but not pushed to or beyond your limits. Exercising for fitness should be invigorating, and when you finish exercising you should feel good, not exhausted from pushing your body to its limits of physical endurance.

The muscle strengthening program should concentrate on the three large muscle groups of your body:

Arms—upper extremity muscle groups including:
1. Biceps (front arm—flexes [bends] arm)
2. Triceps (back arm—extends arm)
3. Deltoid (shoulder) and teres major, minor, etc. (rotator cuff)
4. Pectoralis (anterior chest)

Abdominal and back—mid-muscle groups including:
1. Rectus abdominis, obliques (flexes forward abdomen—tightens and flattens stomach)
2. Erector spinae (extends lower back), trapezius, latissimus, rhomboids (upper back muscles)

Legs—lower extremity muscle groups including:
1. Quadriceps (front thigh—extends knee)
2. Hamstrings (posterior thigh—flexes knee)
3. Tibialis (front lower leg)
4. Gastrocnemius and soleus (posterior lower leg—Achilles)
5. Gluteus maximus (major buttock or "butt" muscle extends hip backward)
6. Iliopsoas and rectus femoris (flexes hip forward)
7. Gluteus medius, minimus, and tensor fascia latae (abducts out the leg)
8. Adductor magnus, longus, brevis, pectineous, and gracilis (adducts in the leg)

Studies have consistently shown that weight training is one of the very best means of increasing your bone density. A wide diversity of equipment is available at sports stores for in home use, and a larger array is available at various exercise facilities. Yet, a simple but complete program for this requires only light free weights consisting of dumbbells or a pair of small adjustable weight barbells and ankle weights. For convention, all references to dumbbells in this chapter also refer to small adjustable weight barbells. The exercises are the same, and the differences in the two entities is technical rather than a practical point that is important when exercising.

Small adjustable weight barbells (bars with adjustable weights on the ends secured by a collar) or dumbbells (bars with weight which cannot be changed) are relatively inexpensive and easily purchased at any sports equipment store. These are used for your upper body muscle groups. Small barbell weight increments may adjust from two to twenty pounds. If you are a female purchasing dumbbells, you will probably require 2, 3, 5, 8, and 10-pound dumbbells. As you progress in muscle strengthening, you may want to increase to 15 and occasionally 20-pound dumbbells. Dumbells are inexpensive, costing only 59¢–99¢ per pound. These can be more expensive if you purchase them in chrome and a with a storage rack.

A method of storage such as a vertical rack is recommended for two reasons. First, it keeps the dumbbells in a single secure place rather than possibly being scattered and a possible obstacle to cause a fall. And second, it keeps them about two feet off the ground so that there may be less chance of injury when you first pick them up to do a muscle-strengthening exercise. There is a tendency for many individuals when first beginning an exercise program to not fully stretch and warm-up and then to bend over from the waist rather than to bend the knees to pick up dumbbells from the floor. Many of you reading this are probably over 50 years old and have had some episode of back pain already if not some degree of low back degenerative disc disease. (Ninety-five percent of us will have back pain at one time or another in our lives.) So be careful and consider storing the dumbbells on a rack, and, of course, do not allow small children to get near or play with them.

Adjustable strap-on (velcro) ankle weights are relatively inexpensive and easily purchased at any sports equipment store. These are used for your lower body muscle groups. Purchase a pair of these with adjustable weight increments up to a total of 20 pounds for the pair (10 pounds each leg). They can be adjusted by removing weight from 2 to 10 pounds per leg. You may be tempted to buy a lighter set with fixed light weight from 2 1/2 to 5 pounds, but instead consider the 20 pound total pair adjustable set. While these lighter weights may increase the intensity of an aerobic exercise such as walking, running, or aerobic dancing, you will find they are not heavy enough for a muscle-strengthening program as you progress and your muscles become stronger. When exercising with ankle weights you will need to wear long legged exercise pants or high socks. If you strap ankle weights on bare skin, they may rub and cause a rash or break your skin and cause an abrasion.

A sturdy chair without arms, a mat for floor exercises, and a towel are required as well.

Various free-standing exercise strength-training gyms are available. These vary from one or two exercise stations to room-sized multi-station personal fitness systems costing $1,000 to $5,000. Home machines with adjustable weight stacks are generally preferred over those with resistance bands. As a band stretches, its resistance increases. This increased resistance can prevent you from following through with a full range of motion. Full range of motion when performing exercises is best so optimal flexibility may be obtained of your muscles, tendons, and ligaments. With free weights or free weight machines, resistance remains constant throughout the entire exercise so maximal range of motion is obtained.

Correct Form
Kris Beyer,
Certified
Personal Trainer
and Owner of
Kris' Physical
Evidence Fitness
Center in
Brooklyn, MI,
teaches
correct form.

Fitness centers and health clubs are located in most every city and provide a diverse choice of various equipment for a good muscle-strengthening program. Most provide a personal fitness trainer who can help you tailor a program to your needs.

A Sample Muscle Strength-Training Program

A typical total body program might include two 45-minute full body exercise sessions per week to include approximately:
- 5 minutes stretching and warm-up
- 35 minutes of 13 muscle-strengthening exercises consisting of 4 lower, 1 mid (abdominal-back), 4 upper, 4 balance exercises
- 5 minutes stretching and cool-down

Monday	Tuesday	Wednesday	Thursday	Friday	Saturday
Full Body			Full Body		
(upper, mid, lower)			(upper, mid, lower)		

Monday	Tuesday	Wednesday	Thursday	Friday	Saturday
Upper, Mid	Lower, Mid	Rest		Upper, Mid	Lower, Mid

A typical split (half) body program might include four 30-minute exercise sessions per week to include approximately:

- 5 minutes warm-up and stretching
- 20 minutes muscle-strengthening exercises, alternating days of exercising the upper and lower major muscle groups
- 5 minutes cool-down and stretching

Always allow a day of rest (48 hours) before rechallenging a muscle with another intense workout with weights to allow for full recovery of the muscles. This 48-hour recovery principle applies to intense training with weights, not to stretching or aerobic exercise such as walking, or to isometric exercises like the abdominal curl. These exercises can be done daily or even several times a day if desired.

Strength trainers refer to a complete movement as a lift. Reps (short for repetitions) are a repeated number of lifts. Sets are a certain number of reps, usually 8 to 12, but sometimes 6 when first beginning a program. For more advanced muscle strengthening, exercisers may perform up to 15 reps. Usually there is at least 15 seconds but sometimes up to 90 seconds of rest between sets. Rest until your muscles feel rested. There is no need to use a watch and no specific rest time between sets is "fixed in stone." For example, you might perform one set of 10 reps of biceps curls, rest for 15 to 90 seconds, and then perform a set of 10 reps of triceps extensions. Do not perform more than 15 reps, as this has been found to tire the muscles too much and results in diminishing returns in muscular strength and muscular endurance. When you are advanced in muscle-strengthening, increase to two sets of each exercise. As weeks progress and your lifting becomes easier as you become stronger, increase the weight of a specific exercise two or three pounds each time. All beginning exercisers should do only one set of each exercise, otherwise the exercise routine will get too long and you'll get discouraged and possibly stop the program. As you progress, you may increase to 2, and then possibly even 3 sets of each exercise. Your strength-training program should begin with lighter weight and a full range of motion, gradually increasing in weight as the weeks progress.

If you are just beginning an exercise program, then start with one set of exercises for each of the major muscles in the three major muscle groups: (1) upper body, (2) mid body back/abdomen, and (3) lower body. This results in at least 13 total sets for a full body exercise program. The reason for the emphasis on one set is because you have time to flow through your whole program this way. This is satisfactory for producing your goal of a moderate increase in muscular strength and endurance for physical fitness. If you really want to tone, shape and build a large muscle or group of muscles, then multiple sets up to three of 15 reps each of a particular exercise would be indicated. But if you want moderate muscle toning and strengthening for fitness, then one challenging set is adequate. The weight can be increased with increasing fitness. Remember, to prevent osteoporosis, focus on moderate muscle-strengthening, not body building.

An average free weight lift such as a biceps curl is done slowly, focusing on the isolated muscle being exercised and taking approximately 7 to 9 seconds:

- 3 to 4 seconds to contract the biceps muscle and slowly raise the weight (called concentric phase)
- 1 second pause (called isometric phase; muscle is held at peak contraction)
- 3 to 4 seconds to relax the biceps muscle and slowly lower the weight (called eccentric phase; muscle contraction is slowly released)
- Relax 2 to 3 seconds then repeat

Breathe out with slightly pursed lips when contracting the muscle to lift the weight, and breathe in with a deep slow relaxed abdominal breath when returning to the relaxed starting position. Develop a rhythm with your abdominal breathing and the lifts. If you find yourself holding your breath as you exercise, then notice this and focus on a slow, relaxed abdominal breath while lowering the weights to relax and return to the starting position. Focus upon a rhythm of exhalation through your mouth with slightly pursed lips as you raise the weight, and focus on a slow, relaxed abdominal breath in as you relax the weight. After a two to three second pause, begin the cycle of muscle contraction and slow exhalation again. Exercise in rhythm with your breathing, not only because it brings oxygen into the lungs and increases oxygen-rich red blood cells to your tissues but also because it slows the repetitions, which creates a better exercise routine. During the 15 to 90 second rest time between reps, practice slow, relaxed abdominal breathing because this type of breathing is maximally efficient, and the oxygen replenishment to your tissues will be much more rapid and effective.

When beginning to exercise, most individuals have a tendency to do the reps too quickly. A slow, deliberate repetition with pauses at the beginning and end challenge the muscle with more constant resistance and helps you obtain a better workout of the muscle you are isolating. Please note, however, that many fitness trainers emphasize a natural fluid motion rather than a slow deliberate motion with pauses between reps. As with many things in life, both have merit depending upon the end result you want: to challenge the muscle more or to increase fluidity of motion. Through practice you will find a rhythm that is correct for you, but always remember not to rush the movement, whether you pause or not.

Exercising in rhythm with slow, relaxed abdominal breathing reduces the speed of your exercise and automatically gives you the proper pace for your exercises. For performing light weight strength training, you do not have to use abdominal breathing, but it makes sense to do so.

■ **Warning: If you breathe too fast and deeply you may develop what is called respiratory alkalosis from breathing off carbon dioxide from the lungs. This may cause you to become lightheaded or dizzy and to possibly fall. While carotid plaque is a common cause of lightheadedness and dizziness, individuals who hyperventilate (have rapid, shallow, upper chest breathing) or breathe too deeply and too fast may experience this. The prevention: breathe slowly!**

If you find that you simply cannot get the hang of abdominal breathing when you exercise, at least do not hold your breath. Rather, breathe freely. Holding your breath momentarily causes increased air pressure in your chest and abdomen which raises your blood pressure and prevents blood from returning to your heart. (Note: This is easy to demonstrate. Just stand in front of a mirror, hold your breath, and notice that the veins of your neck dilate and the veins on the back of your hands become more prominent). If you hold your breath as you do the exercise, then as you breathe out again your blood pressure abruptly falls, which can cause a serious strain on your heart and may even cause a blackout. Counting the reps out loud as you do each one prevents you from holding your breath and is a simple way to be sure that you are breathing freely.

I can't stress enough that, in the beginning, less is better. Increase slowly.

■ **Start low and go slow.**

When performing an exercise, for maximum benefit focus your attention on the specific muscle(s) you are contracting. As you contract the muscle, you might visualize in your mind the muscle contracting and moving your bones. When performing an exercise, only the muscle(s) you are exercising should be contracted. This is called muscle isolation. All your other muscles, particularly the forehead, jaw, upper back, and lower back muscles should be relaxed. If you notice any of these other muscles tightening up, let go of the tension and see the tightness leaving with your next breath. As you breathe out, see the tension leave the muscles and exit your body with the exhaled air.

When you let the weight back down, never allow it to fall down abruptly or bounce at the end of your lift. This is a good way to cause injury. As you lower the weight back down, allow for a slight resistance so there is not a jerky movement.

It is preferable to design your program so that succeeding exercises work on different muscle groups. Thus, a long rest is not required between exercises. If doing a second or third set of the same exercise, you may need to take a longer rest between sets, particularly if you are not physically conditioned.

A Sample 13-Step Exercise Strength-Training Program to Prevent Osteoporosis

A basic muscle-strengthening program to maintain and improve bone health and prevent fractures consists of a simple 4-1-4-4 program:
- 4 upper exercises
- 1 mid (abdominal-back) exercise
- 4 lower exercises
- 4 balance and posture exercises

Begin with eight repetitions (reps) of each exercise and then over the next few weeks increase the number of reps to 10, then 12, then 15. Increase the weight as you feel challenged but not strained. As you become more advanced, you may gradually increase to two sets of 8 reps and then again over the next few weeks increase the number of reps to 10, then 12, then 15.

These exercises can just as well be done on exercise weight machines (commonly called Nautilus machines although there are several manufacturers such as Cybex, Body Masters, and others) at your local fitness center. If you have the money to purchase one of the multistation units for your home, this can be used to perform the exercises, and it can be used in combination with dumbbells or other free weights as well. Some of the exercises may be done on the multistation weight machine and some with free weight. The key is to isolate and exercise specific muscle groups, and there is no one method of doing this that is suited for everyone.

The exercises are shown here for demonstration using simple, inexpensive, ankle weights and adjustable weight dumbbells and a chair. Comparative exercises can be done at your local fitness center or on a more expensive home exercise multistation unit.

■ **Caution: The exercises illustrated in this book are representative of many that can be performed. Discuss these exercises with your physician, physiatrist, physical therapist, or other qualified health professional who is familiar with your medical condition to determine if they are right for you before performing any of them. Any of these exercises should be performed only under the direction and supervision of your health professional.**

Upper Extremity Muscle Group Exercises

1. **Biceps Curl** (alternating arms) with dumbbell. This strengthens the biceps (muscle in front of your upper arm) and the forearm. Both arms may be exercised at the same time for simultaneous curls if you desire, as long as it does not adversely stress your low back.

2. **Lateral Side Raise** with dumbbell. This strengthens the deltoid (the shoulder muscle) and rotator cuff (four muscles that keep your arm in the shoulder socket).

3. **Upward Row** with dumbbell in each hand. (**Note:** This could be done using one heavier dumbbell with both hands palms facing toward your body.) This strengthens the deltoid, the rotator cuff muscles, the trapezius (upper back and lower neck muscle), and the bicep.

4. **Overhead Press** with dumbbell. This strengthens the deltoid and rotator cuff, trapezius, and triceps (muscle in back of your upper arm).

Each of these upper extremity muscle group exercises may be done in the standing or sitting position.

Abdominal and Low Back Muscle-Strengthening Exercise

5. Abdominal and Low Back Isometric Exercise. This isometric exercise strengthens the rectus abdominis, oblique muscles (front abdomen), tightens and flattens the tummy, and is a great low back exercise for strengthening the erector spinae muscle (low back).

This is primarily an abdominal and low back exercise, and primary muscular effort in the performance of the exercise should come from these muscles. As you lift your head, your low back muscles contract so that your low back is flat with the floor and the arch to your low back is gone. In this movement, the pelvis naturally rocks back, an action called the pelvic tilt. Press the small of your low back to the floor. Do not lift your butt off the floor. Your hands may rest on top of your thighs with palms facing down and slide forward as you perform the exercise or they can be placed down at your side. It is important to keep the knees bent and feet flat on the floor while performing this exercise. Just as important, the shoulder blades should not come off the ground. Lift gently and slowly and only until the tops of your shoulders begin to come off the ground. Raising your shoulder blades may cause the spine to flex forward, resulting in an anterior wedge vertebral fracture. Also, do not flex your neck anterior but keep it neutral. You know you are flexing your neck if your chin moves toward your chest. You may need a small pillow under your head if you have osteoarthritis and secondary forward flexion of your neck. If you have neck problems such as degenerative osteoarthritis of the lower neck, common in the older age group, you may want to do this very carefully or perhaps not at all. Perform the exercise so that you hold for three to five seconds at the top of the movement, and then lower slowly, pause, and repeat the movement. Since this is an isometric exercise and does not use weights, a second set may be considered for a good workout. Because weights are not used, this exercise can be done daily without a day of recovery in between. The 48-hour muscle recovery rule does not apply to isometric exercises. Pelvic tilt exercises flatten the low back, also known as decreasing lumbar lordosis. The basic exercise consists of contracting your low back muscles which flattens the arch of your low back and flattens your abdomen. This exercise can be done sitting, standing, or lying on your back. There are many variations of the basic pelvic tilt exercise such as lying on your back and raising your legs, etc. They all have in common flattening the arch of the low back and strengthening the extensor muscles of the low back and abdomen muscles.

Lower Extremity Muscle Strengthening Exercises

6. **Knee Extension** seated with ankle weights. This strengthens the quadriceps (large muscle in front of your thigh). It can be done seated in a chair and with ankle weights or with a weight machine as shown below.

7. **Side Hip Raise** with ankle weights. This strengthens the hip abductors (muscles located along the outside of your thigh).

8. Hip Extension with ankle weights. This strengthen the gluteus maximus (muscle of your buttock), and your hamstrings (muscles in the back of your thigh). It can be done with ankle weights while holding onto a chair or with a weight machine as shown here.

If the hip extension exercise feels uncomfortable or hurts your back, do not do it.

9. Hip Flexion with ankle weights. This strengthens the hip flexors, the muscles in your anterior thigh that cause the thigh to move for-

ward and up, and helps strengthen the abdominals and the quadriceps somewhat.

Balance and Posture Exercises

10. **Toe Stand** without ankle weights. This strengthens the gastrocnemius and soleus (muscles in the back of your leg sometimes called calf muscles). In the beginning, this may be done with hands on a wall or holding onto a high-backed sturdy chair in front of you for balance, but as better strength, posture, and balance is achieved, then it should be done without the hands on the wall or chair. In an advanced program, you should hold light dumbbells. As you progress, you may perform the exercise with one foot on the floor and the other flexed (bent at the knee), and then perform it on a step using a handrail for balance.

Raise up on toes and hold 3–5 seconds

11. **Heel Stand** without ankle weights. This strengthens the anterior tibialis muscle (front of your lower leg). In the beginning, it may be done with hands on a wall or holding onto a high-backed sturdy chair in front of you for balance, but as better strength, posture, and balance is achieved, then it should be done without the hands on the wall or chair. If good strength, posture, and balance is achieved, it may be done in an advanced program holding light dumbbells.

 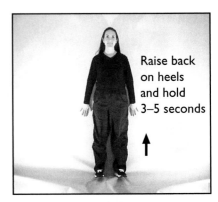

Raise back on heels and hold 3–5 seconds

12. **Squat** without ankle weights. This strengthens the quadriceps (muscle in front of thigh), as well as the back thigh muscles, gluteals, abdominals, and lower back muscle groups. It's an excellent exercise that strengthens multiple muscle groups and may be done with many variations.

For example, it may be performed with your back against a wall for balance, or it may be performed while getting up and down from a chair with arms crossed or with arms outstretched or holding. It may be performed while standing behind and holding onto the back of a sturdy chair for balance, or while holding onto a walker. It may even be performed in an advanced program while holding light dumbbells. To perform against a wall, stand with your back against the wall and your feet 8 to 12 inches away from wall. Keep your back, head, and stomach (low back) flat against the wall. Bend your knees and slide up and down against the wall. When down, you should be in a sitting or "chair" position. Hold the down position for approximately 3 to 5 seconds. You may hold the down position for up to 30 seconds for a better work out. Move your feet closer to the wall for an easier exercise; move your feet slightly farther away from the wall for a harder exercise. For an easier exercise, perform with hands flat against the wall; for an intermediate program, perform with arms crossed over your chest. For an advanced program, exercise with your arms outstretched forward.

Squat and hold 3–5 seconds

13. **Forward Lunge** without ankle weights. This strengthens the quadriceps (muscle in front of thigh), hamstrings (muscles in back of thigh), gluteals (butt), and gastrocnemius and soleus (muscles in back of lower leg also known as calf muscle). The exercise is performed by standing with your feet naturally apart (as wide as your shoulders), with your weight a little back on your heels, and your hands on your hips. With one foot in place, lunge forward about one stride (24 to 30 inches), bending your knees. While you step forward with one foot, the heel of your back foot will come off the ground.

Lunge and hold 3–5 seconds

Do not step too far forward so that you cannot keep your balance or allow your front knee to move forward past your toes. Keep your eyes focused on a point in front of you, because if you look down you may have tendency to lose your balance and fall forward. Step back, pause, then repeat. If you have problems with balance or falling, do not do this exercise. In an advanced program, this exercise may be done with light dumbbells.

Other Exercises

For specific programs of exercises and more in-depth muscle-strengthening information, the exercise and fitness section at your local bookstore has several rows of books on the subject. One of the best, with exercise programs designed specifically for women and osteoporosis, is *Strong Women Stay Young* by Miriam E. Nelson, Ph.D. with Sarah Wernick, Ph.D. (Bantam Books). Another good muscle strengthening book is *Bone-Building Body-Shaping Workout* by Joyce L. Vedral, Ph.D. (Simon & Schuster). Another good book not specifically designed with osteoporosis in mind but with good exercise information is *Fitness and Health* by Brian Sharkey, Ph.D. (Human Kinetics).

Putting it All Together for a Good Exercise Program to Prevent Osteoporosis

A good exercise program to prevent osteoporosis for most individuals is an aerobic weight-bearing exercise (such as walking at least 30 minutes three times a week on alternating days or 20 minutes five times a week) in conjunction with a muscle strengthening program (such as moderate weightlifting with dumbbells/ankle weights) for 45 minutes two times a week with two days between sessions, 30 minutes three times a week with one day between sessions, or a split (half) body program of 20 minutes at least four and preferably six days a week.

An Investment of Only Three Hours a Week

No matter how you look at it, a good exercise program takes approximately three hours per week: one and one-half hours of moderate aerobic weight-bearing exercise, and one and one-half hours of moderate muscle-strengthening exercise. Three hours per week is a small investment of time to ensure an osteoporosis-free lifetime and optimal physical and mental health.

If the aerobic and strength training are done consecutively on the same day, as is often the case, it is best to perform the aerobic weight-bearing exercise (i.e. walking) first to further warm-up the muscles for strength training. If the strength training is done on consecutive days of the week, do not strength-train the same muscle groups two days in a row but rather alternate them. Allow the muscle groups to rest at least one day between workouts. You might do upper extremity muscle groups one day, and lower extremity muscle groups the next day. If you do a full body program, don't lift more than three days a week and leave at least one day of rest between workouts. If you are beginning a muscle strengthening program, you might find it best to work on a split (half) routine of the upper and lower muscle groups individually such as upper extremity with mid body (abdominals and back), and then lower extremity with mid body (abdominals and back) rather than doing the full body program. A full body work-out may be too much in the beginning and cause discouragement and disillusionment. After four to six weeks of easing into the exercise program on a regular basis, incorporate the whole body exercise routine. Also, never exercise seven days a week but always allow the muscles at least one day of rest a week for full recuperation.

If you choose to do a complete total body program (aerobic, muscle-strengthening, balance, and posture) exercises on the same day, the following is a sample Monday-Wednesday-Friday program that will take approximately 75 minutes:
- 5 minutes warm-up and stretching
- 30 minutes walking
- 5 minutes cool-down
- 30 minutes full body strength training
- 5 minutes cool-down and stretching

If you have not exercised for some time and your muscles are extremely weak and flaccid, you might find it best to begin with a light muscle-strengthening program first to strengthen your muscles, and then incorporate the aerobic program into the exercise regimen after your muscles are stronger.

For most individuals, the beginning exercise program should consist of both low level aerobic weight-bearing and low intensity muscle strengthening. The program must start out at a low level and then increase slowly in intensity. For example, it might begin with briskly walking a half mile and then one mile and then gradually increasing to two miles over 30 minutes. It might also start with free-weight exercises utilizing light dumbbells or low-level variable/resistance exercise machines at your local fitness center and slowly increase in intensity and duration as weeks progress.

After you have been into a regular, brisk walking program for 8 to 12 weeks, adding light wrist weights might be a consideration to further enhance the aerobic and muscle strengthening benefits. Ankle weights for walking or running are not recommended as a general rule because they throw off the natural gait and cause a jerky running motion rather than a smooth and rhythmic one.

Write down the exercises you do in an exercise log or on a calendar every time you do them. This is vitally important, particularly in the beginning. This serves as a visual stimulus to continue your program and a permanent log to chart your improvement. It will indicate your progress in distance and time of walking, tell which muscle groups are exercised, give the number of reps and sets, indicate change in weight, and give any other personal endpoints of improvement you may wish to note.

Daily Exercise Record

Date _____   Day of the Week _____

Stretching and Warm-up Time   _____

Walking Time _____ Distance _____

Muscle-strengthening Exercises

Weight	Sets	Reps	Notes
_____	_____	_____	_____
_____	_____	_____	_____
_____	_____	_____	_____
_____	_____	_____	_____
_____	_____	_____	_____
_____	_____	_____	_____
_____	_____	_____	_____
_____	_____	_____	_____
_____	_____	_____	_____
_____	_____	_____	_____
_____	_____	_____	_____
_____	_____	_____	_____
_____	_____	_____	_____

Cool-down and Stretching Time _____

Notes _____

_____

_____

_____

_____

Special Exercise Considerations If You Have Osteoporosis

If you currently have osteopoenia (thin bone) or osteoporosis (brittle bone), you are at risk for fracture and you need to avoid spine-jarring exercise programs such as high impact aerobics, jogging, running, skipping rope, vigorous dancing, and racket sports. These exercises carry a greater possibility of bone fracture. Thin, weakened vertebrae can compress and fracture with very little force. Even the impact of jarring the spine from simple bending, twisting, or jogging may possibly cause a fracture if you have osteoporosis.

If you are over the age of 50 you should think twice about running, jumping on trampolines, jumping rope, and performing high intensity or impact aerobics since there is a much greater potential for injury with these exercises. Increasing age, as mentioned earlier in Chapter 2, is an independent risk factor for the development of osteoporosis and subsequent osteoporotic fracture.

If you have thin or brittle bone, forward stooped (flexed) posture, or osteoporotic compression fracture, do not perform any motion which consists of bending forward at the waist with the back rounded. This includes such exercises as sit-ups, abdominal crunches, toe-touches, and any exercise machine that requires a bending motion forward. These spinal flexion motions might further compress the bone and result in a compression fracture of a spinal vertebrae. You should, however, consider performing more spine extension exercises which strengthen the back extensor (erector spinae) muscles.

Exercises You Should Avoid

If you have thin or brittle bone of the hip, particularly the neck of the femur, then never perform exercises that demand outward movement (abduction) or inward movement (adduction) of the leg against strenuous resistance. This could result in fracture.

■ **Warning: If you have a history of back problems, a very low bone mineral density, or a recent fracture, then you should perform exercises only under the direct supervision of your physician, physiatrist, physical therapist, or other qualified health professional.**

As we increase in age, flexibility exercises become increasingly important. I'm sure you can think of someone now who has lost mobility and, in a sense, "rusted up." If we aren't mobile, then our muscles and bones weaken. All too often there is rapid progressive deterioration in geriatric individuals once mobility is lost. Maintaining flexibility and maximum mobility is a prime consideration in the elderly and for the treatment of osteoporosis.

A secondary benefit of maintaining flexibility, mobility, and muscle strength is that it improves balance and thereby helps to prevent falls. Falls are the major traumatic etiology of osteoporotic fractures in the elderly. Among elderly women, 90% of all hip fractures are attributed to osteoporosis.[1] One of the most important goals in the treatment of everyone with osteoporosis must be to prevent falls.

Preventing falls is the goal of the following exercise program that is aimed at improving your posture and balance as well as your muscle strength.

A Sample 13-Step Exercise Program If You Have Osteoporosis

■ **Caution:** The exercises illustrated in this book are representative of many that can be performed. Discuss these exercises with your physician, physiatrist, physical therapist or other qualified health professional who is familiar with your medical condition to determine if they may be appropriate for you before performing any of them. These exercises should be performed only under the direction and supervision of your health professional. No exercise should hurt when you perform it. If it hurts, then stop it immediately. The exercises may cause some minor muscle soreness but should not cause muscle achiness for more than 24 hours after you perform them.

You might begin with 8 repetitions of each exercise. Increase the reps up to a maximum of 15 as you become stronger, more flexible, and have better sense of balance. Remember, start low and go slow. As you progress from a beginning –> intermediate –> advanced program, you may increase to two sets of each exercise and eventually three, or you might exercise with limited reps twice a day.

1. **Wall Slide.** Place feet 8 to 12 inches away from wall, holding your back, head, and stomach flat against the wall. Bend your knees and slide up and down against the wall. When down, you should be in a sitting or "chair" position with your weight slightly on your heels. Hold the down position for 3 to 5 seconds. You may hold the down position for up to 30 seconds for a better work out. Move your feet closer to the wall for an easier exercise and slightly farther away from the wall for a more difficult exercise. For an easier exercise, perform with your hands flat against the wall; for an intermediate exercise, perform with arms crossed over your chest. For an advanced program, perform with arms outstretched forward.

2. Toe Raises. This exercise may be done holding lightly onto a chair, countertop, walker, or wall for balance. Your knees should be relaxed and not locked or hyperextended. Hold the "up" position for 3 to 5 seconds, and then relax. When advanced, this exercise may be done not holding onto, but rather next to a chair, countertop, walker, or wall to grab if necessary for balance. When advanced, this exercise may be done on one foot with the other flexed. When advanced, this exercise may be done on the edge of a step holding onto the handrail for balance.

3. One Leg Balance. Hold onto a chair, countertop, or walker lightly for balance and bend one leg. Hold for 3 to 5 seconds and relax. You may hold this position for up to 30 seconds as you become more advanced. If you are more advanced, you can do this without holding onto a chair, but keep a chair nearby to grab for balance. While doing this exercise, maintain flat or tight abdominal muscles. Do not move forward when performing this or you may lose your balance.

4. Forward Lower Body Stretch. For balance, rest your hands lightly on the back of a chair. Move your hip forward and lean forward on the bent front knee. Keep the heel of your back foot on the floor, causing tension in the anterior thigh, calf muscle, and Achilles tendon. Hold for 3 to 5 seconds and relax. If you are at an intermediate level of exercise, you may begin in the standing position with your feet together, performing the exercise step forward, while keeping your back heel on the ground. If you are at an advanced level of exercise, you may lift the heel of your back foot off the floor and bend forward slightly more on the front bent knee, similarly to the forward lunge described in the previous program—*Exercises to Prevent Osteoporosis.* Do not stretch too far forward such that you lose your balance or allow your front knee to move forward past your toes. Keep your eyes focused on a point in front of you. If you look down, you may have tendency to lose your balance and fall forward. If you are at a very advanced level of exercise, you may perform the forward lunge exercise described in *Exercises to Prevent Osteoporosis* with a chair or countertop nearby to grab for balance.

5. Chair Raise. Place your feet apart about the width of your hips. Lean forward with your weight on your toes as you stand. Stand up

 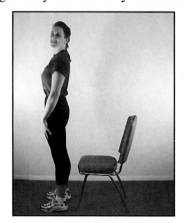

for 3 to 5 seconds, then sit down keeping your weight forward on your toes. In the beginning, you may use your hands on the seat or arms of your chair for assistance. An individual with a walker may find it helpful in the beginning to hold onto their walker when getting up. If you are at an intermediate level of exercise, perform this exercise with your arms crossed over your chest. If you are at an advanced level of exercise, perform this exercise with your arms forward and outstretched.

6. **Sitting Lower Leg Extension Stretch.** Your toes should just lightly brush against the floor. Extend your leg, hold for 3 to 5 seconds and relax. This exercise may be more easily performed with a towel under your knees to lift your legs slightly off the ground. Do not arch your back.

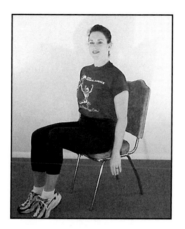 

7. **Sitting Knee Lift Stretch.** Raise your knee, hold for 3 to 5 seconds and relax. Keep your low back and stomach flat, not arched. If you are at an advanced level of exercise, at the top of the exercise, you may also raise your toes up and back.

8. Hip Abduction (Out). Hold lightly onto a chair, from either the side or back. Keep the knee of your supporting leg relaxed, not locked or hyperextended. Move your leg out, hold for 3 to 5 seconds and relax.

9. "Stick 'em Up" Back Extension Stretch. Keep your elbows at 90 degrees, palms forward, as if you were surrendering. Extend your elbows back and bring your shoulder blades together. Hold for 3 to 5 seconds, relax and return to the starting position. Maintain a flat, low back and stomach by exhaling your abdominal breath as you pull your elbows back.

10. Arms Behind Head Back Extension Stretch. Extend your elbows back and bring your shoulder blades together. Hold for 3 to 5 seconds, relax, and return to the starting position. Maintain a flat, low back and stomach by exhaling your abdominal breath as you pull your elbows back.

11. Arms Tucked Into the Side Back Extension Stretch. Extend your elbows back and bring your shoulder blades together. Hold for 3 to 5 seconds, relax, and return to the starting position. Maintain a flat, low back and stomach by exhaling your abdominal breath as you pull your elbows back.

12. Arms Outstretched and Down Back Extension Stretch. Extend your arms straight behind you, pulling your shoulders back also into extension. Extend your arms back and bring your shoulder blades together. Hold for 3 to 5 seconds, relax, and return to the starting position. Maintain a flat, low back and stomach by exhaling your abdominal breath as you pull your elbows back. If you are at an advanced level of exercise, you may clasp your outstretched fingers together and gently pull your extended arms up and back.

13. Overhead Stretch. Extend your hands, arms, and shoulder blades up. Hold for 3 to 5 seconds, relax, and return to the starting position. If possible, avoid rotating your hands or elbows. Keep them in the same position so that when your arms are overhead your palms are facing outward toward your side walls. Maintain a flat, low back and stomach by exhaling your abdominal breath as you extend your arms up.

I have not included exercises that require an individual to get down on the floor, although there are many excellent ones which can be done this way. The reason: compliance. In my experience I have found most individuals 60 years and older do not like and will not perform exercises requiring them to get down on the floor. Many of the elderly, even if they would get down, do not have the strength, due to years of muscle wasting, to get themselves up.

Older, frail individuals with muscle wasting need the exercises the most. So I've included only those exercises in the sitting and standing positions which are most accommodating and easy to perform for the elderly. Consult with your personal physician, physical therapist, or qualified health professional to see if floor exercises are right for you should you decide to do them. You can find some of them in the handbook *Boning Up on Osteoporosis* published by the National Osteoporosis Foundation. A copy can be purchased at the:

National Osteoporosis Foundation
1150 17th Street, N. W., Suite 500
Washington D.C., 20036-4603
1-202-223-2226
1-202-223-2237 (fax)

I have also not included low back extension exercises. The reason for this is that many (if not most) of the elderly I see have moderate or severe degenerative disc disease in their low back at L5S1 (between the 5th lumbar vertebrae and the sacrum), and sometimes L4-5 (between the 4th and 5th lumbar vertebrae). Exercises which increase the arch of the low back such as prone floor leg extensions or standing low back extension bends often cause increasing low back pain and/or sciatica. There's nothing more destructive to someone beginning an exercise program than to hurt his or her back the very first day an exercise program is started. These low back exercises are beneficial for many individuals, however.

An excellent low back exercise which flattens and strengthens the low back is the abdominal and low back isometric exercises described in *Exercises to Prevent Osteoporosis*. The only reason it is not included in the sample exercise program above is that it is a floor exercise. I highly recommend this exercise, however, if you are able to get down and get up from a mat on the floor. Consult with your personal physician, physical therapist, or qualified health professional to see if this and other low back exercises are right for you should you decide to do them. You can find some of them in the handbook *Boning Up on Osteoporosis* published by the National Osteoporosis Foundation.

Making Your Exercise Program Work For You

Exercise in Moderation

When beginning an exercise program, I recommend exercising to tolerance and not overdoing it. If you push yourself beyond the limits you feel capable of, you risk potential serious injury and then become discouraged and decide exercise is not for you. Nagging injuries can lead to frustration and discouragement, particularly in the early stages of an exercise program.

"Exercising to tolerance" is a phrase I find myself using a lot in encouraging elderly individuals to increase physical activity without going beyond their bounds so as to risk injury.

If you do experience an injury, listen to what your body is telling you through the pain. If you should have to miss a regular exercise time due to injury or illness, when you begin exercising again, take as much time as you need to get back to your previous exercise level. Remember, gradual progress is still progress. Avoid pushing too hard too quickly, and you can prevent a more serious strain or injury that can derail your exercise fitness program for weeks.

Some minor muscle soreness and achiness after exercising is normal when first beginning to exercise, particularly if you are considerably "out of shape." Frequently, an individual causes injury in the beginning of a program by overdoing the intensity or exercising too long. The injured muscles and tendons become very stiff and sore 12 to 24 hours after, not necessarily at the time of the injury. It's like the typical motor vehicle accident at which the individual tells the policeman he/she is fine, and the next day wakes up with back pain that "won't quit" and neck spasms so severe the individual can only turn his/her head by turning the whole upper torso.

When to Exercise

There is no fixed time to exercise that is best for everyone, but whatever time you choose, make it a habit. You might set your morning alarm for 30 to 45 minutes earlier and perform moderate exercise while you watch the morning news and wait for the water to heat for the morning oatmeal and coffee. You might find it best to exercise for 30 minutes just before dinner, or perhaps set your wrist watch alarm to alert you to exercise at 7:15 every weeknight.

Do not exercise for one hour after eating a meal to allow for adequate digestion. Do not exercise before going to sleep since exercise invigorates you and makes you more alert.

Steps to Ensure Success

One thing you can be sure of regarding your exercise program—as enthusiastic as you might be right now, there are going to be times when you are going to find excuses not to exercise. Your deconditioned body may find sore ways to protest, your sedentary lifestyle may seduce you, or you may not be able to find the time. Finally, you'll realize you are no longer exercising! Here is a revealing statistic: 68% of people who begin an exercise program are no longer exercising after 30 days! That's greater than two out of three people who quit for one reason or another. What can you do to insure that you will not be one of those 68%? You can follow these guidelines.

• Choose an exercise program you enjoy. The commitment to exercise must be a lifelong commitment. No matter how beneficial an exercise program may be for you, you probably will not stick with it longterm unless it feels good. There is no one ideal exercise program for everyone. The specific type of exercise program you incorporate into your daily life to promote your physical fitness will depend not only on the activities you enjoy and your personality but also on what equipment or facilities are available to you, your own physical health, your capabilities, and your age.

• Keep in mind that you are exercising for better health and not doing grueling, demanding training for athletic competition. You should finish the exercise routine feeling energized and relaxed, not pained or strained.

• Make exercise a part of your daily routine. The easiest way to insure that you persist with your exercise program is to make it a habit. Choose a time of day to exercise daily and set your wristwatch alarm to alert you to stick to it. Write down your time period to exercise in your appointment book. Some individuals find that they prefer to exercise first thing in the morning, so when they leave for work they feel invigorated and alert. Some prefer to exercise during the early part of lunchtime because it reduces their appetite and gives them far more energy for the afternoon than a big meal would. Others prefer late afternoon after work but before dinner. They find that exercise helps them shed tension from work and provides a surge of energy to get them through the evening hours. Still others prefer a walk and light weight routine about an hour or two after supper. They find that this helps them "wind down." Whatever time you choose, make it as much a part of your day as eating, sleeping, or working. Once exercising is a firm part of your daily life, you will find that if you don't exercise one day, you will feel as if something were missing.

- Write out your specific exercise program including specific exercises and short-term exercise goals. Forget about longterm statements like "I'm going to exercise to get in shape" or "I'm going to exercise to improve my health or get a better figure." Stick with concrete, do-able, specific activities. Write out week-by-week what stretching, aerobic weight-bearing, and muscle-strengthening exercises you intend to do. Assess yourself every week. How well have you done? Are the exercises accomplishing what you want them to do? Adjust your exercises accordingly.

- Condition yourself mentally. Professional athletes know that conditioning the psyche is as important as conditioning the body. As mentioned above, two-thirds of individuals who begin an exercise program fail to get beyond the first month. An excellent way to reinforce your exercise program is through visualization. First, visualize the results you desire. For example, visualize yourself with stronger bones, trimmer, more attractive, and energized through exercise. Second, visualize yourself doing and enjoying the exercising.

When you visualize, use all five of your senses to experience actually doing the exercises and enjoying the benefits. See yourself exercising. Touch yourself and feel your muscles becoming firm and your bones strong. See your heart becoming more conditioned, your blood vessels becoming more elastic, your resting pulse rate decreasing, your lungs able to take in more oxygen, your mind becoming more alert. Feel invigorated. See increased oxygen being supplied to every cell of your body by efficient, slow, and relaxed abdominal breathing. See the cholesterol and triglyceride levels decreasing in your bloodstream. See yourself eager to exercise, invigorated, and maintaining the high of exercise in your daily activities long after you've exercised that day.

Most Common Excuses Given Not To Exercise

- "I'm too old to begin to exercise." None of us can afford not to exercise. We must maintain mobility and strength since we either "use it or lose it." Exercise is a pill any of us can swallow. It has no contraindications due to age and can be done in one form or another by everyone. It has been said that the best anti-aging pill is the exercise pill.

- "I get plenty of exercise at work." Upon more intense questioning, I usually find that individuals using this excuse are not getting adequate cardiovascular aerobic fitness exercise and good muscle strengthening/toning exercise.

- "I get plenty of exercise running after the kids." Mere movement may not be enough to stimulate the building of bone.

- "I don't have the time to exercise." These individuals might consider moderate physical activity for 30 minutes six times a week in the form of a treadmill or at least a recumbent exercise bike, with free weights conveniently located in front of the television.

- "I'm too overweight and out of shape to exercise." Being overweight and being physically fit are two entirely different things. Each is totally independent of the other. Overweight individuals can be very physically fit, and you will find your weight problem automatically improving as well.

- "I'm too tired to exercise." Individuals are too tired precisely because they don't exercise! What it takes to break this vicious cycle of tiredness and inactivity is a commitment to make a regular time for exercise and persist through the initial break-in period until your body adjusts.

For All Procrastinators

For all procrastinators, I recommend the following prescription:

Commit now in writing to begin a moderate exercise program for 30 minutes 3 to 5 days a week as discussed above (i.e. walking and light-moderate muscle-strengthening workout) for the next 30 days!

Why 30 days? Because psychologists have found it takes 30 days of practice to unlearn an old habit and replace it with a new habit. So it may take 30 days to unlearn being a couch potato and learn to incorporate a healthy exercise routine into your daily lifestyle. After 60 days, the new habit is well solidified in your psyche.

If You Still Insist On Not Exercising Regularly

If after reading this you still are not motivated to begin a regular exercise program, then I have one thing to say to you: *stay active.* In my 25 years of medical practice I have taken care of several individuals over 100 years of age and many in their 90s. The common thread among these individuals is that they have all stayed mentally and physically active. They have maintained a feisty, vigorous zeal for living, for keeping physically busy, for nurturing active social relationships, and for keeping interested in all aspects of living. I have noticed that as individuals age, material accomplishments and possessions are less valued, and maintaining active relationships with friends and particularly with family, such as grandchildren and great-grandchildren, become the focus of their lives. While this may not be considered by some to be exercise, maintaining an active physical, emotional, and mental life seems to be one of the keys to long healthy living.

Other Benefits of Exercise

The most dramatic effect of exercise on bone density comes if you have led a sedentary lifestyle and have the least activity prior to your beginning an exercise program. The beneficial effects of exercise are also more rapidly lost for you if regular exercise is stopped.

Exercise helps us relieve depression, anxiety, stress, tension, fatigue, and insomnia and helps treat hypertension, diabetes, heart disease, and constipation. It raises your HDL (good) cholesterol and lowers LDL (bad) cholesterol. It decreases your pains from osteoarthritis (wear and tear arthritis) and helps with a host of other illnesses.

Exercise burns up calories and reduces our body fat by promoting the breakdown of storage fat. (Note: Healthy body fat ranges for women over 30 years is 20 to 27% and for men over 30 years is 17 to 23%. Women are considered obese if they have over 32% body fat, and men are considered obese if they have over 25% body fat. Body fat percentage is thought to be a better indicator of health than total weight.) A total body bone mineral density analysis such as we perform with a Bone Mineral Density Test at the Osteoporosis Testing Center of Michigan gives body fat analysis not only for the total body but also for each leg, arm, and the abdomen.

By decreasing body fat, exercise improves Body Mass Index (BMI). (Note: BMI is a height and weight calculation that helps determine weight-related health risks.) If your BMI is 27 kg/m^2 or higher, you have an increased chance of weight-related health risks.[2]

Less than 19: Underweight—at underweight health risk
19–26: Satisfactory—normal healthy weight-to-height ratio
27–30: Overweight—at increased health risk
Greater than 30: Obese—at considerable health risk

As lean body mass improves, your health improves. An increase in muscle mass by strengthening exercise increases lean body mass. Although muscle weighs more than fat, it does not take up as much physical space. This is why individuals who exercise decrease their measurement sizes.

Body Mass Index

Height (in feet and inches)

Weight (in pounds)	5'	5'1"	5"2"	5'3"	5'4"	5'5"	5'6"	5'7"	5'8"	5'9"	5'10"	5'11"	6'	6'1"	6'2"
100	20	19	18	18	17	17	16	16	15	15	14	14	14	13	13
105	21	20	19	19	18	17	17	16	16	16	15	15	14	14	13
110	21	21	20	19	19	18	17	17	16	16	16	15	15	15	14
115	22	22	21	20	20	19	19	18	17	17	17	16	16	15	15
120	23	23	22	21	21	20	19	19	18	18	17	17	16	16	15
125	24	24	23	22	21	21	20	20	19	18	18	17	17	16	16
130	25	25	24	23	22	22	21	20	20	19	19	18	18	17	17
135	26	26	25	24	23	22	22	21	21	20	19	19	18	18	17
140	27	26	26	25	24	23	23	22	21	21	20	20	19	18	18
145	28	27	27	26	25	24	23	23	22	21	21	20	20	19	19
150	29	28	27	27	26	25	24	23	23	22	22	21	20	20	19
155	30	29	28	27	27	26	25	24	24	23	22	22	21	20	20
160	31	30	29	28	27	27	26	25	24	24	23	22	22	21	21
165	32	31	30	29	28	27	27	26	25	24	24	23	22	22	21
170	33	32	31	30	29	28	27	27	26	25	24	24	23	22	22
175	34	33	32	31	30	29	28	27	27	26	25	24	24	23	22
180	35	34	33	32	31	30	29	28	27	27	26	25	24	24	23
185	36	35	34	33	32	31	30	29	28	27	27	26	25	24	24
190	37	36	35	34	33	32	31	30	29	28	27	26	26	25	24
195	38	37	36	35	34	33	32	31	30	29	28	27	26	26	25
200	39	38	37	36	35	34	33	32	31	30	29	28	27	26	26
205	40	39	38	37	36	35	34	33	32	31	30	29	28	27	26
210	41	40	38	37	36	35	34	33	32	31	30	29	28	28	27
215	42	41	39	38	37	36	35	34	33	32	31	30	29	28	28
220	43	42	40	39	38	37	36	35	34	33	32	31	30	29	28
225	44	43	41	40	39	37	36	35	34	33	32	31	31	30	29
230	45	43	42	41	39	38	37	36	35	34	33	32	31	30	30
235	46	44	43	42	40	39	38	37	36	35	34	33	32	31	30

☐ **Less than 19: Underweight—at underweight health risk**

☐ **19–26: Satisfactory—normal healthy weight-to-height ratio**

☐ **27–30: Overweight—at increased health risk**

☐ **Greater than 30: Obese—at considerable health risk**

Durazo-Arvizu[3] and others looked at BMI and mortality in 13,242 black and white individuals in the NHANES I epidemiologic follow-up study in order to estimate the BMI at which minimum mortality occurs. The BMI of minimum mortality was:

BMI of Minimum Mortality

White Women	White Men	Black Women	Black Men
24.3	24.8	26.8	27.1

There are a wide range of BMI values associated with low relative mortality risk.

Exercise reduces our appetite and appreciably increases our metabolism which burns more calories at rest so we stay thinner. After age 20, our basal metabolism decreases approximately 2% every 10 years. This is why as we get older it's easier to gain weight and harder to lose it. Muscle burns more calories per day than fat.

Women also tend to slowly gain weight after menopause. Most gain 6 to 7 pounds 1 to 2 years after their monthly periods stop. Before menopause, the monthly menstrual period blood loss burns up calories. After menopause, this calorie burner is no longer present.

In addition to the beneficial effects of exercise on bone formation and the musculo-skeleton, there are other substantial halo benefits. Whenever we exercise moderately, our body manufactures endorphins and enkephalins which improve our energy level, emotional well-being, and immune system—creating what has sometimes been called the "runner's high." These *feel good* drugs are more powerful than morphine. If we are physically fit, we tend to have more of these present in our system. Exercise improves our self-image, self-esteem, and self-confidence and enables most individuals to experience a greater feeling of mastery over their life.

Physically fit individuals tend to produce fewer catecholamines. These are hormones our body produces in response to stressful situations that tend to produce anxiety, depression, and even illness. Physically fit people are better able to handle stress without adverse effects such as hostility, frustration, and anxiety. A regular exercise program is usually far more effective in the long run in dealing with "nerves" than a tranquilizer. Tranquilizers temporarily cover up the problem, but exercise is a positive energy outlet for dealing with and dissipating the energy put into the problem. Popping pills is passive, but exercise is active involvement in improving your life and well-being. Of course, a short term tranquilizer may be the best way to handle an acute problem, but in the long run exercise will be far more effective as a way to gain real control and mastery over your life.

Regular exercise not only tunes up our body, but tunes up our mind as well. Regular conditioning improves oxygenation of our brain, improving logical thinking abilities, memory, reaction time, coordination, intuition, and creativity.

Although all these health and well-being benefits are achieved through exercise, the number one reason individuals exercise is that they feel better!

In summary,

■ **A program of moderate aerobic weight-bearing exercise, moderate muscle-strengthening exercise, balance exercise, and posture exercise is a universal prescription for the prevention and treatment of osteoporosis.**

Points to Remember

■ Without exercise, even the best diet cannot be metabolized properly.

■ Before starting an exercise program, consult with your physician or qualified health care provider.

■ Your exercise program should be fun and enjoyable; otherwise, long-term compliance will not take place.

■ Learning abdominal breathing and incorporating it into your everyday life as the normal way you breathe is literally a breath of life.

■ Walking is the easiest and best aerobic weight-bearing exercise for most individuals to incorporate into their daily lives.

Chapter 6 Bibliography

1   Melton LJ III, Thamer M. ray NF, et al. *Fractures Attributable to Osteoporosis: Report from the National Osteoporosis Foundation. Journal of Bone and Mineral Research 1997; 12:16–23).*

2   *National Heart, Lung, and Blood Institutes Expert Panel, 1998. NHLBI Obesity Education Initiative Expert Panel on the Identification, Evaluation, and Treatment of Overweight and Obesity in Adults. Clinical Guidelines on the Identification, Evaluation, and Treatment of Overweight and Obesity in adults. The Evidence Report. Bethesda, MD: National Heart, Lung and Blood Institute; 1998*

3   *Durazo-Arvizu RA et. al. Mortality and Optimal BMI in a Sample of the U.S. Population, American Journal of Epidemiology, 1998, April 15; 147 (8): 739–749*

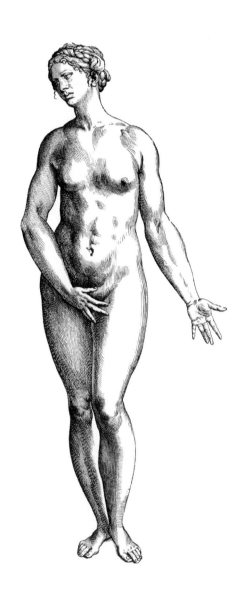

Making an Informed Decision About Estrogen

Chapter 7

Every Woman's Dilemma at Menopause

Every woman faces a key decision at menopause: to take estrogen versus not to take estrogen. For most, it's a perplexing personal struggle of weighing the benefits on one hand and the risks on the other.

Weigh the Risks and Benefits of Estrogen

Risks:
• Breast cancer
• Menstrual bleeding
• Osteoporosis

Benefits:
• Bones
• Heart
• Lipids
• Menopausal symptoms

With data from numerous research studies, it is now well known that the benefits of estrogen during menopause extend far beyond the relief of menopausal symptoms such as hot flashes and irritability—the benefits affect the whole body. Correspondingly, the risks go far beyond possible breakthrough bleeding and tender breasts—they affect the whole body as well.

One hundred years ago, women rarely lived beyond menopause, but today the average woman experiences menopause at age 50, and she can expect to live several decades beyond this. The decision whether or not to take estrogen at menopause will affect the rest of a woman's life.

Estrogen replacement therapy is not right for every woman. Wulf Utian, Executive Director of the North American Menopause Society, sums up the problem: "People are looking for the simple answer, the one-size-fits-all solution. I've got bad news: it doesn't exist."

Approximately 30% of women try estrogen replacement therapy at the time of natural menopause. Twenty percent never fill their first prescription. Over 12 million women currently use hormone replacement therapy, and two-thirds of these have had a hysterectomy. This chapter summarizes important information so you can make an informed decision about the best choice for you.

Understanding Estrogen

The term estrogen actually refers to a group of related estrogen hormones of which the three major ones in humans are estrone (E_1), estradiol (E_2), and estriol (E_3). These act on different target cells in various organs (i.e., uterus, breast, bone, heart, brain, connective tissues, macula of eyes, colon) in varying ways and to varying degrees.

Estrone (E_1)

After menopause, most of the estrogen the body makes is produced by the conversion of androstenedione (produced in the adrenal cortex) to estrone. In postmenopausal women, estrone, especially in its sulfate ester form, is the most common form of circulating estrogen found in the bloodstream.

Estrone can be manufactured in body fat. With increasing fat, there is an increasing amount of androgen bio-chemically able to be converted to bone protecting estrogen, giving individuals who are overweight a lower propensity for the development of osteoporosis. Paradoxically, it probably also is why anorexic young women stop menstruating and subsequently develop premature osteoporosis.

In the liver, estrone can be converted into estriol and also into estradiol. Estradiol can also be converted into estrone. The liver can also convert estrone into a non-active form of estrogen called 2-hydroxy-estrone that is taken out of the blood by the kidneys and excreted in the urine. The conversion into non- active estrogen is a one-way street, as 2-hydroxy-estrone cannot be converted back into an active estrogen.

Estradiol (E_2)

Estradiol, also known as 17-Beta Estradiol or 17 β Estradiol, is the major estrogenic hormone secreted by the human ovary in the pre-

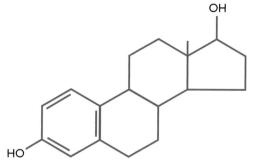

Estradiol (E₂) is the principal intracellular estrogen found in many tissues and is generally considered to be the most potent form of estrogen at the receptor level.

menopausal woman. The ovaries secrete 70 to 500 mcg/day of estradiol depending on the phase of the menstrual cycle. Most of the estradiol is converted in the liver into estrone, which circulates in almost equal proportion to estradiol in the bloodstream. A smaller amount is converted to estriol.

Estradiol is the principal intracellular estrogen found in many tissues and is generally considered to be the most potent form of estrogen at the receptor level.

Estriol (E3)

Estriol normally fluctuates with the menstrual cycle and is thought to be protective against breast cancer. Estriol is considered to be the least potent of the three major estrogens in the body.

These three human estrogens exist in a dynamic equilibrium of metabolic interconversions by the liver to affect tissue-specific receptors.

Target Organ Specificity and Estrogen Receptors

The activity of an estrogen is tissue-specific. Different estrogens manifest different activities in specific target cells of our organs. This relationship is dependent upon the biological potency of the particular estrogen and the receptor affinity for that particular estrogen in the target organ.

Researchers have found that there are at least two different estrogen receptors, and they theorize that there are many more estrogen receptors in our body which have yet to be discovered. Different estrogen receptors have different biological functions and have different tissue-specific distributions. Some tissues have many more estrogen receptors than others, and some estrogens may affect more or exert stronger effects on particular tissue receptors than others.

Some estrogens may selectively bind and activate one receptor and not another or even block another receptor. Researchers have found that some estrogens act as estrogen receptor agonists (facillitators), whereas others function as antagonists (block or counteract the effects). These estrogens are termed Selective Estrogen Receptor Modulators (SERMS). For example, tamoxifen (Nolvadex®), a synthetic estrogen, acts as an estrogen agonist (builds bone) in the bone but as an antiestrogen or antagonist (blocks estrogen effects in the breast, lowering the incidence of breast cancer) in breast tissue.

Raloxifene (Evista®), another synthetic estrogen of the SERM type, exerts considerable estrogen effects as an agonist in bone—but exerts estrogen antagonist (antiestrogen) activity in the breasts and uterus.

The Upside of Hormone Replacement Therapy

Menopausal Vasomotor Symptoms

Estrogen alleviates the acute symptoms associated with the onset of menopause. Hot flashes (flushes), night sweats, mood swings and depression, irritability, and sleep deprivation are all alleviated with estrogen replacement therapy in the climacteric. These menopausal vasomotor symptoms are best treated if estrogen is begun as soon as symptoms appear rather than waiting until they are very severe.

Eighty-five percent of women experience hot flushes at normal menopause, and generally most women experience them with surgical menopause. Approximately 500,000 women in the United States have a hysterectomy and bilateral oopherectomy (ovariectomy-removal of ovaries) yearly, and after their surgery they will be estrogen deficient. Not all accept estrogen replacement therapy.

The most common reason women seek medical care at menopause is for hot flashes. Hot flashes tend to lessen after the first two postmenopausal years. The sudden feeling of intense heat spreading over the face, head, and chest usually lasts thirty seconds to several minutes and are so severe as to interfere with the quality of life in about 15% of women.

Prevention of Osteoporosis

Estrogen replacement therapy (ERT), also known as hormone replacement therapy (HRT) if estrogen and progesterone are used in combination, is approved by the FDA and recommended by the National Osteoporosis Foundation as the initial pharmacological option for both the prevention and management of osteoporosis. In estrogen epidemiologic studies, it appears to give a 50% to 80% decrease in vertebral fractures and a 25% decrease in non-vertebral fractures in five years of use. Estrogen acts by inhibiting the osteoclastic breakdown of bone. In medical literature, the beneficial effects of estrogen on bone are well documented.[1]

Robert Lindsay, MD, Ph.D, and past President of the National Osteoporosis Foundation, said, "Osteoporosis in postmenopausal women needs to be recognized and handled by the primary care physician…. We believe that hormone replacement therapy remains the gold standard and probably should be the number one choice for consideration."[2]

Since the greatest amount of bone loss in a woman's lifetime tends to occur within the first five years after menopause, estrogen therapy for maximum benefit is best begun at menopause or, in the case of surgical menopause, at the time of bilateral oophorectomy (removal of the ovaries). Dr. Lindsay found that estrogen slows bone loss irrespective of whether the replacement is started at zero, three, or even six years after surgical bilateral oopherectomy.[3]

Women not taking estrogen at menopause often lose 3% to 5% of bone mineral density annually during the next five years and can lose up to 7% a year. After menopause, the fracture rate in women increases dramatically due to this accelerated bone mineral density loss. It makes sense then to start estrogen replacement as early as possible at the time of menopause to prevent bone loss.

■ **Estrogen is best started at menopause when bone mineral density levels are still high. It's easier to keep bone than to build new bone.**

Studies have consistently demonstrated that postmenopausal women on estrogen have consistently higher bone mineral densities than those who do not take estrogen. Women on adequate estrogen replacement therapy typically increase their bone mass by approximately 3% in the first year. Estrogen consistently protects against bone density loss after menopause and preserves bone mass density and strength.

Studies have shown that even in the elderly the initiation of estrogen significantly builds bone mineral density mass and protects against future fractures. Even if you are 70 or 75 years of age, you may begin taking estrogen (at low dose and gradually increased as tolerated) and realize significant bone protective benefit.

Studies have also demonstrated that once estrogen is stopped, the benefits on bone mineral density from estrogen also stop. In other words, the estrogen replacement benefits do not persist after estrogen is withdrawn. Most physicians recommend at least 10 to 15 years of estrogen replacement therapy after normal menopause at age 50. The more years a woman takes estrogen, the more increase in bone mineral density achieved with subsequent decrease in risk of fractures. When weighing whether or not to take ERT, you should consider that a lifetime protection from osteoporosis may require a lifetime commitment to taking estrogen.

Coronary Artery Disease

The incidence of cardiovascular disease rises rapidly at menopause until age 60. Women who do not take estrogen after menopause have the same incidence of cardiovascular disease as their male counterparts. It is well known that estrogen has a very significant beneficial effect on the prevention of coronary artery disease in previously healthy women. Retrospective observational studies indicate that coronary heart disease mortality is decreased by approximately 50% in women taking estrogen. The mechanism for this cardioprotective protection is thought to be:

Improved lipid profile. Estrogen raises high density lipo-protein (HDL; good, "happy", cholesterol) by up to 15%, and lowers low density lipo-protein (LDL; bad, "lousy", cholesterol) by up to 20%. The greater the estrogen dose, the greater the improvement in HDL and the lower the LDL. Estrogen appears to decrease the deposition of low-density lipo-protein in the coronary arteries and therefore is considered to exert anti-oxidant properties. It also decreases total cholesterol by up to 25%.

Improved endothilium-dependent vasodilatation. Estrogen appears to increase coronary artery diameter and coronary blood flow. It reduces coronary vasospasm by increasing the production of endothelial-derived relaxing factor (nitric oxide) and decreasing the production of endothelin, a coronary artery vasoconstrictor.

Estrogen causes changes in blood coagulation factors. It increases the breakdown of fibrin (fibrinolysis), a coagulated protein that produces the coagulation of blood. Estrogen decreases fibrinogen (blood clotting factor I). In the presence of thrombin and ionized calcium fibrinogen is converted into fibrin and plasminogen activator inhibitor (PAI).

For women who have a history of pre-existing coronary artery disease, the situation is quite different. Women with known coronary artery disease who were taking estrogen were found to have a 50% increase in the number of heart attacks in the first year of taking estrogen (Heart and Estrogen/Progestin Replacement Study [HERS)]).[4] Interestingly, after four years of taking estrogen, the increase in risk of heart attacks declined to equal those not taking estrogen. Further studies are being done on this important aspect of estrogen replacement, including one called the Women's Health Initiative,[5] a study of 27,500 women receiving estrogen replacement therapy.

Long-term estrogen users have approximately a 20% less risk of death than women who do not take estrogen. The Nurses Health Study[6] of greater than 59,000 women with hormone use found that if coronary risk factors are considered, estrogen users have approximately a 50% lower death rate than women who do not take estrogen.[7]

Vaginal Dryness and Painful Intercourse

The decrease in estrogen at menopause produces a thinner, more fragile vaginal epithelium. There is also decreased vaginal lubrication in response to sexual stimulation, which can lead to a dryer, more painful intercourse, itching, and occasionally post-coital (sex) bleeding from fragile, cracked vaginal mucosa. During sexual activity, bruising and irritation of the thin vaginal mucosa can cause more frequent cystitis (bladder infections) known as postmenopausal cystitis and sometimes an increase in incidence of a chronic inflammation of the bladder wall known as interstitial cystitis. The friable vaginal mucosa and atrophic vulva is also susceptible to increased vaginal infection and inflammation. For most women, the vaginal pH before menopause is about 4.5 to 5. After menopause, it is more alkaline, about pH 7. This change in pH can make the vaginal mucosa more susceptible to subsequent infections such as bacterial vaginitis, trichomoniasis, chlamydia, or yeast (moniliasis, candidiasis).

When talking with you, your doctor may refer to the above as postmenopausal or atrophic vaginitis. Estrogen helps to maintain a stronger, more moist, and healthier vaginal lining.

Collagen Loss in the Skin and Supporting Tissues

Declining estrogen levels cause declining collagen levels in the skin and supporting tissues of the body. Collagen loss in the skin and supporting structures in your body causes thinning and wrinkling of your skin, including facial skin and weakness in the supporting tissues. The average postmenopausal woman loses approximately 2% of skin collagen per year in the immediate ten-year postmenopausal period. Some women can lose up to 30% of skin collagen during the first five years after menopause. Preventive treatment for collagen loss is best if initiated at menopause before significant collagen loss has occurred.

Collagen loss also causes a weakness in the tissues supporting the bladder, urethra, and uterus, causing more susceptibility to a fallen bladder and stress incontinence, rectocele (protrusion of rectal wall into vagina) and subsequent constipation or impaction, and more susceptibility to a fallen uterus and possible subsequent need for a hysterectomy. This is generally known as urogenital atrophy. Postmenopausal women often find themselves going to the bathroom more often or leaking small amounts of urine when laughing, coughing, sneezing, or exercising. This stress incontinence, which occurs when there is increased pressure on the bladder and weakened supporting tissues, is an embarrassing problem, and many women do not want to talk about it, even to their physicians.

Collagen loss also occurs in the vascular system and muscles, making these tissues more susceptible to the changing effects of aging.

Cognitive Function

Estrogen generally causes a feeling of improved mood, increased energy, and improved memory by increasing adrenergic function. Estrogen's neuro-protective effects and improvement in cognitive abilities may be due to its effect on estrogen receptor neurons and neurotransmitters in the brain.

Alzheimer's Disease

Evidence is growing that estrogen replacement therapy during menopause may delay the onset of and the progression of Alzheimer's disease, a slow, progressive deterioration of mental functioning, for upwards of two years. Alzheimer's affects approximately four million Americans and is probably the number one reason for institutionalization of individuals in nursing homes.

The Incidence of Alzheimer's Increases with Age		
Age 80	➡	40 percent of the population
Age 85	➡	50 percent of the population

Alzheimer's is a particular threat to older women. This disease seems to manifest itself at an earlier age in women than in men, and 72% of the population over 85 years of age are women. Half of these have Alzheimer's of one degree or another. Some studies seem to indicate a lower risk of developing Alzheimer's dementia in postmenopausal women, indicating a 40% to 60% reduction in the risk of Alzheimer's in women on estrogen replacement therapy.

In addition to delaying the possible onset of Alzheimer's disease, some studies indicate an improvement in cognitive function in individuals with Alzheimer's and a slowing in the progressive rate of cognitive function decline. In Alzheimer's disease, crucial neurotransmitters, including serotonin and acetylcholine, are depleted, and neurons crucial to brain functioning are damaged. Estrogen appears to stimulate the regeneration of damaged neurons and the production of important neurotransmitters, serotonin and acetylcholine. Some estrogens appear to affect estrogen receptors in the nervous system and be neuroprotective.

Parkinson's Disease

Evidence is growing that postmenopausal women receiving estrogen replacement therapy may reduce their risk of developing Parkinson's disease.

Colon Cancer

There is evidence to suggest that postmenopausal estrogen replacement therapy gives some benefit in the prevention of colon cancer. There are 48,600 new cases of colon cancer in women each year, resulting in 24,000 deaths yearly.[7] There seems to be a relationship between the length of time of estrogen use with decreasing colon cancer risk.[8]

Multiple studies indicate that women who use estrogen replacement therapy may have up to a 20% reduction in colon cancer and a 15% reduction in rectal cancer. The exact mechanism of how it does this is unknown, but it is known that there are estrogen-specific receptors in the colon.

Teeth

Estrogen replacement therapy during menopause may decrease the risk of future tooth loss. Thirty-two percent of American women over age 65 have lost their teeth for various reasons. Although periodontal disease is the major cause of tooth loss, researchers suspect that there may be a relationship between osteoporotic bone loss in the jaw and tooth loss.

Prevention of Eyesight Loss

Estrogen may help to prevent the development of eyesight loss from age-related macular degeneration (AMD), the leading cause of blindness in the United States. It affects approximately 35% of the population aged 75 and older and is responsible for up to 60% of new cases of blindness. There is a high association between age-related macular degeneration and smoking.

The Rotterdam study compared the risk of macular degeneration in those with early versus those with late menopause.[9] They found that women with early menopause had a 90% increase in macular degeneration. The Eye Disease Case Control Study found that those taking estrogen in the menopause had a 70% decrease in the risk of developing macular degeneration.[9]

The Downside of Hormone Replacement Therapy

The most common reason given by women for not beginning estrogen replacement therapy at menopause is the perception that estrogen therapy is harmful.[10]

The three major concerns that women have regarding estrogen replacement therapy, in decreasing order of concern are:

- The risk of breast cancer
- The risk of endometrial (uterine) cancer
- The risk of blood clots (deep venous thrombosis, pulmonary emboli, and strokes)

Other concerns are:

- Continuation of the menstrual periods/continuation of fertility
- Breast tenderness and/or fibrocystic breast changes
- Endometriosis
- Bloating
- Spotting
- Return of menstrual bleeding or monthly menstrual periods

- Hair loss
- Fluid retention
- Gall stones

In addition, many women are hesitant to take estrogen because it is not a "natural" therapy.

Risk of Breast Cancer

Fear of breast cancer is the greatest concern women have about taking estrogen. Approximately 15% of women who start estrogen replacement therapy stop it because of the fear of cancer.

Many research studies have examined the relationship between estrogen replacement therapy during menopause and breast cancer. The results have not always been consistent. Epidemiological data was reanalyzed from 51 investigative centers on over 160,000 women.[11] Women who were former users of estrogen and had stopped it had a relative risk (RR) of breast cancer of 1.07; women who had ever used estrogen replacement had a relative risk of 1.14, and current users of estrogen had a relative risk of 1.35.

For every 100 postmenopausal women, approximately four are expected to develop breast cancer. The relative risk of developing breast cancer in postmenopausal women due to estrogen use increases to slightly more than 5 of 100 postmenopausal women receiving estrogen for approximately 13 years.

This means that 1.2 additional women are at risk for developing breast cancer out of every 100 with estrogen use.

Interestingly, although estrogen replacement therapy increases slightly the risk of developing breast cancer, studies demonstrate a decreasing death rate from breast cancer in women taken estrogen. The increased survival rate in women on estrogen is attributed to a lower frequency of late-stage disease. There is evidence to support the fact that estrogen replacement does not cause cancer but rather accelerates the growth of a malignant locus already there and thus presents clinically at a less virulent and less aggressive stage.

Breast Cancer and Estrogen in the Postmenopausal Woman

- **4 (3.9) out of 100 without estrogen use**
- **5 (5.1) out of 100 with estrogen use**

Some recent studies suggest that postmenopausal women taking estrogen replacement therapy in combination with progesterone may have a higher risk of developing breast cancer. The Women's Health Initiative, a study begun in 1993 by the National Institute of Health (NIH) involving 27,000 women ages 50–79, is investigating this. The women are being followed for 8–12 years so preliminary results should be available in several more years.

All postmenopausal women receiving estrogen should have an annual mammogram and perform a monthly breast self-examination.

Risk of Endometrial (Uterine) Hyperplasia and Endometrial Cancer

A woman who has not had a hysterectomy and receives postmenopausal estrogen alone has a slightly higher risk of developing endometrial hyperplasia, which may lead to endometrial cancer. Women receiving unopposed estrogen have a 20% chance of developing endometrial hyperplasia after one year of therapy and a 61% chance of developing endometrial hyperplasia after three years. If estrogen is used without progesterone in the postmenopausal woman for more than one year, the risk of endometrial cancer increases.[12] A postmenopausal woman not taking estrogen has approximately a one in 1000 chance of developing endometrial cancer, and if she takes estrogen for more than one year, she has a 5 to 10 in 1000 chance of developing endometrial cancer.[13]

If progesterone is added to the treatment regimen, this risk decreases to be comparable to that of women not taking estrogen.[14]

Some treatment regimens (i.e. Prempro®, Combipatch®, Femhrt®, Ortho-Prefest®) contain estrogen and progesterone combination. With these, there is no thickening of the uterine wall nor the secondary monthly shedding of the endometrium which creates a menstrual period. Sometimes physicians give estrogen several days of the month, for example days 1 to 25, and give progesterone several days of the month, for example, days 16 to 25 (10 days for the month). Other cycles are also used. Premphase® (conjugated estro-

---

Uterine Cancer and Estrogen Replacement Without Progesterone in the Postmenopausal Woman

- 1 in 1,000 women without estrogen
- 5–10 in 1,000 women with estrogen

gens and medroxyprogesterone acetate) is another alternative to regulate monthly menstrual cycles. Your doctor will work with you to develop the best treatment program for you.

Risk of Blood Clots including Deep Venous Thrombosis (DVT), Pulmonary Embolism (PE), and Strokes

There is a modest increased risk of developing deep venous thrombosis (DVT) in women taking estrogen replacement therapy.[15] This risk seems to be concentrated in women who just begin estrogen replacement therapy and not in those who have been taking it for a long time.[16] There is a slight increase in pulmonary emboli in postmenopausal women taking hormone replacement therapy. Researchers in the Harvard nurses health study found that among women currently taking hormone replacement therapy aged 50 to 59, five additional cases/100,000 persons could be attributable to HRT.[17]

The risk of stroke with hormone replacement therapy is controversial. In the well-known Framingham Study, researchers reported a small increase in stroke in women taking estrogen replacement therapy;[18] however, the majority of studies have found no relationship, and four studies have found a lowering of the risk of stroke in postmenopausal women taking hormone replacement therapy.

Other Concerns

Breast tenderness is the most common reason given by women for premature discontinuation of estrogen treatment. The other two reasons are weight gain and the restarting of menstrual periods.

There is an increase in gallbladder disease in women taking oral estrogen. Women who have gallbladder dysfunction or gall stones would be better off to use an estrogen patch. The estrogen in this form bypasses the liver and goes directly to the tissues.

Some other concerns associated with estrogen and estrogen/progesterone combinations include headaches, mood changes, acne, nausea, bloating and fluid retention, hair loss, and occasionally leg cramping.

Another concern is that the continuation of the menstrual periods at menopause with cyclic estrogen/progesterone will continue the possibility of pregnancy. Many women want continuous suppression so as to have complete peace of mind that they are no longer fertile. This peace of mind is so connected with the absence of menstrual periods that combined continuous estrogen/progesterone therapy at menopause can be extremely reassuring. Many women at menopause do not want to tolerate withdrawal bleeding anymore for obvious reasons. They want to be done with their menstrual periods and that reproductive phase of their life and look forward to late mid-life and the golden years.

Contraindications to Estrogen Therapy

Absolute contraindications to estrogen therapy are known or suspected breast cancer, known or suggested pregnancy, estrogen dependent neoplasia (cancer), undiagnosed abnormal vaginal bleeding (may possibly indicate uterine cancer), active thrombophlebitis or history of thromboembolic disorders (deep vein thrombosis, stroke, pulmonary emboli), and active liver disease.

Having a first-degree relative with breast cancer such as your mother or sister has in the past been considered an absolute contraindication; however, in light of recent research studies, this is no longer so. A small but not statistically significant increase in breast cancer has been found in women with a family history of breast cancer. While it is still considered a possible contraindication, the risks must be weighed against the benefits for the individual with her particular symptoms. For many women in this situation, a selective estrogen receptor modulator such as Evista® (Raloxifene) may be a strong consideration.

In the MORE (Multiple Outcomes of Raloxifene) study of 5129 women, breast cancer risk was decreased by 76% during three years of treatment with raloxifene.[19] Raloxifene has no stimulatory effect on the uterus.

Estrogens are given intermittently (i.e., 25 days on, 5 off) or continuously depending upon your individual requirements as determined by your physician.

Premarin® is the most widely prescribed form of estrogen. It consists of conjugated equine estrogens and is obtained exclusively from natural sources. Premarin® consists of dozens of estrogens extracted from the urine of pregnant mares.

Common Estrogens

Trade Name	Common Estrogen Dose (in milligrams per day)

Premarin®
(conjugated esterified equine estrogens) 0.3, 0.625, 0.9, 1.25, 2.5

Prempro®
(0.625 conjugated estrogens + 2.5 (5) mg MPA (medroxyprogesterone
acetate) daily for full 28 days of the month).. 0.625

Premphase®
(0.625 conjugated estrogens daily for full
28 days of the month + 5 mg. MPA, days 15–28)... 0.625

Cenestin®
(Synthetic conjugated estrogens) 0.625, 0.9

Estrace®
(micronized 17 beta estradiol)...0.5, 1, 2

Estraderm®
(transdermal 17 beta estradiol bi-weekly patch) 0.05, 1

Estratab®
(esterified estrogen, estrone, equilin) 0.3, 0.625, 1.25, 2.5

Estratest®
(esterified estrogens and methyltestosterone) .... 1.25(Est) + 2.5(MT)

Estratest®HS
(esterified estrogens and methyltestosterone) ....0.625(Est) + 1.25(MT)

Menest™
(esterified estrogens) 0.3, 0.625, 1.25, 2.5

Estinyl®
(ethinyl estradiol, 0.02 mg. or 0.05 mg.)..............0.05 one to three times per day

Ogen®
(estropipate, piperazine estrone sulfate) 0.625, 1.25, 2.5

Ortho-Est®
(estropipate, sodium estrone sulfate)...0.625, 1.25

Ortho-Prefest®
(17 beta estradiol 1 mg. + intermittant
(every three days) 0.09 mg. norgestimate)................................. 1(Est) + 0.09(Nor)

Alora®
(17 beta estradiol biweekly transdermal patch) 0.05, 0.075, 0.1

Fempatch®
(17 beta estradiol transdermal patch)... 0.025 weekly

Climara®
(17 beta estradiol transdermal patch)......................0.025, 0.05, 0.075, 0.1 weekly

Vivelle®
(17 beta estradiol transdermal patch)................0.0375, 0.05, 0.075, 0.1 biweekly

Combipatch®
(17 beta estradiol and norethindrone (progesterone))..... 0.05(Est) + 0.14(Nor)
0.05(Est) + 0.25(Nor)

Femhrt®
(ethinyl estradiol 5 mcg./norethindrone
acetate 1 mg.) .... continuous combined HRT
0.05(Est) + 0.25(Nor)

Hence Premarin's name derivation: pre (pregnant), mar (mares), in (urine). Estrone is the major estrogen in Premarin.® Premarin® has a low amount of 17α estradiol. Other estrogens present in smaller quantities in it, but not normally present in humans, are equilin, 17α dihydroequilin, equilenin, and 17α dihydroequilenin.

■ **Because Premarin® is the most common estrogen replacement therapy used in the United States, most studies of benefits and risks of estrogen have been performed using this form of replacement.**

Estrogen skin patches (transdermal estrogen) have some different effects from estrogen taken orally. Estrogen taken by patches bypasses the liver, so the beneficial effects on cholesterol, HDL and LDL may not be present. Patches can be used, however, with caution if an individual has a history of blood clots.

Women who smoke may benefit from the patch because smokers break down estrogen by mouth faster than non-smoking women. The patches are easy to use and are worn on the abdomen or hip. Some are affixed once a week, some every 3 to 4 days. The major drawback is skin irritation.

Estrogen increases a woman's risk of developing blood clots, and since women who smoke have a particularly increased risk of developing deep venous thrombosis, all women taking estrogen therapy should consider taking one baby aspirin, or preferably one enteric coated aspirin (i.e. Ecotrin®), a day to help prevent blood clots. As mentioned earlier, if a women has had a history of thrombophlebitis or has a strong family history of thrombophlebitis or pulmonary embolism, then, as a general rule, estrogen should not be used. If it is deemed necessary to use it (for example, if a woman has very severe menopausal symptoms), then transdermal estrogen is preferred over the oral tablets because it bypasses the liver and seems to have less effect in the clotting factors involved in blood clotting. Estrogen should be used only with great caution and only if clearly needed if an individual has had a heart attack.

Starting Estrogen Dose

A woman who is over 65 years old may not tolerate starting estrogen at more than 0.3 mg/day conjugated estrogens or a low dose estrogen patch. This is because estrogen metabolism (break down) slows with age. On the other hand, a young woman who has had surgical menopause (removal of the ovaries) may require starting at higher dosages such as 0.625, 0.9, or 1.25 mg/day conjugated estrogens or a stronger estrogen patch and may need titration upwards if menopausal symptoms require.

Minimum Effective Estrogen Dose to Build Bone

The dose of estrogen that may be required for you is best determined in consultation with your physician. The effects of estrogen on bone seem to have an almost linear improvement with increasing dose. The more the dose is increased, the more the improvement on bone mass density and the lower the fracture risk.

Researchers found that a net bone loss occurred in postmenopausal women taking Ethinyl Estradiol estrogen replacement with < 15 mg daily, that no gain or loss occurred between 15–25 mg, and a net gain ocurred with > 25 mg per day.[12]

The minimum effective average dose to prevent bone loss and build better bone of some of the more commonly used preparations is:

- Premarin® (conjugated estrogens; estrone & equilin estrogens) 0.625 mg
- Estrace® (micronized estradiol) 0.5 mg
- Ogen® (estropipate) 0.625 mg
- Estraderm® (estradiol transdermal) 0.05 mg

Estrogen in Combination With Progesterone or Testosterone

Estrogen demonstrates substantial benefit for both the prevention and the management of osteoporosis. Estrogen is sometimes combined with progesterone (i.e., Prempro®, Combipatch® transdermal, Ortho-Prefest®, Femhrt®), or combined with testosterone (Estratest® tabs) depending upon your needs. The combination with progesterone offers protection against the risk of endometrial (uterine) hyperplasia and the resulting uterine cancer, and the combination with testosterone offers improvement in persistent postmenopausal symptoms (i.e., hot flashes, night sweats, irritability, mood alterations, and decreased sexual desire).

The addition of progesterone, most commonly medroxy progesterone, has some other side effects such as fluid retention, mood changes and bloating. Micronized progesterone (trade name Prometrium®) may minimize some of these side effects.

Ortho-Prefest® (1 mg 17 β Estradiol + 0.09 mg norgestimate) intermittant delivers a combination of constant estrogen and intermittent low dose norgestimate (Progesterone) via a novel constant estrogen/pulsed progestin regimen, designed to maximize estrogen replacement benefits while minimizing progestin-related side effects. The Ortho-Prefest® regimen provides for a single oral tablet to be taken once daily. The pink tablet containing 1.0 mg estradiol is taken on days one through three of therapy; the white tablet containing 1.0 mg estradiol and 0.09 mg norgestimate is taken on days four through six of therapy. This pattern is then repeated continuously to produce the constant estrogen/intermittent progestin regimen of Ortho-Prefest®.

Most continuous treatments with medroxy progesterone are 2.5 mg of medroxy progesterone daily with estrogen (i.e., Prempro®, 0.625/2.5.) If spotting appears, then the medroxyprogesterone component is increased (i.e., Prempro®, 0.625/5 mg). Frequently, newly menopausal women have increased spotting with the continuous low dose so the cyclical regimen may be preferred initially. Approximately 20% of women who take a combination estrogen/progesterone on a continuous basis will experience irregular menstrual bleeding during the first several months. If spotting continues despite increased progesterone component, then referral for further evaluation and possible endometrial (uterine) biopsy should be considered. Femhrt® is a continuous combined hormone replacement therapy consisting of ethinyl estradiol 5 mcg and norethindrone acetate 1mg. In studies over 2 years, Femhrt® improved BMD 9.4% over untreated patients.

Several cyclical treatments are used for estrogen/progesterone combination therapy, such as taking estrogen day 1 through 25 of each month and progesterone days 16 through 25 of each month as well. Premphase® is a replacement hormone combination that consists of estrogen (Premarin® 0.625 mg) days 1 to 14 of the month and an estrogen/progesterone combination (Premarin® 0.625 mg and medroxyprogesterone acetate MPA® 5 mg.) days 15 to 28 of each month. Monthly periods may continue in the menopause; however, this does not mean that the woman is fertile and can become pregnant.

Evidence indicates that progesterone may have more of a protective effect on bone than previously realized. Research is currently being done to investigate this. Progesterone effects are being studied when taken by mouth and transdermally (the patch). When taken by mouth, it is transported to the liver where approximately 80% to 90% of it is conjugated by glucouronic acid and excreted into the bile. Progesterone is a raw material that can be used by the body for the production of cortisone and estrogen.

Addition of Testosterone and Surgical Menopause

All younger women who have had their ovaries surgically removed may want to strongly consider testosterone (androgen) replacement. Testosterone is important for sexual desire (libido), for the preservation of muscle mass and strength, and for the relief of severe vasomotor menopausal symptoms (i.e., hot flashes, night sweats, mood swings, and irritability). It also helps to prevent bone mineral loss and subsequent osteopoenia/osteoporosis.

The ovaries in a normal, healthy woman produce estrogen (estradiol), progesterone, and androgens (testosterone and androstenedione). Peak production occurs at about age 35 and thereafter declines gradually until natural menopause. At menopause there is an abrupt decline in estrogen and progesterone production (although there is still some production) but only a small decline in testosterone and androstenedione production.

With surgical menopause, however, a different situation occurs. All hormone production by the ovaries (estrogen, progesterone, and the androgens) is abruptly gone. Age-matched women who have had normal menopause have almost twice the plasma testosterone than women who have had surgical menopause.

Even if a woman has not had surgical menopause, the addition of testosterone may be a consideration should you have loss of sex drive or vasomotor symptoms not responsive to estrogen. Testosterone even helps to prevent osteoporosis. Remember, testosterone can be converted into bone-protecting estrogen. Overweight individuals have more testosterone in their fatty tissues that can be converted into bone-protecting estrogen.

Pap Smear and Mammogram

All postmenopausal women who have not had surgical removal of their uterus and who are receiving estrogen therapy should have a yearly pap smear. All women 50 years and older should have a yearly mammogram.

Natural Estrogens

Many women do not like to take prescription medications at all but want the preventive and treatment effects of estrogen. Other women may want or agree to take only natural or herbal remedies. For them, natural estrogens should be considered.

Natural estrogens, also called phytoestrogens, are found primarily in plants. They have a weak, hormone-like action. Their chemical structure is similar to the estrogens in our body, but the phytoestrogens are less potent than the major estrogens found in our body. Over 200 members of the estrogens have been discovered in over 300 plants, animals, and humans.

The most common type of phytoestrogen found in nature is the isoflavones. Plant estrogens (phytoestrogens) are similar to the three most common human estrogens (estradiol, estrone, and estriol) but are not identical. The isoflavones are thought to increase bone mass but have not been linked to an increase in cancer. Researchers are not sure how effective they are or what dose is necessary for protective effects. And to complicate matters, researchers are not sure even what amounts are found in various food sources which have them.

Soy is the most common source of phytoestrogens in the United States. Phytoestrogens (particularly the isoflavone group of which genistein is found in soy and daidzein) are found in high quantities in soy beans (i.e. soy milk [approximately 41.5 mg per 8 ounces], tofu, tempeh). Soy estrogens are considered to be much less potent than the body's primary estrogen 17 (Estradiol).

Soy milk can be substituted for regular milk at breakfast, lunch, or dinner. Japanese women, who consume on the average 45 mg of soy a day, have 25% of the breast cancer incidence of American women, who consume an average of only 5 mg of soy a day. Japanese women who immigrate to the United States often conform to the high-fat American diet, and their incidence of breast and endometrial cancer increases. Soy is also available as soy extracts sold in capsules. Up to 400 mg per day may be recommended, with the average daily dose being 200–400 mg per day.

Black Cohosh, a perennial herb growing in the northeastern United States, contains phytoestrogens. It has been prescribed for years by European physicians for the treatment of hot flashes and menstrual cramps. Black Cohosh is sold as a capsule and in a concentrated liquid form.

Phytoestrogens are also thought to be found in red clover, don quai, comfrey, alfalfa, false unicorn, ginseng, licorice, pfaffia, sage and other herbs.

Structures of 17ß-Estradiol and the two primary isoflavones found in soy, Genistein and Daidzein.

These plant hormones are also found in wild yams, flax seed, nuts, whole grains, fresh fruits, dried fruits, vegetables, legumes, cooking herbs and honey. Estrogen herbal supplements are popular at many natural health food stores as a supplement for the treatment of menopausal symptoms such as hot flashes, night sweats, and mood swings. These estrogen plant hormones do seem to help with the vasomotor menopausal symptoms. Further research needs to be done into plant phytoestrogens before their value, or lack of value, is determined for the prevention and treatment of osteoporosis.

You must also keep in mind that herbal products are not regulated by the FDA, which means that the safety and effectiveness of a herb does not have to be proven. Equivalency standards do not have to be met by manufacturers nor are there any dosage or potency controls. The amount of active drug in each dose may vary because the manufacturer may not have good quality control standards, and the amount of active drug per milligram dose may vary with different manufacturers. The purity of the herb is not necessarily assured, either, as there may be the possibility of contamination with other compounds. For example, the leaves of a plant herb may be collected, distilled, and manufactured in capsules. The active ingredient may not necessarily have been identified, and there may be contamination with a host of other chemicals that may have various effects on receptors in different parts of the body. Contrary to a popular belief, herbs and herbal supplements are not inert or benign just because they are natural.

Points to Remember

- The decision whether or not to take estrogen at menopause will affect the rest of a woman's life.

- Estrogen is best started at menopause when bone mineral density levels are still high. It's easier to keep bone than to build new bone.

Chapter 7 Bibliography

1   Kanis, J.A. Estrogens, the Menopause, and Osteoporosis. Bone 19,
    no. 5 supplement (November 1996), 185S–190S.

    Cauley, J.A., Seeley, D.G., Ensrud, K, et. al. For the Study of Osteoporotic
    Fractures Research Group. Estrogen Replacement Therapy and Fractures in
    Older Women. Annual Internal Medicine, 1995, 129, 9–16.

    Ettinger, B.F., H. K. Genant, and C. E. Cann. Long Term Estrogen Replacement
    Therapy Prevents Bone Loss and Fractures. Annals of Internal Medicine 102
    (1985): 319–324.

    Lindsay, R., Aitkin, J.M., Anderson, J.B., et. al. Long-term Prevention of
    Postmenopausal Osteoporosis By estrogen, Lancet 1:1038–1041, 1976.

    The Writing Group for the PEPI Trial. Effects of Hormone Therapy on Bone
    Mineral Density. JAMA 276 (1996): 1389–1396.

2   Interview with R. Lindsay, M.D., Ph.D., Modern Medicine, Volume 67
    (January 1999): 36–42.

3   Lindsay, R., et al. Prevention of Spinal Osteoporosis in Oophorectomized
    Women. Lancet (1980): 1151–1153.

4   Grady, D., S. M. Rubin, D. B. Petiti, et al. Hormone Therapy to Prevent Disease
    and Prolong Life in Postmenopausal Women. Annals of Internal Medicine 117
    (1992): 1016–1017.

5   Women's Health Initiative Study Group. Design of the Women's Health
    Initiative Clinical Trial and Observational Study. Control Clinical Trials 19
    (1998): 61–109.

6   Grodstein, F., M. J. Sampfer, J. E. Manson, et al. Postmenopausal Estrogen
    and Progesterone Use and the Risk of Cardiovascular Disease. New England
    Journal of Medicine 335 (1996): 453–461.

7   American Cancer Society. Cancer Facts and Figures. 1997.

8   Calle, E.E., H. L. Miracle-McMahil, M. J. Thun, C. W. Heath Jr. Estrogen
    Replacement Therapy and Risk of Fatal Colon Cancer in a Prospective Cohort
    of Postmenopausal Women. Journal of the National Cancer Institute 87 (1995):
    517–523.

9   Vingerling, J.R., I.Dielemans, C. M. Witterman, A. Hofman, D. E. Grobbee,
    T. V. M. de Jong. Macular Degeneration and Early Menopause: A Case-Control
    Study. British Medical Journal 310 (1995): 1570–1571.

10 Eye Disease Case Control Study Group. Risk Factors for Neovascular Age-
    Related Macular Degeneration. Archives of Opthalmology 110 (1992):
    1701–1708.

11 Salmone, L. M., A. R. Pressman, D. G. Seeley, J. A. Cauley. Estrogen
    Replacement Therapy. Archives of Internal Medicine 156 (1996): 1293–1297.

12 Ziel HK, Finkle WD. Increased Risk of Endometrial Carcinoma among Users of
    Conjugated Estrogens. New England Journal of Medicine 1975;293:1167–1170.

13 Smith, D. C. , R. Prentice, D. J. Thompson, et al. *Association of Exogenous Estrogen and Endometrial Carcinoma. New England Journal of Medicine 293 (1975): 1164–1167.*

14 Persson, I, et al. *Cancer Incidence and Mortality in Women Receiving Estrogen and Estrogen-Progestin Replacement Therapy—Long Term Follow-up of a Swedish Cohort. International Journal of Cancer 67 (1996): 327–332.*

15 Daly, E., M. P. Vessey, M. M. Hawkins, J. L. Carson, P. Gough, S. Marsh. *Risk of Venous Thromboembolism in Users of Hormone Replacement Therapy. Lancet 348 (1996): 977–980.*

16 Jick, H., L. E. Derby, M. W. Myers, C. Vasilakis, K. M. Newton. *Risk of Hospital Admission for Idiopathic Venous Thromboembolism Among Users of Postmenopausal Estrogens. Lancet 348 (1996): 981–983.*

17 Grodstein, et al, 1996 in *The Harvard Nurses Health Study.*

18 Wilson, P. W. F., R. J. Garrison, W. P. Castelli. *Postmenopausal Estrogen Use, Cigarette Smoking, and Cardiovascular Morbidity in Women Over 50: The Framingham Study. New England Journal of Medicine 313 (1985): 1038–1043.*

19 Cummings, et al.. *The Effect of Raloxifene on Risk of Breast Cancer in Post-menopausal Women—Results from the MORE Randomized Trial. JAMA 281 (1999): 2189–2197.*

20 Horsman, et al. *The Effect of Estrogen Dose on Postmenopausal Bone Loss. New England Journal of Medicine 309 (1983): 1405–1407.*

TAB. I.

C. Grignion Sculp.   Imprint. S. & J. Knapton, London. 1737.

Medications Used to Treat Osteoporosis

Building Bone Mass and Building Better Quality Bone

In considering the pharmacologic treatment of osteoporosis, it is well known that improvement in bone mass density alone sometimes does not fully account for the significant decrease in actual fractures seen. Often a substantial decrease in fractures is achieved with only a modest improvement in bone density.

It is postulated that medications may improve the microscopic architecture of the trabecular structure of bone, possibly making bone stronger with only a moderate improvement in bone mineral density. By improving the microarchitecture of bone, the macroarchitecture is strengthened as well, resulting in a decreased tendency for fractures. Medications may work through an improvement in bone quality and possibly bone turnover, as well as an increase in bone mass; current research into the pharmacologic treatment of osteoporosis is looking at these factors.

When to Begin Treatment with Pharmacologic Options

The National Osteoporosis Foundation recommends the following:

- Initiate therapy to reduce fracture risk in postmenopausal women with BMD T-Scores below –2 in the absence of risk factors and in women with T-Scores below –1.5 if other risk factors are present.

- Women over age 70 with multiple risk factors (especially those with previous non-hip, non-spine fractures) are at a high enough risk of fracture to initiate treatment without BMD testing.

The National Osteoporosis Foundation is adamant in emphasizing that the "recommendations developed in this report are intended to serve as a reference point for clinical decision making with individualized patients. They are not intended to be rigid standards, limits, or rules. They can be tailored to individual cases to incorporate facts that are beyond the scope of this guide. Because these are recommendations and not rigid standards, they should not be interpreted as quality standards. Nor should they be used to limit coverage for treatments."

When the NOF developed their guidelines in 1998, they only had data from large studies of Caucasian women to use. The NOF was not suggesting that osteoporosis affects only white postmenopausal women; the data just was not available from which to make recommendations for premenopausal women, women of other races, or men. Nor did it address secondary causes of osteoporosis for the same reasons.

This data is being compiled now by such studies as the National Osteoporosis Risk Assessment (NORA) Study. The NOF will make further guidelines when adequate, appropriate data has been compiled from which to draw conclusions. NORA is the largest study ever of its kind and involved over 4,000 primary care physicians across the country. Over 200,000 postmenopausal women were tested, women who had no prior history of osteoporosis and no BMD testing in the prior twelve months. These women were given a risk factor questionnaire and received a baseline BMD test using a screening peripheral device. The conclusions from the data—regarding osteoporosis fracture risk predictors, age, ethnicity, and other indicators—are being studied and written for publication.

The more independent risk factors for osteoporosis a woman has in addition to menopause, the earlier intervention should be considered. Given that many postmenopausal women have at least four risk factors (i.e., Caucasian, lifelong calcium deficiency, inactivity, advanced age) for osteoporosis, by the NOF guidelines most postmenopausal women with a T-score below –1.5 should be considered for pharmacological intervention.

But what about that gray area of a postmenopausal woman with a T-score of –1.1 to –1.4? She may "fall between the cracks" of the treatment recommendations. For example, a 52-year-old postmenopausal lifelong calcium deficient, inactive, Caucasian woman with a T-score of –1.4 may not necessarily be a candidate for pharmacological treatment if the recommendations are strictly adhered to.

However, her T-score does not fall in the normal range, and she does not have strong bone; thus, she is at risk for impending osteoporosis and fracture. This woman is also at high risk for rapid bone loss of 3 to 5% and possibly 7% a year. The majority of clinicians would probably agree that aggressive prevention intervention is indicated. Most clinicians would consider the possibility of pharmacological intervention in a newly diagnosed recent postmenopausal woman with a T-score of less than –1. It's a lot easier to keep bone strong than to try and rebuild it again. The old cliché applies: An ounce of prevention is worth a pound of cure.

Each individual should be assessed in a clinical context by her or his individual T-score, clinical history, and personal risk factors for fracture to determine what the prevention and treatment measures should be initiated. For example, if a postmenopausal woman has bone loss in the spine, this fits the pattern of postmenopausal bone loss. However, if a postmenopausal woman has a normal spine BMD but low BMD at the hip, then secondary causes of osteoporosis should be considered and investigated.

Fosamax® (Alendronate)

Fosamax is approved by the FDA for both the prevention and treatment of osteoporosis and for the treatment of glucocorticoid-induced osteoporosis in men and women. It inhibits the osteoclastic breakdown of bone, causing a significant increase in bone mineral density.

Fosamax is a powerful alternative for the prevention and treatment of osteoporosis in women who cannot take or are unwilling to take estrogen replacement therapy or in whom estrogen replacement therapy is not adequate. Fosamax is not approved for use in premenopausal women. Fosamax is also beneficial for the prevention and treatment of osteoporosis in men.

Fosamax is often used in combination with hormone replacement therapy for a powerful combined effect. This combination therapy seems to have a synergistic effect, resulting in greater gains in bone mass than either estrogen or Fosamax alone. Although combination therapy is not yet recommended by the NOF, early research studies are very promising, and approval for this combination therapy will probably be forthcoming in the near future.

Fosamax has been approved for the prevention of osteoporosis at a dose of 5 mg per day and for the treatment of osteoporosis at a dose of 10 mg per day. Merck will probably be approved by the FDA soon for a 70 mg. tablet once a week.

The Fracture Intervention Trial (FIT Study)[1] involved 2,027 women who had at least one baseline vertebral fracture. One-half were treated with Fosamax, and the other one-half were given a placebo (no treatment). In the comparison, Fosamax treated women demonstrated a 47% reduction in recurrent vertebral fractures over three years.

U.S. (478 women) and multinational (516 women) studies[2] compared the effects of Fosamax on vertebral fracture incidence in women with a BMD T-Score of at least –2 SD. In patients treated with Fosamax as compared to those given a placebo over three years, there was a significant increase in BMD and a 48% reduction in vertebral fractures.

In both studies, Fosamax reduced the number of two or more vertebral fractures by 90%. The FIT study also found that Fosamax reduced the proportion of women experiencing hip fractures by 51% and wrist fractures by 48%. Other osteoporosis treatment studies involving Fosamax have yielded similar results.

In postmenopausal women under the age of 60 who do not have pre-existing osteoporosis, studies have demonstrated that Fosamax universally prevents bone mineral density loss.

Fosamax is a member of the bisphosphonate class of therapeutic medications. One to two percent of it is absorbed, so for maximum absorption in the gastrointestinal tract, it must be taken in the morning after an overnight fast with a full glass of water (at least 8 ounces), one half-hour before taking in any other liquids, food or medications. The individual must remain upright after taking it for 30 minutes to minimize the possibility of esophageal reflux, since there have been some reported cases of chemical esophagitis (irritation of the esophagus). Most of these cases seem to be related to use of little or no water. Most individuals who take Fosamax find it best to keep it in the bathroom since most individuals go to the bathroom when they get up in the morning, take the Fosamax immediately with 8 oz. of water, then take a shower or bath and fix breakfast. At least 30 minutes elapses between the time they get up and take Fosamax and the time they sit down for breakfast.

Fosamax is not recommended if an individual has a history of esophageal stricture or difficulty in swallowing. It is also not recommended for individuals who have decreased renal function with a creatinine clearance of less than 35 ml per minute, since it is excreted unchanged by the kidneys. No significant drug interactions have been found. Fosamax is now available as a wax-polished oval 10 mg tablet.

Fosamax® is manufactured by Merck Pharmaceutical Co., Research Triangle Park, NC
Customer Services 1-800-290-4259

Miacalcin®

Miacalcin is a synthetic calcitonin similar to the salmon calcitonin molecule. Like human calcitonin, it inhibits bone resorption by direct action on osteoclasts, but it is 40–50 times more potent and has a longer duration of action than human calcitonin.

Miacalcin (Calcitonin-salmon) nasal spray is approved by the FDA for the treatment of postmenopausal osteoporosis in females greater than five years postmenopause. It is specifically indicated for women with low bone mass who refuse or cannot tolerate estrogen or for whom estrogen is not an option. The recommended dose is one spray (200 I.U.) per day intranasally.

Miacalcin is not yet approved for the prevention of osteoporosis. The clinical distinction between prevention and treatment of osteoporosis is often very blurred in primary care offices. Clinically, many physicians are using Miacalcin for prevention of osteoporosis as well as treatment.

The PROOF Study (Prevention of Recurrence of Osteoporotic Fractures) involved 1,175 women who had a least one baseline vertebral spine fracture and a spinal bone mass density greater than 2 standard deviations (SD) below the mean for a healthy young adult. The three year interim results released September 1997[3] of the eventual five-year multicenter trial demonstrated a 37.4% reduction in recurrent vertebral fractures. Interestingly, the spinal BMD increased by

1.26% in the Miacalcin treated individuals, which did not vary statistically from those treated with placebo.

Miacalcin particularly fulfills a niche in osteoporosis treatment in the elderly in nursing homes and assisted living facilities. For many of these very elderly requiring ongoing care, the stricter oral regimen of Fosamax and inability to eat or lie down after taking it is not practical for nurses or nurses aides, and estrogen and or Evista® may be contraindicated (i.e., create blood clots or stroke). For these individuals, the easy compliance of one spray a day in the nose makes it a convenient choice.

Side effects are minimal and, if present, most likely consist of local irritation of the nasal mucosa causing dryness, crusting, and occasionally a minor nosebleed. To minimize nasal irritation, alternate nostrils should be used each day. The spray pump vials must be refrigerated before first use. Before the first use, the spray bottle must be assembled and the spray pump primed by pressing it a few times. After being opened, the bottles need no longer be refrigerated but may be stored at room temperature. No significant drug interactions have been reported.

No effects on cortical bone of the hip and wrist have yet been demonstrated. Therefore, if an individual has a low hip or forearm BMD, Miacalcin would not be a preferred therapeutic medication (unless future studies prove differently).

Miacalcin is generally thought to be less effective than Fosamax, Actonel, or estrogen for the management of osteoporosis. It is, however, an alternative to Fosamax or Actonel when Fosamax or Actonel cannot be taken such as a lifestyle that does not permit it to be taken as directed orally in the morning, and/or estrogen is contraindicated.

Miacalcin can be taken by both men and women.

Miacalcin® is manufactured by Novartis Pharmaceuticals
East Hanover, NJ
Customer Services 1-888-644-8585

Evista (raloxifene) is a selective estrogen receptor modulator (SERM) approved by the FDA for the prevention and treatment of osteoporosis.

A North American Study (544 women), European Study (601 women), and International Study (619 women who had undergone a hysterectomy) each showed improvement in BMD in Evista-treated women. All women were treated also with 600 mg calcium/day. The calcium-supplemented placebo groups lost approximately 1% of BMD over 24 months, whereas the Evista-treated groups each gained BMD.

The MORE (Multiple Outcomes of Raloxifene Evaluation) studied 7,705 women with postmenopausal osteoporosis receiving Evista over 24 months.[4] All women also received 500 mg calcium/day and vitamin D 400 IU/day. Bone mass density at the hip (femoral neck) and the lumbar spine each increased by 2.5%. Spinal fractures in women who had no previous history of a spinal fracture decreased by 52%. In women with previous spinal fractures, raloxifene decreased the likelihood of having another spinal fracture by 32%.

Evista works like an estrogen by decreasing the osteoclastic breakdown of bone, but in some other tissues of the body that estrogen normally affects, Evista has estrogen-antagonist (opposite) actions (i.e., on the uterus and breasts). A secondary benefit is the lowering of total cholesterol by 6% and LDL cholesterol levels by 11% without increasing triglycerides. Recent studies have shown promise that Evista may be particularly effective in reducing the risk of breast cancer. A recent study of postmenopausal women with osteoporosis demonstrated a 76% decrease in invasive breast cancer during three years of treatment with raloxifene. In postmenopausal women, Evista apparently delays the onset of or prevents breast cancer without increasing the risk of developing endometrial cancer. If future clinical studies bear this out, then this may be a particularly beneficial effect for women at risk for breast cancer.

Evista is given at a dose of 60 mg per day orally. Side effects can include an increase in hot flashes (approximately 25% of individuals taking it begin or experience an accentuation of hot flashes) and, just like estrogen, it may cause blood clots so it cannot be used by individuals with a history of active thrombophlebitis or thrombo-lembolic disease, pulmonary emboli, or stroke.

Evista® is manufactured by Eli Lilly
Indianapolis, IN
Customer Services 1-800-545-5979

Actonel®

Actonel® (risedronate) was approved by the FDA in April 2000 for the prevention and treatment of osteoporosis in postmenopausal women and for the prevention and treatment of glucocorticoid-induced osteoporosis in men and women who are either initiating or continuing systemic glucocorticoid treatment (≥ 7.5 mg. predni-sone or equivalent) for chronic diseases (i.e. rheumatoid arthritis). It is also approved by the FDA for the treatment of Paget's disease of bone.

Actonel® is a member of the bisphosphonate class of medications which inhibit bone resorption. The usual dosage is 5 mg./day orally. Actonel® is an oval-shaped, film-coated tablet that transits the esoph-agus in approximately three seconds, so it is well-tolerated by the gastrointestinal system. Actonel® is well-tolerated, even in patients with gastrointestinal (GI) disease, including those with ulcers, esoph-agitis, and chronic heartburn. Actonel® can be taken by individuals taking nonsteroidal anti-inflammatory drugs (NSAIDS) or aspirin, or in individuals with ongoing GI disease. In clinical trials, the incidence of GI side effects was no greater than that of patients taking a placebo (sugar pill). In studies, rates of withdrawal from taking Actonel® because of tolerability problems were equivalent to the placebo.

In North America and Europe, four studies for up to three years involving a total of 4,875 postmenopausal women with osteoporo-sis demonstrated a 41 to 49 percent reduction in recurrent vertebral fractures and a 33 to 39 percent reduction in non-vertebral fractures. Bone mineral density increased from 5 to 7 percent.

Actonel® consistently demonstrates a reduction in vertebral fracture incidence in just one year of treatment compared to a control group in both postmenopausal women and in individuals with glucocorti-coid-induced osteporosis.

Without treatment, one-in-six patients beginning glucocorticoid therapy will experience a vertebral fracture within the first year, and up to 50 percent of patients on chronic glucocorticoid therapy will suffer a fracture. Actonel® is the first therapy to be approved by the FDA for the prevention of glucocorticoid-induced osteoporosis. Actonel® reduces glucocorticoid-induced osteoporosis fractures within the first year by up to 70 percent.

Actonel® is a member of the bisphosphonate class of therapeutic medications. One to two percent of it is absorbed, so for maximum absorption in the gastrointestinal tract, it must be taken in the morning with a six- to eight-ounce glass of water after an overnight fast, and one half hour before taking any other liquids, foods, or medications. Do not lie down for 30 minutes after taking Actonel®. Most individuals find it convenient to keep Actonel® in the bathroom where they can easily find when they get up in the morning. By taking Actonel® with six to eight ounces of water and then showering and fixing breakfast, a person will usually have allowed 30 minutes to elapse prior to eating.

Actonel® is not recommended for individuals who have severely decreased renal function, since it is excreted in the kidneys. No significant drug interactions have been found. Actonel® can be used by both men and women. Proctor & Gamble will probably have a higher-dose, once-a-week tablet in the future as studies are currently underway investigating this dosing regimen.

> Actonel® is manufactured by
> Procter & Gamble Pharmaceuticals
> Cincinnati, OH
> Customer Services 1–800–436–4151

■ **Studies are currently underway evaluating the synergistic (combined) effects of two or more medications. Preliminary results appear very encouraging for enhanced beneficial treatment effects.**

Other Medications

There are several other medications that may benefit osteoporosis but are not approved for the prevention or treatment of osteoporosis by the FDA.

Nolvadex® (tamoxifen) is approved by the FDA for the prevention of recurrent breast cancer. Tamoxifen acts as a nonsteroidal antiestrogen in the breasts, helping to prevent breast cancer, but it also has positive estrogen-like effects on bone. Tamoxifen significantly increases bone mineral density and reduces fractures in postmenopausal women. In a recent study, patients taking tamoxifen 10 mg by mouth twice a day increased the BMD of their lumbar spine by 0.0565 g/cm^2 over one year.

> Nolvadex® is manufactured by Zeneca Pharmaceuticals
> Wilmington, DE
> Customer Services 1-800-456-5678

Didronel® (etidronate) is approved by the FDA for the treatment of Paget's disease of bone (osteitis deformans, a progressive bone disease characterized by abnormal and accelerated bone metabolism) and for myositis ossificans (heterotropic ossification, characterized by abnormal growth of bone in a localized area). Etidronate is a member of the bisphosphonate class of medications like Fosamax, which has been found to inhibit the osteoclastic breakdown of bone and increase bone mineral density. Multiple studies have demonstrated significant increases in spine and hip BMDs and decrease fracture rates in individuals receiving etidronate.

> Didronel® is manufactured by Procter & Gamble
> Pharmaceuticals
> Cincinnati, OH
> Customer Services 1-800-836-0658 or (513) 983-1100

Fluoride increases bone mineral density by stimulating the osteoblastic bone forming cells to produce more bone. Several small studies evaluating sodium fluoride have demonstrated significant increases in BMD, however, fracture reduction results have been variable, and there is a significant question as to whether the bone made is strong bone. At this time, fluoride should not be used for the prevention or treatment of osteoporosis.

Points to Remember

- **Medications to treat osteoporosis may work through an improvement in bone quality and possibly bone turnover, as well as an increase in bone mass.**

- **The more independent risk factors for osteoporosis in addition to menopause, the earlier intervention should be considered for a woman.**

- **Each individual should be assessed in a clinical context by her or his individual T-score, clinical history, and personal risk factors for fracture to determine what prevention and treatment measures should be.**

Chapter 8 Bibliography

1   Black, D. M. et al., Randomized Trial of Effect of Alendronate on Risk Fracture
    in Women with Existing Vertebral Fractures, Fracture Intervention Trial
    Research Group. Lancet 348, No. 9041 (December 1996): 1535–1541.

2   Liberman, U. A., et al. Effect of Oral Alendronate on Bone Mineral Density
    and the Incidence of Fractures in Postmenopausal Women.
    New England Journal of Medicine 333 (1995): 1437–1443.

3   Chestnut, C. et al., Salmon-Calcitonin Nasal Spray Prevents Vertebral
    Fractures in Established Osteoporosis. Further Interim Results of the PROOF
    Study. ECO Abstracts 1998.

4   Ettinger B., et al. ECO Abstracts, MORE Study 1998.

5   Watts, Nelson, Risedronate Effective in Treating Osteoporosis. Report at the
    Annual Meeting of the Endocrine Society, 1999, Family Practice News, July 15,
    1999, Vol. 29, No. 14.

Appendix A

Personal Osteoporosis Risk Assessment

Osteoporosis Testing Center of Michigan
© Raymond E. Cole, D.O., C.C.D.

Name_____ Date _____

The more you answer "yes" to these questions, the greater your risk of osteoporosis.

General Personal Information

[YES] [NO] Are you female?

[YES] [NO] Are you Caucasian or of Northern European ancestry?

[YES] [NO] Are you Asian or Hispanic?

[YES] [NO] Do you have a thin, small-boned frame?

[YES] [NO] Do you have a very lean build, weigh less than 127 pounds, or have a body fat percentage that is less than 15 percent of your total body weight?

[YES] [NO] Are you over the age of 50?

[YES] [NO] Are you over the age of 65?

Personal Physical Characteristics

YES   NO   Have you lost over an inch in height?

YES   NO   Do you have dowager's hump (forward stooping over of your mid-spine)?

YES   NO   Do you have frequent low back pain?

YES   NO   Have you ever broken a bone and had a vertebral compression fracture or experienced a fracture of your hip, wrist, pelvis, rib, or foot as an adult?

YES   NO   Have you ever had a stress fracture?

Family History

YES   NO   Does your mother have a diagnosis of osteoporosis?

YES   NO   Does your sister or brother have osteoporosis?

YES   NO   Does your grandmother have osteoporosis?

YES   NO   Do you have an immediate female family member who has broken a bone as an adult?

Nutrition

YES   NO   Is your diet low (less than 3 servings a day) in sources of calcium such as milk and other dairy products?

YES   NO   Is your diet high in animal protein (more than 3 times a week) such as red meat?

YES **NO**	Are you a strict vegetarian, or do you have a diet primarily weighted toward vegetables and fruits alone?
YES **NO**	Do you have poor nutrition or poor eating habits such as skipping meals?
YES **NO**	Do you drink two or more cola-type beverages daily?
YES **NO**	Do you drink three or more cups of coffee per day?
YES **NO**	Do you obtain less than 800 IUs per day of Vitamin D?
YES **NO**	Do you obtain less than twenty minutes of natural sunlight a day?

Social History

YES **NO**	Do you smoke cigarettes now or have you smoked cigarettes regularly in the past?
YES **NO**	Do you drink two or more alcoholic beverages a day or do you drink alcohol to excess?

Exercise and Body Conditioning

YES **NO**	Do you consider your muscles weak?
YES **NO**	Do you perform aerobic weight-bearing (i.e. walking) and muscle strengthening/toning exercises less than three times weekly?

YES	NO	Are you physically inactive in your work or daily routines?
YES	NO	Is your health so poor that you are not able to perform your Activities of Daily Living (ADLs) such as getting dressed, bathing, and preparing meals?
YES	NO	Have you experienced a fall or are you at increased risk for falling (i.e. unstable from poor health/frailty, postural dizziness, blacking out, fainting spells)?

Female History

YES	NO	Are you a postmenopausal woman?
YES	NO	Have you had a hysterectomy with surgical removal of your ovaries?
YES	NO	Have both your ovaries been removed before natural menopause?
YES	NO	Did you experience menopause before the age of 45?
YES	NO	Did your first menstrual period begin after the age of 15?
YES	NO	Are you past your menopause and not taking hormone replacement therapy?
YES	NO	Have your menstrual periods stopped because of intensive exercise?
YES	NO	Have your menstrual periods stopped for one reason or another for over a year?

YES	NO	Are your menstrual periods scarce and irregular?
YES	NO	Have you not had children (nulliparity)?

Male History

YES	NO	Do you have a decrease in testosterone (commonly known as the male hormone) or experience impotence (difficulty in or inability to achieve penile erection or ejaculate?
YES	NO	Do you have decreased testicular function (male hypogonadism)?
YES	NO	Are you receiving Lupron, (a Gonadotropin-releasing hormone) to treat prostate cancer?

Medication History

YES	NO	Do you take steroid or cortisone-like drugs (i.e. prednisone)?
YES	NO	Do you take thyroid hormone medication which might be excessive?
YES	NO	Do you take anticonvulsants for seizures or epilepsy such as phenobarb or phenytoin (Dilantin®)?
YES	NO	Do you regularly take aluminum containing antacids such as Maalox® or Mylanta® ?
YES	NO	Do you take Loop diuretics or water pills such as Lasix®, Bumex®, or Edecrin®?

YES	NO	Do you take Lithium, isoniazid, methotrexate, or heparin?
YES	NO	Have you had chemotherapy for cancer?
YES	NO	Do you take multiple medications or practice polypharmacy?

Medical History

YES	NO	Have you ever had an X-ray report which said you had demineralization or loss of bone density?
YES	NO	Do you have hyperthyroidism (overactive thyroid)?
YES	NO	Do you have hyperparathyroidism (overactive parathyroids)?
YES	NO	Do you have insulin-dependent diabetes mellitus?
YES	NO	Do you have rheumatoid arthritis?
YES	NO	Do you have chronic obstructive pulmonary disease such as emphysema or chronic bronchitis?
YES	NO	Do you have Paget's disease of bone?
YES	NO	Do you have multiple myeloma, lymphoma, or leukemia?
YES	NO	Do you have an eating disorder such as bulimia or anorexia?

YES	**NO**	Do you have liver disease?
YES	**NO**	Have you had part of your stomach removed or had stomach by-pass surgery?
YES	**NO**	Do you have a malabsorption syndrome such as Crohn's disease or sprue?
YES	**NO**	Do you have a chronic intestinal disease such as irritable bowel disease (IBS)?
YES	**NO**	Do you have lactose intolerance or any other nutritional disorders which interfere with intestinal absorption?
YES	**NO**	Do you have chronic renal insufficiency or failure?
YES	**NO**	Do you have sarcoidosis or multiple sclerosis?
YES	**NO**	Do you have pernicious anemia, endometriosis, thalassemia, hyperprolactonemia, systemic mastomy-cosis, congenital porphyria, hemophilia, osteogenesis imperfecta, malacia, Ehrlers-Danlos syndrome, or homocystinuria?
YES	**NO**	Do you have prolonged immobilizaion or partial or complete paralysis of an extremity?
YES	**NO**	Have you had an organ transplant?
YES	**NO**	Do you have multiple chronic medical conditions which are causing you poor health, frailty, and lack of abiltiy to perform your normal daily activities?

Frequently Asked Questions About Hip and Spine DEXA Bone Densitometry

Appendix B

1. Why do I need this examination?

This examination measures your bone mineral density and compares your measurements to those of a normal, healthy 30-year old woman. Your physician can use this information to make a diagnosis about your bone status and fracture risk and to give you osteoporosis prevention and treatment recommendations.

2. Is the examination safe?

The examination is highly safe. It is not an X-ray; the radiation emitted is less than 1/10th the dose of a normal chest X-ray, or about as much radiation as you would get if you were in the sun all day. If you are pregnant, be sure and inform the technologist or your physician when this test is ordered.

3. Will the examination hurt?

The technologist will make every effort to make you comfortable during the exam. There will be no shots or injections, there is nothing to ingest, and there is no pressure from the machine. The machine is open; you will not be enclosed during the exam.

4. Is there any special preparation involved?

For spinal/hip densitometry only, you do not need to undress for the examination, although it is helpful if you wear loose fitting clothing without metal zippers, preferably elastic waist pants. For a total body exam, you will need to undress and wear a special gown that the center provides. It is helpful if you do not wear jewelry (necklaces, watch, or rings) to the exam as you will need to remove all metal items.

5. **Do I need to alter my eating habits in preparation for the test?**

There is no pre-examination preparation you must do before arriving for the exam. You need not fast from either food or liquids before taking the exam.

6. **How long will the examination take?**

The spinal/hip only examination takes approximately ten minutes; the total body exam takes about fifteen minutes. Upon arrival, you will be asked to fill out a questionnaire giving the technologist and your physician information about your risk factors for osteoporosis. If the technologist answers questions and gives you your results, the total exam may take up to forty-five minutes.

7. **What is the examination like?**

During the exam, you will lie on an open table with a mechanical arm extending over you the width of the table. During this exam, the arm will travel over the portion of your body being scanned. It will never touch your body.

8. **When will I get the results from the exam?**

At the Osteoporosis Testing Center of Michigan, the technologist can give you your results immediately following the exam, but you will need to get a prevention and treatment plan from your recommending physician.

Appendix C
Individual Case Studies and Treatment Recommendations

Introduction

The case studies in this section show the results of three different diagnoses related to osteporosis:

- Normal bone mineral density

- Osteopoenia

- Severe osteoporosis

The pages shown are actual reports from the LUNAR® Prodigy system used at the Osteoporosis Testing Center and demonstrate the level of detail available in the diagnosis of osteoporosis.

Case Study 1: Normal Bone Mineral Density

Osteoporosis Testing Center of Michigan
107 W. Chicago St.
Brooklyn, MI 49230
FAX : (517) 592-2540   Phone : (517) 592-9355

DXA Bone Density Test Report

Test Date : 09/20/1999	Report Date : 12/14/1999
Doctor :	Patient :
Phone :	Patient ID:
FAX :	DOB:
Procedure : Bone Density Test	Home Phone :
Device : Prodigy	Work Phone :

On 09/20/1999 we performed an initial DEXA bone density test. The assessment is based upon the T-score as recommended by the World Health Organization[1] with modification[2]. The fracture risk assessment is based upon the patient's Z-score using the prospective data published from the ongoing Study of Osteoporosis Fractures[3]. Please call me if you have any questions about this report.

Indications for the Bone Density Test
The bone density test was performed to evaluate the need for treatment of bone loss in this estrogen deficient woman.
The bone density test was indicated to determine the need for treatment of bone loss in a patient with multiple risk factors for osteoporosis.
The bone density test was performed to screen the patient for osteopenia and osteoporosis.

Present Therapy
Estrogen

RISK FACTORS

Female Gender	Post-Menopause	Caucasian Descent
Excessive Colas	Excessive protein	Hx Nephrolithiasis
S/P Hysterectomy		

Assessment

The patient's bone density test in the lumbar spine was normal.
Please note that the values of the PA Spine bone density for L2-L4 may be somewhat elevated due to artifactual interferance from degenerative osteoarthritic changes (see image).
The patient's bone density test in the right hip was normal.
The patient's bone density test in the left hip was normal.

Bone Density Test Measurements

Test Date	Key Site	BMD gm/cm^2	T-Score	%Young Normal	Z-Score	% Age Matched
09/20/1999	PA Spine	1.451	2.095	121%	3.885	147%
09/20/1999	Total Left Hip	0.939	-0.510	94%	0.788	111%
09/20/1999	L. Fem. Neck	1.001	0.176	102%	1.749	127%
09/20/1999	Total Right Hip	0.925	-0.622	93%	0.677	110%
09/20/1999	R. Fem. Neck	1.078	0.819	110%	2.392	136%

HEIGHT   WEIGHT

Test Date	In Inches	In Meters	In Pounds	In Kilograms
09/20/1999	64.173	1.630	119.048	54.000

Recommendations

A daily intake of approximately 1000 mg of elemental calcium from either dietary or supplementary sources is suggested for this patient.

Recommend Vitamin D3 400 IU/day (most multiviamins ie. Centrum have this amount) to increase the absorption of calcium. A multivitamin also helps supply trace minerals necessary for bone formation. Foods high in calcium are milk, yogurt, cheese, ice cream, tofu, vegetables(brocccoli, soybeans, collards, turnip greens, bok choy), fish and shellfish (oysters, sardines, salmon, shrimp), oranges, orange juice fortified with calcium, almonds, etc. Many low-fat foods are calcium rich such as low-fat or skim milk, low-fat cheese, low-fat yogurt, etc., for the weight conscious individuals.

Because of the patient's history of kidney stones, calcium citrate would be the preferred type of calcium supplement.

Recommend a moderate exercise program to include stretching and aerobic weight-bearing exercise (such as walking 30-minutes 3x's a week on alternating days or 20-minutes 5x's a week); In conjunction with a muscle-strengthening program, (such as light weight lifting with dumbells for 40-45 minutes 2x's a week with at least three days between sessions, or 30-minutes 3x's a week with at least one day between sessions or 20-minutes five days a week).

General considerations to reduce ones risk of Osteoporosis fracture are: avoiding long acting sedative hypnotic agents (increase risk of falls), reducing caffeine (ie.coffee, chocolate) and absence of nicotine (ie. smoking) intake, maintaining healthy vision (so as not to be predisposed to falls) and instituting maximum therapeutic measures available to maintain and improve Bone Mineral Density.

A follow-up bone density test is recommended in 24 months.

The patient has been instructed to follow up with you next week to discuss the test results, and for continuing treatment.

Sincerely,

Raymond E. Cole D.O., C.C.D.

Raymond E. Cole D.O., C.C.D.

(1) Kanis JA, Melton LJ, Christiansen C, Johnson CC, Khaltaev N. The diagnosis of osteoporosis. J Bone Min Res 1994;9:1137-1141.
(2) Modified WHO Criteria: T-score > -1.0 = Normal, T-score < -1.0 but > -2.0 = osteopenia, T-score < -2.0 = osteoporosis
(3) Cummings SR, Black Dm, Nevitt MC, Browner W, Cauley J, Ensrud K, Genant HK, Palermo L, Scott J, Vogt TM. Bone density at various sites for prediction of hip fracture. Lancet 1993;341:72-75.

Osteoporosis Testing Center
107 West Chicago Street
Brooklyn, MI 49230

	DUALFEMUR BONE DENSITY			
Attendant:	Measured:	09/20/1999	10:02:15 AM	(2.05)
63.7 Years 01/20/1936	Analyzed:	09/20/1999	10:04:57 AM	(2.05)
64.3 in. 119.2 lbs. White Female	Printed:	12/06/1999	12:37:56 PM	(2.05)
Physician:				_fid2xo7vx.dfe

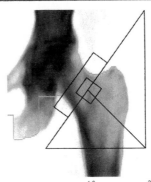

Reference: Total[11]

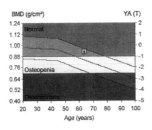

Region	BMD (g/cm²) [1,6]	Young-Adult (T) [2,7]	Age-Matched (Z) [3]
Total Lt.	0.939	-0.5	0.8
Total Rt.	0.925	-0.6	0.7
Total Avg.	0.932	-0.6	0.7
Total Diff.	0.013	-	-

Image not for diagnosis

76.3.0:50.00:12.0 0.00:11.04 0.60x1.05 13.4:29.2
0.00:0.00 0.00:0.00

1 — Statistically 68% of repeat scans fall within 1SD (± 0.020 g/cm² for Total)
2 — USA, Femur Reference Population, Ages 20-40
3 — Matched for Age, Weight (females 25-100 Kg), Ethnic
6 — Standardized BMD for Total Rt. is 875 mg/cm², Total Lt. is 888 mg/cm²
7 — Total T-Score difference is 0.1. Asymmetry is None.
11 — WHO T-Score categories are: >-1.0 SD = Normal; -1.0 to -2.5 SD = Osteopenia;
    <-2.5 SD = Osteoporosis

LUNAR® Prodigy
10221

Osteoporosis Testing Center
107 West Chicago Street
Brooklyn, MI 49230

Attendant:

63.7 Years 01/20/1936

64.3 in. 119.2 lbs. White Female

Physician:

DUALFEMUR BONE DENSITY

Measured:	09/20/1999	10:02:15 AM	(2.05)
Analyzed:	09/20/1999	10:04:57 AM	(2.05)
Printed:	12/06/1999	12:37:56 PM	(2.05)

_fid2xo7vx.dfe

ANCILLARY RESULTS

Region	BMD [1,6] (g/cm²)	Young-Adult [2,7] (%)	(T)	Age-Matched [3] (%)	(Z)	Est. BMC [4] (g)	Est. Area [4] (cm²)
Neck Lt.	1.001	102	0.2	127	1.7	4.8	4.8
Neck Rt.	1.078	110	0.8	136	2.4	5.2	4.9
Neck Avg.	1.040	106	0.5	131	2.1	5.0	4.8
Neck Diff.	0.077	-	-	-	-	0.4	0.0
Wards Lt.	0.830	91	-0.6	130	1.5	2.1	2.6
Wards Rt.	0.910	100	0.0	143	2.1	2.4	2.6
Wards Avg.	0.870	96	-0.3	137	1.8	2.3	2.6
Wards Diff.	0.080	-	-	-	-	0.2	0.0
Troch Lt.	0.700	89	-0.8	102	0.1	7.0	10.1
Troch Rt.	0.649	82	-1.3	95	-0.3	8.3	12.8
Troch Avg.	0.674	85	-1.1	98	-0.1	7.7	11.4
Troch Diff.	0.051	-	-	-	-	1.2	2.7
Shaft Lt.	1.082	-	-	-	-	15.8	14.6
Shaft Rt.	1.128	-	-	-	-	15.5	13.8
Shaft Avg.	1.105	-	-	-	-	15.7	14.2
Shaft Diff.	0.046	-	-	-	-	0.3	0.8
Total Lt.	0.939	94	-0.5	111	0.8	27.7	29.5
Total Rt.	0.925	93	-0.6	110	0.7	29.1	31.4
Total Avg.	0.932	93	-0.6	110	0.7	28.4	30.4
Total Diff.	0.013	-	-	-	-	1.4	1.9

1 — Statistically 68% of repeat scans fall within 1SD (± 0.020 g/cm² for Total)
2 — USA, Femur Reference Population, Ages 20-40
3 — Matched for Age, Weight (females 25-100 Kg). Ethnic
4 — Results for investigational use only.
6 — Standardized BMD for Total Rt. is 875 mg/cm², Total Lt. is 888 mg/cm².
7 — Total T-Score difference is 0.1. Asymmetry is None.

LUNAR Prodigy
10221

Osteoporosis Testing Center
107 West Chicago Street
Brooklyn, MI 49230

AP SPINE BONE DENSITY

Attendant:
63.7 Years 01/20/1936
64.3 in. 119.2 lbs. White Female
Physician:

Measured:	09/20/1999	9:59:29 AM	(2.05)
Analyzed:	09/20/1999	10:06:45 AM	(2.05)
Printed:	12/06/1999	12:37:08 PM	(2.05)
			_fid2r67vx.dfs

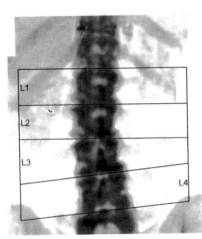

Reference: L2-L4[11]

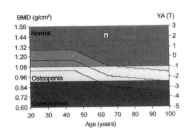

Region	BMD[1,6] (g/cm²)	Young-Adult[2] (T)	Age-Matched[3] (Z)
L1	1.287	1.3	3.1
L2	1.471	2.3	4.0
L3	1.528	2.7	4.5
L4	1.367	1.4	3.2
L2-L4	1.451	2.1	3.9

Image not for diagnosis
76.3.0:50.00:12.0 0.00:9.30 0.60x1.05 14.9:23.8
0.00:0.00 0.00:0.00

1 — Statistically 68% of repeat scans fall within 1SD (± 0.010 g/cm² for L2-L4)
2 — USA, AP Spine Reference Population, Ages 20-40
3 — Matched for Age, Weight (females 25-100 Kg), Ethnic
6 — Standardized BMD for L2-L4 is 1,382 mg/cm².
11 — WHO T-Score categories are: >-1.0 SD = Normal; -1.0 to -2.5 SD = Osteopenia;
     <-2.5 SD = Osteoporosis

Prodigy
10221

Osteoporosis Testing Center
107 West Chicago Street
Brooklyn, MI 49230

		AP SPINE BONE DENSITY		
Attendant:	Measured:	09/20/1999	9:59:29 AM	(2.05)
63.7 Years 01/20/1936	Analyzed:	09/20/1999	10:06:45 AM	(2.05)
64.3 in. 119.2 lbs. White Female	Printed:	12/06/1999	12:37:08 PM	(2.05)
Physician:				_fid2r67vx.dfs

ANCILLARY RESULTS

Region	BMD [1,6] (g/cm²)	Young-Adult [2] (%)	Young-Adult [2] (T)	Age-Matched [3] (%)	Age-Matched [3] (Z)	Est. BMC [4] (g)	Est. Area [4] (cm²)	Est. Width [4] (cm)	Est. Height [4] (cm)
L1	1.287	114	1.3	141	3.1	15.6	12.1	3.8	3.1
L2	1.471	123	2.3	149	4.0	17.6	12.0	4.0	3.0
L3	1.528	127	2.7	155	4.5	20.1	13.2	4.2	3.1
L4	1.367	114	1.4	139	3.2	20.2	14.7	4.6	3.2
L1-L2	1.378	120	1.9	147	3.7	33.2	24.1	3.9	6.1
L1-L3	1.431	122	2.2	150	4.0	53.3	37.3	4.0	9.2
L1-L4	1.413	120	1.9	146	3.7	73.5	52.0	4.2	12.5
L2-L3	1.501	125	2.5	152	4.3	37.7	25.1	4.1	6.1
L2-L4	1.451	121	2.1	147	3.9	57.9	39.9	4.3	9.3
L3-L4	1.443	120	2.0	146	3.8	40.3	27.9	4.4	6.3

Z-Score for Vertebral Height (L2-L4)

Compared to young adult (Z):	-2.1
Adjusted for stature (Z):	-2.3

1 — Statistically 68% of repeat scans fall within 1SD (± 0.010 g/cm² for L2-L4)
2 — USA, AP Spine Reference Population, Ages 20-40
3 — Matched for Age, Weight (females 25-100 Kg), Ethnic
4 — Results for investigational use only.
6 — Standardized BMD for L2-L4 is 1,382 mg/cm².

LUNAR Prodigy 10221

Case Study 2: Osteopoenia

Osteoporosis Testing Center of Michigan
107 W. Chicago St.
Brooklyn, MI 49230
FAX : (517) 592-2540   Phone : (517) 592-9355

DXA Bone Density Test Report

Test Date : 10/21/1999
Doctor :
Phone :
FAX :
Procedure : Bone Density Test
Device :   Prodigy

Report Date :
Patient :
Patient ID:
DOB:
Home Phone :
Work Phone :

On 10/21/1999 we performed an initial DEXA bone density test. The assessment is
based upon the T-score as recommended by the World Health Organization[1] with modification[2]. The fracture
risk assessment is based upon the patient's Z-score using the prospective data published from the ongoing
Study of Osteoporosis Fractures[3].   Please call me if you have any questions about this report.

Indications for the Bone Density Test
The bone density test was performed to evaluate the need for treatment of bone loss in this estrogen
deficient woman.
The bone density test was indicated to determine the need for treatment of bone loss in a patient with
multiple risk factors for osteoporosis.
The bone density test was performed to screen the patient for osteopenia and osteoporosis.

RISK FACTORS

| Female Gender | Post-Menopause | Caucasian Descent |
| Dairy Intake Low | Excessive Coffee | Hx Hypertension |

Assessment

**Please note that the values of the PA Spine bone density for L2-L4 may be somewhat elevated due to
artifactual interferance from degenerative osteoarthritic changes (see image).
The patient's bone density test in the lumbar spine was diagnostic of osteopenia.**

**The patient's bone density test in the left hip was diagnostic of osteopenia.
The patient's bone density test in the right hip was diagnostic of osteopenia.**

Bone Density Test Measurements

Test Date	Key Site	BMD gm/cm^2	T-Score	%Young Normal	Z-Score	% Age Matched
10/21/1999	PA Spine	1.006	-1.615	84%	-0.275	97%
10/21/1999	Total Left Hip	0.812	-1.565	81%	-0.423	94%
10/21/1999	L. Fem. Neck	0.775	-1.711	79%	-0.352	95%
10/21/1999	Total Right Hip	0.817	-1.525	82%	-0.382	95%
10/21/1999	R. Fem. Neck	0.800	-1.498	82%	-0.139	98%

Test Date	HEIGHT In Inches	In Meters	WEIGHT In Pounds	In Kilograms
10/21/1999	65.354	1.660	165.345	75.000

Recommendations

A total intake of approximately 1500 mg of elemental calcium from dietary and supplementary sources is suggested for this patient.

Foods high in calcium are milk, yogurt, cheese, ice cream, tofu, vegetables(brocccoli, soybeans, collards, turnip greens, bok choy), fish and shellfish (oysters, sardines, salmon, shrimp), oranges, orange juice fortified with calcium, almonds, etc. Many low-fat foods are calcium rich such as low-fat or skim milk, low-fat cheese, low-fat yogurt, etc., for the weight conscious individuals.

Recommend vitamin D3 400 IU/day (most multivitamins i.e. Centrum have this amount) to increase the absorption of calcium. A multivitamin also helps supply trace minerals necessary for bone formation.

Recommend a moderate exercise program to include stretching and aerobic weight-bearing exercise (such as walking 30-minutes 3x's a week on alternating days or 20-minutes 5x's a week); In conjunction with a muscle-strengthening program, (such as light weight lifting with dumbells for 40-45 minutes 2x's a week with at least three days between sessions, or 30-minutes 3x's a week with at least one day between sessions or 20-minutes five days a week).

General considerations to reduce ones risk of Osteoporosis fracture are: avoiding long acting sedative hypnotic agents (increase risk of falls), reducing caffeine (ie.coffee, chocolate) and absence of nicotine (ie. smoking) intake, maintaining healthy vision (so as not to be predisposed to falls) and instituting maximum therapeutic measures available to maintain and improve Bone Mineral Density.

Recommend consideration for hormone replacement therapy and/or pharmacologic therapy.

A follow-up bone density test is recommended in 24 months.

The patient has been instructed to follow up with you next week to discuss the test results, and for continuing treatment.

Sincerely,

Raymond E. Cole D.O., C.C.D.

Raymond E. Cole D.O., C.C.D.

(1) Kanis JA, Melton LJ, Christiansen C, Johnson CC, Khaltaev N. The diagnosis of osteoporosis. J Bone Min Res 1994;9:1137-1141.
(2) Modified WHO Criteria: T-score > -1.0 = Normal, T-score < -1.0 but > -2.0 = osteopenia, T-score < -2.0 = osteoporosis
(3) Cummings SR, Black Dm, Nevitt MC, Browner W, Cauley J, Ensrud K, Genant HK, Palermo L, Scott J, Vogt TM. Bone density at various sites for prediction of hip fracture. Lancet 1993;341:72-75.

Osteoporosis Testing Center
107 West Chicago Street
Brooklyn, MI 49230

DUALFEMUR BONE DENSITY

Attendant:	Measured:	10/21/1999 8:33:33 AM	(2.05)
71.0 Years 10/04/1928	Analyzed:	10/21/1999 8:37:21 AM	(2.05)
65.5 in. 166.0 lbs. White Female	Printed:	12/06/1999 2:31:27 PM	(2.05)
Physician:			_fjydgs7vx.dfe

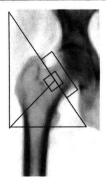
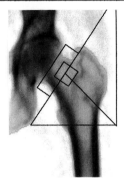

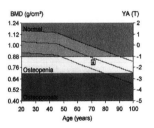

Reference: Total[11]

Region	BMD (g/cm²)[1,6]	Young-Adult (T)[2,7]	Age-Matched (Z)[3]
Total Lt.	0.812	-1.6	-0.4
Total Rt.	0.817	-1.5	-0.4
Total Avg.	0.815	-1.5	-0.4
Total Diff.	0.005	-	-

Image not for diagnosis

76:3.0:50.00:12.0 0.00:13.56 0.60x1.05 15.5:43.0
0.00:0.00 0.00:0.00

1 — Statistically 68% of repeat scans fall within 1SD (± 0.020 g/cm² for Total)
2 — USA, Femur Reference Population, Ages 20-40
3 — Matched for Age, Weight (females 25-100 Kg), Ethnic
6 — Standardized BMD for Total Rt. is 769 mg/cm², Total Lt. is 764 mg/cm².
7 — Total T-Score difference is 0.0. Asymmetry is None.
11 — WHO T-Score categories are: >-1.0 SD = Normal; -1.0 to -2.5 SD = Osteopenia; <-2.5 SD = Osteoporosis

LUNAR Prodigy

10221

Osteoporosis Testing Center
107 West Chicago Street
Brooklyn, MI 49230

	DUALFEMUR BONE DENSITY		
Attendant:	Measured:	10/21/1999 8:33:33 AM	(2.05)
71.0 Years 10/04/1928	Analyzed:	10/21/1999 8:37:21 AM	(2.05)
65.5 in. 166.0 lbs. White Female	Printed:	12/06/1999 2:31:27 PM	(2.05)
Physician:			_fjydgs7vx.dfe

ANCILLARY RESULTS

Region	BMD [1,6] (g/cm²)	Young-Adult [2,7] (%)	(T)	Age-Matched [3] (%)	(Z)	Est. BMC [4] (g)	Est. Area [4] (cm²)
Neck Lt.	0.775	79	-1.7	95	-0.4	3.9	5.0
Neck Rt.	0.800	82	-1.5	98	-0.1	3.7	4.7
Neck Avg.	0.787	80	-1.6	96	-0.2	3.8	4.9
Neck Diff.	0.026	-	-	-	-	0.1	0.3
Wards Lt.	0.535	59	-2.9	82	-0.9	1.5	2.8
Wards Rt.	0.478	52	-3.3	73	-1.4	1.2	2.5
Wards Avg.	0.507	56	-3.1	77	-1.2	1.3	2.6
Wards Diff.	0.058	-	-	-	-	0.4	0.4
Troch Lt.	0.671	85	-1.1	94	-0.4	9.0	13.5
Troch Rt.	0.681	86	-1.0	95	-0.3	10.0	14.6
Troch Avg.	0.676	86	-1.0	94	-0.4	9.5	14.1
Troch Diff.	0.010	-	-	-	-	0.9	1.2
Shaft Lt.	0.954	-	-	-	-	14.0	14.7
Shaft Rt.	0.965	-	-	-	-	13.5	14.0
Shaft Avg.	0.960	-	-	-	-	13.8	14.4
Shaft Diff.	0.010	-	-	-	-	0.5	0.7
Total Lt.	0.812	81	-1.6	94	-0.4	26.9	33.2
Total Rt.	0.817	82	-1.5	95	-0.4	27.2	33.3
Total Avg.	0.815	81	-1.5	94	-0.4	27.1	33.3
Total Diff.	0.005	-	-	-	-	0.3	0.2

1 — Statistically 68% of repeat scans fall within 1SD (± 0.020 g/cm² for Total)
2 — USA, Femur Reference Population, Ages 20–40
3 — Matched for Age, Weight (females 25-100 Kg), Ethnic
4 — Results for investigational use only.
6 — Standardized BMD for Total Rt. is 769 mg/cm², Total Lt. is 764 mg/cm².
7 — Total T-Score difference is 0.0. Asymmetry is None.

LUNAR Prodigy 10221

Osteoporosis Testing Center
107 West Chicago Street
Brooklyn, MI 49230

AP SPINE BONE DENSITY

Attendant:

71.0 Years 10/04/1928

65.5 in. 166.0 lbs. White Female

Physician:

Measured:	10/21/1999	8:29:46 AM	(2.05)
Analyzed:	10/21/1999	8:38:25 AM	(2.05)
Printed:	12/06/1999	2:30:34 PM	(2.05)

_fjydbj7vx.dfs

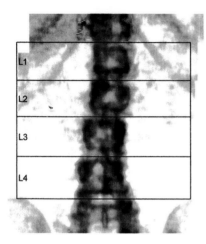

Reference: L2-L4[11]

BMD (g/cm²) YA (T)

Normal

Osteopenia

Osteoporosis

Age (years)

Region	BMD[1,6] (g/cm²)	Young-Adult[2] (T)	Age-Matched[3] (Z)
L1	0.907	-1.9	-0.5
L2	0.968	-1.9	-0.6
L3	1.068	-1.1	0.2
L4	0.983	-1.8	-0.5
L2-L4	1.006	-1.6	-0.3

Image not for diagnosis

76:3.0:50.00:12.0 0.00:11.64 0.60x1.05 18.8:32.8

0.00:0.00 0.00:0.00

1 — Statistically 68% of repeat scans fall within 1SD (± 0.010 g/cm² for L2-L4)

2 — USA, AP Spine Reference Population, Ages 20-40

3 — Matched for Age, Weight (females 25-100 Kg), Ethnic

6 — Standardized BMD for L2-L4 is 958 mg/cm².

11 — WHO T-Score categories are: >-1.0 SD = Normal; -1.0 to -2.5 SD = Osteopenia; <-2.5 SD = Osteoporosis

 Prodigy 10221

Osteoporosis Testing Center
107 West Chicago Street
Brooklyn, MI 49230

Attendant:

71.0 Years 10/04/1928

65.5 in. 166.0 lbs. White Female

Physician:

	AP SPINE BONE DENSITY		
Measured:	10/21/1999	8:29:46 AM	(2.05)
Analyzed:	10/21/1999	8:38:25 AM	(2.05)
Printed:	12/06/1999	2:30:34 PM	(2.05)
			_fjydbj7vx.dfs

ANCILLARY RESULTS

Region	BMD [1,6] (g/cm²)	Young-Adult [2] (%)	(T)	Age-Matched [3] (%)	(Z)	Est. BMC [4] (g)	Est. Area [4] (cm²)	Est. Width [4] (cm)	Est. Height [4] (cm)
L1	0.907	80	-1.9	94	-0.5	10.8	11.9	3.6	3.4
L2	0.968	81	-1.9	93	-0.6	11.4	11.8	3.7	3.2
L3	1.068	89	-1.1	103	0.2	14.7	13.8	3.9	3.5
L4	0.983	82	-1.8	95	-0.5	16.9	17.2	4.6	3.7
L1-L2	0.937	82	-1.8	95	-0.4	22.2	23.7	3.6	6.6
L1-L3	0.985	84	-1.5	98	-0.2	37.0	37.5	3.7	10.1
L1-L4	0.985	83	-1.6	97	-0.3	53.9	54.8	3.9	13.8
L2-L3	1.022	85	-1.5	98	-0.1	26.2	25.6	3.8	6.7
L2-L4	1.006	84	-1.6	97	-0.3	43.1	42.8	4.1	10.5
L3-L4	1.021	85	-1.5	98	-0.2	31.7	31.1	4.3	7.2

Z-Score for Vertebral Height (L2-L4)

Compared to young adult (Z):	0.1
Adjusted for stature (Z):	-0.1

1 — Statistically 68% of repeat scans fall within 1SD (± 0.010 g/cm² for L2-L4)
2 — USA, AP Spine Reference Population, Ages 20-40
3 — Matched for Age, Weight (females 25-100 Kg), Ethnic
4 — Results for investigational use only.
6 — Standardized BMD for L2-L4 is 958 mg/cm².

LUNAR Prodigy
10221

Osteoporosis Testing Center of Michigan
107 W. Chicago St.
Brooklyn, MI 49230
FAX : (517) 592-2540   Phone : (517) 592-9355

DXA Bone Density Test Report

Test Date : 08/06/1999   Report Date : 12/16/1999
Doctor :   Patient :
Phone :   Patient ID:
FAX :   DOB:
Procedure : Bone Density Test   Home Phone :
Device :   Prodigy   Work Phone :

On 08/06/1999 we performed an initial DEXA bone density test. The assessment is
based upon the T-score as recommended by the World Health Organization[1] with modification[2]. The fracture
risk assessment is based upon the patient's Z-score using the prospective data published from the ongoing
Study of Osteoporosis Fractures[3]. Please call me if you have any questions about this report.

Indications for the Bone Density Test
The bone density test was performed to evaluate the need for treatment of bone loss in this estrogen
deficient woman.
The bone density test was indicated to determine the need for treatment of bone loss in a patient with
multiple risk factors for osteoporosis.
The bone density test was performed to screen the patient for osteopenia and osteoporosis.

Present Therapy
Calcium Supplementation
RISK FACTORS

Female Gender	Post-Menopause	Caucasian Descent
Lifestyle Sedentar	Loss of Height	Dairy Intake Low
Excessive protein	Recent wrist fx	

Assessment
The patient's bone density test in the lumbar spine was diagnostic of osteoporosis.
The patient's bone density test of the left hip was diagnostic of osteoporosis.
The patient's bone density test in the right hip was diagnostic of osteoporosis.
**The patient has a recent history of a fragility fracture, therefore meets the W.H.O. criteria for severe
osteoporosis.**

Bone Density Test Measurements

Test Date	Key Site	BMD gm/cm^2	T-Score	%Young Normal	Z-Score	% Age Matched
08/06/1999	PA Spine	0.641	-4.659	53%	-2.502	68%
08/06/1999	Total Left Hip	0.621	-3.200	62%	-1.400	79%
08/06/1999	L. Fem. Neck	0.621	-3.000	63%	-1.000	84%
08/06/1999	Total Right Hip	0.626	-3.100	62%	-1.400	79%
08/06/1999	R. Fem. Neck	0.626	-2.900	64%	-1.000	84%
08/06/1999	Total Body	0.910	-2.685	81%	-0.664	94%

	HEIGHT		WEIGHT	
Test Date	In Inches	In Meters	In Pounds	In Kilograms

08/06/1999   59.055   1.500   112.435   51.000

Recommendations

A total intake of approximately 1500 mg of elemental calcium from dietary and supplementary sources is suggested for this patient.

Recommend Vitamin D3-800 mg. to increase the absorption of calcium. A multiple vitamin also helps supply trace minerals necessary for bone formation.

Foods high in calcium are milk, yogurt, cheese, ice cream, tofu, vegetables(brocccoli, soybeans, collards, turnip greens, bok choy), fish and shellfish (oysters, sardines, salmon, shrimp), oranges, orange juice fortified with calcium, almonds, etc. Many low-fat foods are calcium rich such as low-fat or skim milk, low-fat cheese, low-fat yogurt, etc., for the weight conscious individuals.

Recommend a moderate exercise program to include stretching and aerobic weight-bearing exercise (such as walking 30-minutes 3x's a week on alternating days or 20-minutes 5x's a week); In conjunction with a muscle-strengthening program, (such as light weight lifting with dumbells for 40-45 minutes 2x's a week with at least three days between sessions, or 30-minutes 3x's a week with at least one day between sessions or 20-minutes five days a week).

General considerations to reduce ones risk of Osteoporosis fracture are: avoiding long acting sedative hypnotic agents (increase risk of falls), reducing caffeine (ie.coffee, chocolate) and absence of nicotine (ie. smoking) intake, maintaining healthy vision (so as not to be predisposed to falls) and instituting maximum therapeutic measures available to maintain and improve Bone Mineral Density.

Recommend consideration for hormone replacement therapy and/or pharmacologic therapy.

Given these findings and the markedly high risk for fracture, a thorough medical evaluation looking for secondary causes of osteoporosis is suggested. Long -term treatment to restore bone mass is needed to reduce the high risk of fracture. In this case, a follow-up bone density test is indicated in about 12 months.

The patient has been instructed to follow up with you next week to discuss the test results, and for continuing treatment.

Sincerely,

Raymond E. Cole D.O., C.C.D.

Raymond E. Cole D.O., C.C.D.

(1) Kanis JA, Melton LJ, Christiansen C, Johnson CC, Khaltaev N. The diagnosis of osteoporosis. J Bone Min Res 1994;9:1137-1141.
(2) Modified WHO Criteria: T-score > -1.0 = Normal, T-score < -1.0 but > -2.0 = osteopenia, T-score < -2.0 = osteoporosis
(3) Cummings SR, Black Dm, Nevitt MC, Browner W, Cauley J, Ensrud K, Genant HK, Palermo L, Scott J, Vogt TM. Bone density at various sites for prediction of hip fracture. Lancet 1993:341:72-75.

Osteoporosis Testing Center
107 West Chicago Street
Brooklyn, MI 49230

TOTAL BODY BONE DENSITY

Attendant:

71.0 Years 07/26/1928

59.0 in. 112.0 lbs. White Female

Physician:

Measured:	08/06/1999	1:40:18 PM	(2.05)
Analyzed:	12/06/1999	12:21:37 PM	(2.05)
Printed:	12/06/1999	12:21:48 PM	(2.05)
			_fg20vi7vx.dfb

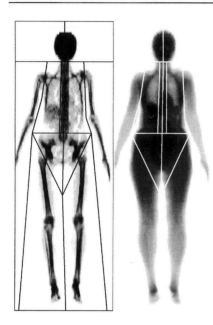

Reference: Total[11]

Region	BMD (g/cm²) [1]	Young-Adult (T) [2]	Age-Matched (Z) [3]
Head	1.950	-	-
Arms	0.695	-	-
Legs	0.898	-	-
Trunk	0.658	-	-
Ribs	0.521	-	-
Pelvis	0.756	-	-
Spine	0.722	-	-
Total	0.909	-2.7	-0.7

Image not for diagnosis

76:0.1:153.85:31.2 0.00:-1.00 4.80x13.00 10.0:38.3
0.00:0.00 0.00:0.00

1 — Statistically 68% of repeat scans fall within 1SD (± 0.010 g/cm² for Total)
2 — USA, Total Body Reference Population, Ages 20-40
3 — Matched for Age, Weight (females 25-100 Kg), Ethnic
11 — WHO T-Score categories are: >-1.0 SD = Normal; -1.0 to -2.5 SD = Osteopenia; <-2.5 SD = Osteoporosis

LUNAR Prodigy
10221

Osteoporosis Testing Center

107 West Chicago Street
Brooklyn, MI 49230

				TOTAL BODY BONE DENSITY		
Attendant:			Measured:	08/06/1999	1:40:18 PM	(2.05)
71.0 Years 07/26/1928			Analyzed:	12/06/1999	12:21:37 PM	(2.05)
59.0 in. 112.0 lbs. White Female			Printed:	12/06/1999	12:21:48 PM	(2.05)
Physician:						_fg20vi7vx.dfb

ANCILLARY RESULTS

Region	BMD [1] (g/cm²)	Young-Adult [2] (%)	(T)	Age-Matched [3] (%)	(Z)	Est. BMC [4] (g)	Est. Area [4] (cm²)
Head	1.950	-	-	-	-	376.8	193.2
Arms	0.695	-	-	-	-	191.7	275.8
Legs	0.898	-	-	-	-	577.4	643.1
Trunk	0.658	-	-	-	-	353.3	536.6
Ribs	0.521	-	-	-	-	103.4	198.4
Pelvis	0.756	-	-	-	-	126.0	166.6
Spine	0.722	-	-	-	-	123.9	171.6
Total	0.909	81	-2.7	94	-0.7	1,499.2	1,648.7

BODY COMPOSITION

Region	Tissue %Fat	Region %Fat	Tissue (g)	Fat (g)	Lean (g)	Est. BMC [4] (g)
Arms	32.7	31.3	4,216	1,379	2,837	191.7
Legs	44.0	42.5	17,026	7,488	9,539	577.4
Trunk	35.6	35.0	23,330	8,294	15,036	353.3
Total	37.3	36.1	47,761	17,799	29,962	1,499.2
Left arm	32.7	31.3	2,151	704	1,448	99.3
Left leg	44.0	42.5	8,525	3,750	4,775	289.4
Left trunk	35.5	35.0	11,265	4,004	7,261	173.2
Left total	37.2	36.0	23,682	8,806	14,876	771.2
Right arm	32.7	31.3	2,065	675	1,390	92.4
Right leg	44.0	42.5	8,502	3,738	4,764	287.9
Right trunk	35.6	35.0	12,065	4,290	7,775	180.1
Right total	37.3	36.3	24,079	8,993	15,086	728.0

1 — Statistically 68% of repeat scans fall within 1SD (± 0.010 g/cm² for Total)
2 — USA, Total Body Reference Population, Ages 20-40
3 — Matched for Age, Weight (females 25-100 Kg), Ethnic
4 — Results for investigational use only.

LUNAR Prodigy 10221

Osteoporosis Testing Center
107 West Chicago Street
Brooklyn, MI 49230

Attendant:

71.0 Years 07/26/1928

59.0 in. 112.0 lbs. White Female

Physician:

DUALFEMUR BONE DENSITY

Measured:	08/06/1999	1:32:29 PM	(2.05)
Analyzed:	08/06/1999	1:33:27 PM	(2.05)
Printed:	12/06/1999	12:16:06 PM	(2.05)
			_fg20me7vx.dfe

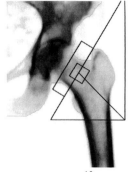

Reference: Total[11]

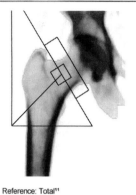

BMD (g/cm²)   YA (T)

Normal

Osteopenia

Age (years)

Region	BMD (g/cm²) [1,6]	Young-Adult (T) [2,7]	Age-Matched (Z) [3]
Total Lt.	0.621	-3.2	-1.4
Total Rt.	0.626	-3.1	-1.4
Total Avg.	0.624	-3.1	-1.4
Total Diff.	0.005	-	-

Image not for diagnosis

76:3.0:50.00:12.0 0.00:11.64 0.60x1.05 12.5:36.2

0.00:0.00 0.00:0.00

1 — Statistically 68% of repeat scans fall within 1SD (± 0.020 g/cm² for Total)

2 — USA, Femur Reference Population, Ages 20-40

3 — Matched for Age, Weight (females 25-100 Kg), Ethnic

6 — Standardized BMD for Total Rt. is 582 mg/cm², Total Lt. is 577 mg/cm².

7 — Total T-Score difference is 0.0. Asymmetry is None.

11 — WHO T-Score categories are: >-1.0 SD = Normal; -1.0 to -2.5 SD = Osteopenia; <-2.5 SD = Osteoporosis

LUNAR Prodigy 10221

Osteoporosis Testing Center
107 West Chicago Street
Brooklyn, MI 49230

Attendant:

71.0 Years 07/26/1928

59.0 in. 112.0 lbs. White Female

Physician:

DUALFEMUR BONE DENSITY

Measured:	08/06/1999	1:32:29 PM	(2.05)
Analyzed:	08/06/1999	1:33:27 PM	(2.05)
Printed:	12/06/1999	12:16:06 PM	(2.05)
			_fg20me7vx.dfe

ANCILLARY RESULTS

Region	BMD [1,6] (g/cm²)	Young-Adult [2,7] (%)	(T)	Age-Matched [3] (%)	(Z)	Est. BMC [4] (g)	Est. Area [4] (cm²)
Neck Lt.	0.621	63	-3.0	84	-1.0	3.0	4.8
Neck Rt.	0.626	64	-2.9	84	-1.0	2.8	4.5
Neck Avg.	0.624	64	-3.0	84	-1.0	2.9	4.7
Neck Diff.	0.005	-	-	-	-	0.1	0.2
Wards Lt.	0.483	53	-3.3	83	-0.8	1.2	2.5
Wards Rt.	0.459	50	-3.5	79	-1.0	1.0	2.3
Wards Avg.	0.471	52	-3.4	81	-0.9	1.1	2.4
Wards Diff.	0.024	-	-	-	-	0.2	0.2
Troch Lt.	0.500	63	-2.6	78	-1.3	6.3	12.6
Troch Rt.	0.496	63	-2.7	77	-1.3	6.3	12.6
Troch Avg.	0.498	63	-2.7	77	-1.3	6.3	12.6
Troch Diff.	0.004	-	-	-	-	0.0	0.1
Shaft Lt.	0.736	-	-	-	-	9.8	13.4
Shaft Rt.	0.754	-	-	-	-	9.7	12.9
Shaft Avg.	0.745	-	-	-	-	9.8	13.1
Shaft Diff.	0.018	-	-	-	-	0.1	0.5
Total Lt.	0.621	62	-3.2	79	-1.4	19.1	30.7
Total Rt.	0.626	63	-3.1	79	-1.4	18.8	30.0
Total Avg.	0.624	62	-3.1	79	-1.4	18.9	30.4
Total Diff.	0.005	-	-	-	-	0.3	0.7

1 — Statistically 68% of repeat scans fall within 1SD (± 0.020 g/cm² for Total)
2 — USA, Femur Reference Population, Ages 20-40
3 — Matched for Age, Weight (females 25-100 Kg), Ethnic
4 — Results for investigational use only.
6 — Standardized BMD for Total Rt. is 582 mg/cm², Total Lt. is 577 mg/cm².
7 — Total T-Score difference is 0.0. Asymmetry is None.

LUNAR Prodigy
10221

Osteoporosis Testing Center
107 West Chicago Street
Brooklyn, MI 49230

AP SPINE BONE DENSITY

Attendant:	Measured:	08/06/1999	1:28:38 PM	(2.05)
71.0 Years 07/26/1928	Analyzed:	08/06/1999	1:48:54 PM	(2.05)
59.0 in. 112.0 lbs. White Female	Printed:	12/06/1999	12:14:24 PM	(2.05)
Physician:				_fg20fn7vx.dfs

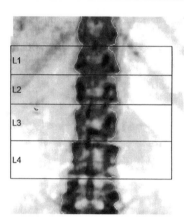

Reference: L2-L4[11]

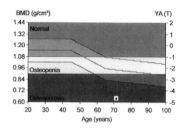

Region	BMD[1,6] (g/cm²)	Young-Adult[2] (T)	Age-Matched[3] (Z)
L1	0.656	-3.9	-1.8
L2	0.628	-4.8	-2.6
L3	0.667	-4.4	-2.3
L4	0.628	-4.8	-2.6
L2-L4	0.641	-4.7	-2.5

Image not for diagnosis

76:3.0:50.00:12.0 0.00:10.86 0.60x1.05 13.8:23.5
0.00:0.00 0.00:0.00

1 — Statistically 68% of repeat scans fall within 1SD (± 0.010 g/cm² for L2-L4)
2 — USA, AP Spine Reference Population, Ages 20-40
3 — Matched for Age, Weight (females 25-100 Kg), Ethnic
6 — Standardized BMD for L2-L4 is 610 mg/cm².
11 — WHO T-Score categories are: >-1.0 SD = Normal; -1.0 to -2.5 SD = Osteopenia;
     <-2.5 SD = Osteoporosis

LUNAR® Prodigy
10221

Osteoporosis Testing Center
107 West Chicago Street
Brooklyn, MI 49230

AP SPINE BONE DENSITY

Attendant:	Measured:	08/06/1999	1:28:38 PM	(2.05)
71.0 Years 07/26/1928	Analyzed:	08/06/1999	1:48:54 PM	(2.05)
59.0 in. 112.0 lbs. White Female	Printed:	12/06/1999	12:14:24 PM	(2.05)
Physician:				_fg20fn7vx.dfs

ANCILLARY RESULTS

Region	BMD [1,6] (g/cm²)	Young-Adult [2] (%)	(T)	Age-Matched [3] (%)	(Z)	Est. BMC [4] (g)	Est. Area [4] (cm²)	Est. Width [4] (cm)	Est. Height [4] (cm)
L1	0.656	58	-3.9	75	-1.8	5.8	8.8	3.4	2.6
L2	0.628	52	-4.8	67	-2.6	6.0	9.6	3.6	2.6
L3	0.667	56	-4.4	71	-2.3	7.6	11.4	3.5	3.3
L4	0.628	52	-4.8	67	-2.6	8.3	13.3	3.9	3.4
L1-L2	0.641	56	-4.2	72	-2.1	11.8	18.3	3.5	5.2
L1-L3	0.651	56	-4.3	71	-2.2	19.3	29.7	3.5	8.4
L1-L4	0.644	55	-4.5	70	-2.3	27.7	42.9	3.6	11.8
L2-L3	0.649	54	-4.6	69	-2.4	13.6	20.9	3.6	5.9
L2-L4	0.641	53	-4.7	68	-2.5	21.9	34.2	3.7	9.2
L3-L4	0.646	54	-4.6	69	-2.5	15.9	24.6	3.7	6.6

Z-Score for Vertebral Height (L2-L4)

Compared to young adult (Z):	-2.3
Adjusted for stature (Z):	-1.2

1 — Statistically 68% of repeat scans fall within 1SD (± 0.010 g/cm² for L2-L4)
2 — USA, AP Spine Reference Population, Ages 20-40
3 — Matched for Age, Weight (females 25-100 Kg), Ethnic
4 — Results for investigational use only.
6 — Standardized BMD for L2-L4 is 610 mg/cm².

LUNAR ® Prodigy
10221

Glossary of Terms

ABSORPTIOMETER: A medical testing machine to measure bone density.

ADENOSINE TRIPHOSOHATE (ATP): High energy compound formed from oxidation of carbohydrate or fat, energy supply of muscle and other body tissues.

ADIPOSE TISSUE: Body tissue in which fat is stored, sometimes called fatty tissue.

AEROBIC EXERCISE: Utilizes our body's maximum ability to take oxygen in through the lungs, transport it to our muscles, and utilize it for work output. Typically, a steady, rhythmic exercise utilizes oxygen for energy in our body's large muscle groups for a prolonged period of time and can be achieved through brisk walking, running and bicycling. It is commonly thought of as causing one's heart rate (measured by one's pulse) to reach 60–85% of maximum heart rate for twenty minutes or longer. It is very healthy for our cardiovascular and pulmonary systems.

AGILITY: Ability to move quickly and easily while maintaining skillful control of our body.

ALVEOLI: Small air sacs in our lungs where oxygen and carbon dioxide exchange places.

AMENORRHEA: Lack of or abnormal cessation of menstrual periods.

ANDROGENS: Male sex hormones, hormones which produce male characteristics, i.e. testosterone, androsterone, dehydroepiandrosterone(DHEA).

ANAEROBIC EXERCISE: Exercise that primarily burns energy from sources other than oxygen because the intense exercise is too strenuous for the normal flow of oxygen from the lungs. Involves absence of oxygen, nonoxidation metabolism. Short bursts of intense exercise utilizing the body's stores of fat and carbohydrate for energy with a by-product of lactic acid build-up in the muscles and blood. For example, moderate walking is aerobic and the oxygen supply from the lungs can keep up with the demand in the muscles and tissues; however, if the intensity is increased to very strenuous prolonged running in which the supply of oxygen from the lungs cannot keep up with the demand of the muscles and tissues, the exercise would become anerobic with associated shortness of breath (from carbon dioxide build-up in the lungs) and fatigue and sore muscles from lactic acid build-up in the muscles.

ANOREXIA NERVOSA: An eating disorder characterized by an inappropriate body image that one is fat, and a subsequent excessive dieting, loss of appetite, refusal to eat, and severe weight loss. Primarily found in teenage girls and young women and may cause amenorrhea and subsequent osteoporosis.

ARTERIOSCLEROSIS/ ATHEROSCLEROSIS: Narrowing and hardening of the arteries by lipid deposits. Usually present in some degree in the elderly.

ARTHRITIS: Inflammation, pain and swelling of the joints.

ATROPHIC: Wasting away.

BALANCE: Capacity to maintain one's equilibrium while moving. Involves visual input, imput from the semicircular canals in our middle ears, and imput from receptors in our muscles.

BILATERAL SALPINGIO-OOPHORECTOMY: Surgical removal of both of the ovaries and fallopian tubes.

BISPHOSPHONATE: A chemical compound which binds to bone tissue and impedes resorption by rendering bone more resistant to resorption by osteoclasts (bone-resorbing cells).

BODY COMPOSITION: Relative amount of fat and lean tissue.

BONE DENSITOMETRY: A medical test that measures the bone density.

BONE MASS MEASUREMENT ACT (BMMA): Presidential Legislative Act effective July 1, 1998 for medicare recipients which provides payment for BMD testing in qualified medicare beneficiaries.

BONE MINERAL DENSITY: The ratio of bone mass to volume, indicating bone compactness. Bone density increases rapidly through adolescence, more slowly until about age 35 and then plateaus and declines. Bone density is measured most frequently in the spine, hip, wrist, forearm and/or heel for the detection and diagnosis of osteoporosis.

BONE FORMATION: That part of a bone-remodeling cycle in which osteoblasts synthesize a protein matrix of fibers upon which crystals of calcium and phosphorus are embedded during mineralization to provide strength and rigidity.

BONE MASS: Amount of mineral measured in the bone.

BONE MATRIX: Meshwork of protein upon which bone minerals are deposited.

BONE REMODELING: A continuous process in which small amounts of bone are removed and replaced by new tissue. During the resorption phase, old bone is dissolved and eliminated by osteoclasts. This is followed by the formation phase, in which protein fibers and calcium are deposited by the bone-forming osteoblasts.

BONE RESORPTION: The breakdown part of bone's life cycle, during which the old and damaged bone tissue is resorbed. Osteoporosis occurs when resorption is greater than formation.

BRONCHIOLE: Medium size airways. Undergoes spasm sometimes making breathing difficult, as in exercise-induced asthma.

CAFFEINE: An alkaloid drug with a stimulating action, found in coffee, tea, and cola type soft drinks. Consuming excessive caffeine is a risk factor for osteoporosis because of its diuretic properties which increase the urinary loss of calcium.

CALCIFEROL: Vitamin D 2, derived from plants.

CALCIFEDIOL: 25 hydroxy-vitamin D3, a form of Vitamin D produced in the liver.

CALCITONIN: A naturally-occurring hormone secreted by the thyroid gland which inhibits bone resorption. Salmon-calcitonin, a synthetic formation, is used to slow the bone resorption rate in osteoporotic patients.

CALCIUM: A metallic element needed for normal development and functioning of the body and used in bone structure (85% of bone's strength).

CALCIUM CARBONATE: A form of calcium found in limestone and oyster shells and used in many calcium supplements.

CALCIUM CITRATE: Type of calcium used in calcium supplements, which is man-made. Used specifically if you have a history of kidney stones or abnormality of stomach absorption.

CALCIUM PHOSPHATE: A form of calcium occurring naturally in milk. It is also available in calcium supplements.

CALORIE: Amount of heat required to raise 1 kilogram of water 1 degree Celsius.

CAPILLARIES: Smallest blood vessels (between arterioles and venules) where oxygen, nutrients, and hormones are transported into our tissues and carbon dioxide and wastes are removed from our tissues.

CARBOHYDRATE: A basic source of energy derived from green plants (simple and complex). Carbohydrates are stored as glycogen primarily in the liver and muscle. Carbohydrate excesses are stored as fat.

CARDIAC: Heart. Relating to the heart.

CARDIAC OUTPUT: Volume of blood pumped by the heart each minute.

CARDIORESPIRATORY ENDURANCE: Aerobic fitness or maximal oxygen intake.

CARDIOVASCULAR SYSTEM: Heart and blood vessels

CERVICAL SPINE: Neck. The first seven bones (vertebrae) at the top of the spinal column.

CHANGE OF LIFE: Menopause. Average age for a woman is 50.

CHOLESTEROL: A type of fatty substance found in the body. In increased amounts in the bloodstream, it has been shown to cause atherosclerosis and increase the risk of heart disease. It can be made in the liver, is a common cause of gallstones, and is a precursor of many steroid hormones.

CLIMACTERIC: Menopausal symptoms.

COLLAGEN: An insoluble protein found in connective tissue including skin, bone, ligaments and cartilage. Collagen represents about 30% of total body protein.

COLLES' FRACTURE: Transverse wrist fracture with displacement of fractured bony part of the radius backward. Often seen in osteoporotic individuals who have attempted to break their fall by extending their hand outward.

COMPRESSION FRACURE: Fracture of a vertebrae in the spine in which the bone collapses or is crushed.

COMPUTERIZED AXIAL TOMOGRAPHY: CT or CAT scan. A type of X-ray that utilizes a three-dimensional image. Can be used to measure bone density.

CONJUGATED EQUINE ESTROGEN: Type of estrogen replacement from the urine of pregnant mares. It contains many different estrogens. Premarin, is a conjugated equine estrogen.

CONTRACTION: Tension of a muscle.

CONTRACEPTION: To prevent conception or pregnancy.

CONTRACEPTIVE: Used to prevent a pregnancy (birth control pill, Intrauterine Device (I.U.D.), sponge, condom, etc.)

COOL DOWN: A cool down exercise used to disperse heat, attain good circulation, and allow the muscles some recovery time.

COORDINATION: Harmonious flow of muscle groups working together in the performance of an undertaking for smooth motion.

CORTICAL BONE: Also known as compact bone because it has a densely packed, hard, solid matrix structure. Cortical bone is very solid and strong, usually found toward the surface of all bones and gives long bones like the leg, hip, and arm their strength. Cortical bone makes up approximately 80% of the skeleton. Cortical bone has a slower metabolic rate than trabecular bone so it is remodeled at a much slower rate than trabecular bone.

CORTICOSTEROIDS: Refers to steroid-type substances produced in the adrenal gland and/or medications that have a steroid-type response.

DENSITOMETRY: Test used to measure the bone mass or density.

DORSAL SPINE: Thoracic spine.

DUAL PHOTON ABSORPTIOMETRY (DPA): A bone mass measurement test that uses photons (units of electromagnetic energy) at two energy levels from a radionuclide source to measure the total cortical and trabecular mineral content of the hip, spine and full body.

DUAL-ENERGY X-RAY ABSORPTIOMETRY (DEXA): Photons generated by an X-ray tube at two energy levels. DEXA provides faster and precise measurements of the hip, spine and full body with minimal radiation exposure.

ELECTROCARDIOGRAM (ECG, EKG): A graphic recording of the electrical activity of the heart. A sort of electrical "picture" of the heart.

ENDOMETRIUM: The lining of the uterus.

ENDORPHINS: Chemical substances produced mostly in the brain that may have pain-lessening properties similar to those of opiates.

ENDURANCE: The ability to keep going or to resist fatigue.

ENZYME: A protein secreted by cells, inducing chemical changes in other substances.

ERT: The abbreviation for estrogen replacement therapy. The replacement of estrogen after menopause.

ESTRADIOL (E2): The major estrogenic hormone secreted by the human ovary in the pre-monopausal woman. Generally considered to be the most potent form of the three major female estrogens at the receptor level.

ESTRIOL (E3): An estrogen found in women thought to be the least potent of the three major estrogens in a woman's body.

ESTROGEN: A female sex hormone produced mainly by the ovaries which influences bone density by slowing the rate of bone resorption, improving retention of calcium by the kidneys, and improving the absorption of dietary calcium by the intestine.

ESTROGEN RELACEMENT THERAPY (ERT): A therapy that restores estrogen lost when natural estrogen production in the ovaries is dramatically reduced due to the onset of natural or surgically-induced menopause.

ESTRONE (E): An estrogen found in women. Less active than estradiol. Estrone can be manufactured in body fat. After menopause, is the most common form of estrogen found in the bloodstream in women.

EXTENSION: Brings the limbs into a straightened condition. Movement of a joint causes the limbs above and below it to move away from one another. The opposite of flexion. Extension of the spine means the spine is arched backward during this type of exercise.

FAT: Stored energy source; stored in adipose tissue for future use when extra calories are ingested. Oxidized with the release of energy.

FATIGUE: A condition of tiredness usually brought on by over-activity.

FITNESS: Combination of aerobic capacity, muscular strength, and endurance that enhances health.

FLEXIBILITY: The ability for the body to maintain a range of motion moving the body parts.

FLEXION: Bending. Movement of a joint causes the limbs above and below it to come together. Flexion of the spine means the spine bends forward from the waist and is rounded during this type of exercise.

FRACTURE: Broken bone.

FREQUENCY: Number of times per day or week.

FSH: The abbreviation for follicle-stimulating hormone. A hormone made in the pituitary gland which stimulates the maturation of the follicle in the ovary, which will release an egg.

FDA: The abbreviation for the Food and Drug Administration.

GLUCOSE: A sugar which is the most important carbohydrate in the body metabolism. It's an indispensable energy source for brain and nervous tissue.

GLYCOGEN: The form in which carbohydrates are stored in the liver and muscles for future use, to be converted to glucose.

GONAD: Reproductive glands. The term can mean either ovaries in a woman or testes in a man.

GROWTH HORMONE (GH): A hormone produced in the anterior pituitary gland that may indirectly stimulate bone formation and subsequently has a positive effect on the treatment of osteoporosis.

HEART ATTACK: Myocardial infarction. Death of heart muscle.

HEART RATE: Frequency of heart contraction.

HIGH-DENSITY LIPOPROTEIN (HDL) CHOLESTEROL: A carrier molecule that takes cholesterol to the liver for removal; commonly known as "good cholesterol."

HIP FRACTURE: Fracture of the upper femur at the hip.

HORMONE: A substance produced in one organ that controls or affects the functions of other organs in the body, like estrogen.

HOT FLASHES: (flushes). An intense warmth from within which can develop suddenly, often awakening a menopausal woman at night. Estrogen deficiency is usually the cause. This may be one of the first signs of menopause.

HRT: Hormone replacement therapy. Use of both estrogen and progesterone in the postmenopausal woman.

HYDROXYAPATITE: Hard crystalline mineral salts in bone

HYPERTENSION: High blood pressure.

HYSTERECTOMY: Surgical removal of the uterus.

IDIOPATHIC: A disease in which the cause is not known.

IMPACT EXERCISE: Exercise that causes an impact or jolt in the bones like jogging and jumping rope.

INTENSITY: Degree of difficulty. With increasing intensity, the speed, rate, or level of activity is increased.

ISOMETRIC: Contraction against an immovable object so that the muscle is tensed but does not actually shorten but maintains a constant length. Pushing against a wall or immovable object would be an isometric exercise.

ISOTONIC: Contraction against a constant resistance. The muscle shortens and lengthens during this type of exercise. Lifting free weights such as barbells or dumbbells would be an isotonic exercise.

LACTIC ACID: A metabolic by-product of anerobic (non-oxygen) exercise, with intense or vigorous exercise. It is an anerobic by-product of glycogen metabolism and accumulates in the muscles and inhibits their enzymatic activity causing fatigue and soreness.

LACTOSE: A type of disaccharide sugar found only in milk products which, when broken down in the body, yields glucose and galactose. Milk contains 4-7% lactose. Milk sours because bacteria have converted the lactose into butyric acid and lactic acid.

LACTOSE INTOLERANCE: A condition in which the body has the inability to absorb lactose. This causes diarrhea, abdominal pain, or bloating after consuming milk products. This condition often causes individuals to avoid dairy products, which may contribute to calcium deficiency.

LEAN BODY WEIGHT: Total body weight minus fat weight.

LDL: The abbreviation for low-density lipoprotein. This is a type of cholesterol that may cause arterioscerosis. This has earned the title "bad cholesterol."

LH: The abbreviation for luteinizing hormone, a hormone produced in the pituitary gland, that signals the ovary to release the egg.

MAGNESIUM: A metallic element necessary for healthy growth and development of the skeleton, muscle, and nervous tissue. Required to convert the inactive form of vitamin D to the active form vitamin D3. Deficiency is common in the elderly.

MAMMOGRAM: An X-ray procedure used to detect breast abnormalities and cancer.

MEDROXYPROGESTERONE ACETATE: Abbreviated MPA. Synthetic progesterone used in hormone replacement for postmenopausal women. Also used as a contraceptive and to control abnormal menstrual bleeding.

MENARCHE: Beginning of the first menstrual period in a young girl.

MENOPAUSE: The time of a woman's last menstrual period, marking the end of her reproductive years. Levels of estrogen fall at this time as the ovaries have ceased their reproductive function.

MUSCULAR FITNESS: Healthy strength, muscular endurance, and flexibility.

NUTRITION: The utilization of food, this including ingestion, absorption, and metabolism. Provides the body with adequate energy (calories) as well as needed minerals, fluids, and nutrients. Some nutrients are stored in the body and can be drawn upon when intake is not sufficient.

OBESITY: Usually pertains to excessive body fat (more than 20% of total body weight for men and more than 30% for women.)

OOPHORECTOMY: The surgical removal of the ovaries.

ORAL CONTRACEPTIVES: Birth control pills

OS CALSIS: Heel bone. Also called the calcaneus.

OSTEOARTHRITIS: A disease in which the lining of the joints is inflamed, causing pain, swelling, and redness of the joints. It can sometimes be very debilitating.

OSTEOBLAST: A cell which plays a key role in forming new bone for bone growth, repair of damaged bone and replacement of old bone.

OSTEOCLAST: A cell which resorbs and removes old bone tissue.

OSTEOMALACIA: A disease of the bone in which the bone is unable to properly incorporate calcium into the structure resulting in soft bone.

OSTEOPOENIA: Decrease in bone density level below normal range, yet not low enough to be termed osteoporotic. By WHO diagnostic criteria a T-Score between –1 and –2.5 standard deviations below normal. An individual with osteopenia is considered to be at risk for osteoporotic fracture.

OSTEOPOROSIS: By WHO definition a disease characterized by low bone density and deterioration of the structure of the bone tissue leading to enhanced bone fragility and an increased susceptibility to fractures. By WHO diagnostic criteria, a T-Score of –2.5 or below.

OVARY: The female reproductive gland where female eggs are made and released. Estrogen, progesterone, and some testosterone are produced in this gland.

OVARIECTOMY: Surgical removal of the ovaries.

OVULATION: The release of the mature egg by the ovary.

PARATHYROID HORMONE (PTH): Hormone secreted by the parathyroid gland. PTH regulates the level of calcium in the blood by adjusting the activity of cells in bone (osteoblasts and osteoclasts) and in the kidney. Through the action of PTH and vitamin D, the body maintains a constant and consistent level of calcium in the blood.

PEAK BONE MASS: The stage at which bones have reached maximum density and strength and after which the rate of bone removal exceeds the rate of bone renewal.

PITUITARY GLAND: A gland at the base of the brain which secretes various hormones, i.e. luteinizing hormone, growth hormone.

PLAQUE: Atheromatous blockage of arteries.

POSTMENOPAUSAL OSTEOPOROSIS: Bone loss accelerated by estrogen deficiency that occurs at menopause. This is now called Type I ssteoporosis.

PRIMARY OSTEOPOROSIS: A category of osteoporosis that includes postmenopausal or Type I, and age-related osteoporosis also known as senile or Type II.

PROGESTERONE: A hormone produced in the ovaries after ovulation occurs.

PUBERTY: The age at which the reproductive organs develop and they become capable of reproduction.

QUANTITATIVE COMPUTED TOMOGRAPHY (QCT): A computerized testing of pinpoint (X-rays) which, when quantified, provides a measurement of trabecular bone density in the spine, the area where bone density changes can be most rapid.

RECEPTOR: A structure in a specific cell which, acted upon by a hormone or a local factor, produces a chemical reaction within the cell.

REPETITION: Also known as a REP. One complete movement of an exercise. From starting position to performance of the exercise back to starting position.

RESORPTION: A physiological process involving the remodeling of bone during which old bone is dissolved and eliminated by osteoclasts.

RESPIRATION: Intake of oxygen and exhalation of carbon dioxide. (The act of breathing).

RISK FACTOR: Factors that may put you at a higher risk for a certain disease. Risk factors for osteoporosis put you at high risk for the development of osteoporosis.

SECONDARY OSTEOPOROSIS: A category used to indicate that bone loss is the result of a disease rather than the primary natural causes of osteoporosis, menopausal estrogen deficiency and age.

SENILE OSTEOPOROSIS: Bone loss relating to aging. Called Type II osteoporosis.

SET: A number of repetitions (complete movements) performed without a rest. For example, one set of biceps curls might consists of 8 reps.

STEROIDS: A class of chemical compounds that have the same basic chemical structure. The estrogens, testosterone, progesterone, and cortisone are all steroids.

STRENGTH: Ability to exert force with a muscle.

STRENGTH TRAINING: Increasing the strength of a muscle through training.

SURGICAL MENOPAUSE: Refers to menopause by the surgical removal of the ovaries in a woman who is still having menstrual periods.

TESTOSTERONE: A predominantly male sex hormone. The most potent of the naturally occurring androgens. Made in the adrenal cortex, the male testes, and the female ovaries. In females, has been found to have a relationship with the female sex drive.

THIAZIDE: Type of diuretic that is often used to treat edema or high blood pressure i.e. hydrochlorthiazide. Thiazides reduce the amount of calcium lost in the urine.

THORACIC SPINE: The 12 vertebrae that make up the upper back from the base of the neck to just above the waist. Also called the dorsal spine.

TONE: Normal tension in healthy firm muscle.

TRABECULAR BONE: Also known as spongy bone because it has a porous, sponge-like structure. Comprises the interior of vertebral bodies and smaller amounts in the ends of long bones. This portion of bone may be preferentially lost in postmenopausal osteoporosis. Makes up about 20% of all bone. It has a faster metabolic rate than cortical (compact or hard) bone, so it is remodeled at a much faster rate than cortical bone.

TRACE MINERALS: Minerals needed in very small amounts to stay healthy. Examples are manganese, boron, copper, and strontium.

TRANSDERMAL: Delivery of medication through the skin.

TRIGLYCERIDE: Fat made up of three fatty acids and glycerol.

UNIVERSAL MACHINE: A type of weight machine in which weights are on rails or tracks and lifted by pulleys and levers.

URETHRA: Tube in which urine flows from the urinary bladder out of the body.

UTERUS: The womb. The hollow muscular organ in a woman's body in which a baby develops before being born.

VAGINA: Female genital canal. Passageway from the uterus to the outside of the body.

VALSALVA MANEUVER: Holding your breath with extreme effort, causing increased pressure in the abdominal and thoracic cavities.

VERTEBRAE: Bones of the spine.

VITAMIN D: Enables calcium to be absorbed in the intestine and stimulates the kidneys to reabsorb calcium from the urine and keep it in the bloodstream. Some Vitamin D is stored in an inactivated form in our skin and some is stored in our liver.

VITAMIN K: Involved in the synthesis of osteocalcin. A deficiency is thought to contribute to the development of osteoporotic fractures.

WEIGHT BEARING EXERCISE: Working against gravity. Exercise that requires you support the weight of your body. Walking is a weight-bearing exercise. Swimming is not considered a weight-bearing exercise because of the water's buoyancy.

WEIGHT TRAINING: A regiment of dumbbells, barbells, or machines to improve muscle strength and endurance.

WOMB: The uterus

ZINC: A trace mineral. Zinc deficiency is thought to contribute to the development of osteoporosis.

Osteoporosis Resources

Organizations

National Osteoporosis Foundation
1150 17th Street N.W., Ste. 500
Washington, DC 20036-4603
202-223-2226
800-223-9994

North American Menopause Society
c/o Cleveland Menopause Clinic
29001 Cedar Rd. #600
Cleveland, Ohio 44124
216-844-8748

The Arthritis Foundation
National Office
1314 Spring St., N.W.
Atlanta, Georgia 30309
404-872-7100
800-283-7800

Administration on Aging
300 Independence Avenue, SW
Washington, DC 20201
202-619-0641

National Arthritis and Musculoskeletal and Skin Diseases Information Clearing House
Box AMS
Bethesda, Maryland 20982
301-496-4000

Osteoporosis and Related Bone Diseases National Resource Center
1150 17th St, NY, Suite 500
Washington, DC 20036-4603
800-624-BONE
Fax 202-223-2237

National Dairy Council
10255 W. Higgins Rd. Suite. 900
Rosemont, IL 60018
847-803-200

American College of Obstetricians and Gynecologists
409 12th St. S.W.
Washington, DC 20024
202-638-5577

American Academy of Orthopedic Surgeons
6300 N. River Rd.
Rosemont, Illinois 60018
847-7186

Health and Medical Research Foundation
4900 Broadway
San Antonio, Texas 78209
210-824-4200

American Association of Retired Persons
601 E. Street, NW
Washington, DC 20201
202-434-2277

National Center for Nutrition and Dietetics
American Dietetic Association
216 West Jackson Blvd.
Chicago, IL 60606-6995
800-366-1655

National Chronic Pain Outreach Association
7979 Old Georgetown Road
Bethesda, MD 20814
301-652-4948

Support Groups Services
National Osteoporosis Foundation
Chicago Office
c/o AMA
515 North State Street
Chicago, Illinois 60610
312-464-5110
312-464-5863 (fax)

Office on Smoking and Health
National Center for Chronic Disease Prevention
US Department of Health and Human Services
1600 Clifton Road NE
Atlanta, Georgia 30333
404-639-3311

Women's Sports Foundation
Eisenhower Park
East Meadow, New York 11554
516-542-4700
516-542-4716 (fax)

American Heart Association
7272 Greenville Avenue
Dallas, Texas 75231
214-373-6300

American Anorexia/Bulimia Association
165 West 46th Street 1108
New York, New York 10036
212-575-6200

Aids for Arthritis
3 Little Knoll Court
Medford, New Jersey 08055
609-654-6918

Older Women's League
666 Eleventh Street NW, Suite 700
Washington, DC 20001
202-783-6686 or 1-800-TAKE-OWL

Women's Health America
429 Gammon Place
PO 9690
Madison, Wisconsin 53715
608-833-9102

National Women's Health Resource Center
Suite 325, 2440 M St. N.W.
Washington, DC 20037
202-293-6045

National Women's Health Network
#2 10th Street NW, Suite 402
Washington, DC 20004
202-347-1140

National Clearinghouse for Alcohol and Drug Information
P.O. Box 2345
Rockville, MD 20847-2345
301-468-2600 or 800 662-4357

National Women's Health Network
514 10th Street NW, Suite 400
Washington, DC 20004
202-347-1140

American Society for Bone and Mineral Research
1200 19th Street, NW, Suite 300
Washington, DC 20036
202-857-1161
Fax: 202-223-4579

Foundation for Osteoporosis Research and Education
27th Street, Suite 103
Oakland, CA 94612
888-266-3015
Fax: 510-208-7174

International Society for Clinical Densitometry
ISCD Headquarters
1200 19th Street, NW Suite 300
Washington, DC 20036-2422
202-828-6056
202-857-1102 (fax)

National Institute on Aging Information Center
PO Box 8057
Gaithersburg, Maryland 20898-8057
800-222-2225

Exercise-Related Resources

Aerobics & Fitness Association of America
15250 Ventura Blvd., Ste. 200
Sherman Oaks, California 91403
800-445-4950

American College of Sports Medicine
P.O. Box 1440
Indianapolis, IN 46206-1440
317-637-9200

American Council on Exercise
P.O. Box 910449
San Diego, CA 92191-0049
216-929-7227
800-537-5512

American Orthopedic Society for Sports Medicine
6300 N. River Road, Ste. 200
Rosemont, Illinois 60018
847-292-4900

Cybex
2100 Smithtown Ave.
Ronkonkoma, New York 11779
516-585-9000

FDA Consumer
5600 Fisher's Lane
Room 15A19
Rockville, MD 20857
301-443-3220

Gym Source
40 E. 52nd Street
New York, New York 10022
212-688-4222

National Academy of Sports Medicine
699 Hampshire Road, Ste. 105
Westlake Village, California 91361
805-449-1370

National Strength and Conditioning Association
P.O. Box 38909
Colorado Springs, Colorado 80937-8909
719-632-6722

Parabody
14150 Sunfish Lake Blvd.
Ramsey, MN 55303-4803
612-323-4500
800-328-9714
612-323-4794 (fax)

Paramount Fitness Corp.
6450 E. Bandini Blvd.
Los Angeles, California 90040-3185
213-721-2121
800-721-2121

President's Council on Physical Fitness & Sports
Washington, DC
202-690-9000

Universal Gym Equipment
515 N. Flager Dr.
4th Floor Pavillion
W. Palm Beach, Florida 33401
561-833-2320
800 843-3906
561-802-5620 (fax)

York Barbell
Box 1707
York, Pennsylvania
717-767-6481
800 358-YORK

Internet Sites

American Society for Bone and Mineral Research
E-mail: asbmr@dc.sba.com
Web: www.asbmr.org

Foundation of Osteoporosis Research and Education
E-mail: relations@fore.org
Web: www.fore.org

International Society for Clinical Densitometry
E-mail: ascd@dc.sba.com
Web: www.iscd.org

The North American Menopause Society
E-mail: info@menopause.org
Web: www.menopause.org

Osteoporosis National Resource Center
(osteoporosis and related bone disease)
E-mail: orbdnrc@nof.org
Web: www.osteo.org

Osteoporosis Links
Web: http://www.pslgroup.com/OSTEOPOROSIS.HTM

National Osteoporosis Foundation
Web: www.nof.org

LOEL (Local Osteoporosis Education Link)
Web: http://www.LOEL.net

Major Bone Density Testing Scanner Manufacturers

Lunar Corp.
1726 Heartland Trail
Madison. WI 53717-1915
800-334-5831

Hologic
590 Lincoln St.
Waltham, Massachusetts 02154
800-343-XRAY

Norland Corp.
Customer Service Department
W6340 Hackbarth Road
Fort Atkison, WI 53538
800-444-8456

Osteometer (peripheral forearm unit)
MediTech/XMA
800-325-8880

Schick (ACCU DEXA peripheral finger unit)
31-00 47th Avenue
Long Island City, NY 11101
888-818-4BMD

McCUE (peripheral heel ultrasound unit)
Parsonage Barn
Compton, Winchester
Hampshire SO21 2AF
United Kingdom
+44 (0) 1962 715239

CIRS (QCT software)
800-617-1177

Image Analysis (QCT software)
800-548-4849

Mindways Software, Inc. (QCT software)
282 Second Street, 4th Floor
San Francisco, CA 94105
415-247-9930

Pharmaceutical Companies Involved in Osteoporosis Research and Treatment

Merck & Co.
P.O. Box 4
West Point, Pennsylvania 19486-004
800 672-6372

Procter & Gamble Pharmaceuticals, Inc..
Sharon Woods Technical Center
11520 Reed Hartman Highway
Cincinnati, Ohio 45241
800-448-4878

Eli-Lilly and Co.
Lilly Corporate Center
Indianapolis, Indiana 46285
800-545-5979

Wyeth-Ayerst Laboratories
Division of American Home Products Corp.
P.O. Box 8299
Philadelphia, Pennsylvania 19101
800-934-5556

Novartis Pharmaceuticals Corporation
59 Route 10
East Hanover, New Jersey 07936
888-669-6682

Bristol-Myers Squibb Company
345 Park Avenue
New York, New York 10154
800-468-7746

Pharmacia & Upjohn
95 Corporate Drive
Bridgewater, New Jersey 08807-1265
888-768-5501

Rhone-Poulenc Rorer Pharmaceuticals, Inc.
500 Arcola Road
Collegeville, Pennsylvania 19426-0107
1-610-454-8110
800-340-7502

Books About Osteoporosis for Suggested Reading

Boning Up on Osteoporosis.
Published by the National Osteoporosis Foundation
NOTE: I highly recommend this for general guidelines.

National Osteoporosis Foundation Physician's Guide to Prevention and Treatment of Osteoporosis.
Published by the National Osteoporosis Foundation

The Osteoporosis Handbook.
Sydney Lou Bonnick, M.D., F.A.C.P.
Taylor Publishing
NOTE: I highly recommend this as a general reference for everyone's osteoporosis library.

Osteoporosis: Prevention, Diagnosis and Management.
Morris Notelovitz, M.D., Ph.D.
Professional Communications, Inc.

Osteoporosis: Diagnostic and Therapeutic Principles.
Edited by Clifford J. Rosen, M.D.,
Humana Press

The Osteoporosis Book.
Nancy E. Lane, M.D.
Oxford University Press

Strong Women Stay Young.
Miriam E. Nelson, Ph.D.
Bantam Books
NOTE: I highly recommend this as an osteoporosis exercise reference book.

Reference Sources For Chapter Topics

Part I	All About Osteoporosis

Chapter I	What is Osteoporosis?

Kanis, J. A. **Diagnosis of Osteoporosis.** *Osteoporosis Int.* 7 (1997): S108–S116.

Miller, P. D. and K.D. Harper. **World Health Organization Criteria for the Diagnosis of Osteoporosis Should be Endorsed.** *Osteoporosis Index* 1 (Rev 1995): 3–19.

NIH Consensus Development Conference. **Diagnosis, Prophylaxis and Treatment of Osteoporosis.** *Am J Med.* 94 (1993): 646–650

WHO Study Group. **Assessment of Fracture Risk and Its Application to Screening for Postmenopausal Osteoporosis: Report of a WHO Study Group.** *WHO Technical Report* Series 843, Geneva, Switzerland: World Health Organization, 1994: 1–129.

The Scope of the Problem

Barrett-Connor, E. **The Economic and Human Costs of Osteoporotic Fracture.** *American Journal of Medicine* 98 (Suppl 2A) 1995: 2A3S–2A8S.

Black, D. M., et al. **Appendicular Bone Mineral and a Woman's Lifetime Risk of Hip Fracture.** *J Bone Miner Res* 7 (1992): 639–645.

Brunelli, M.P. and T. A. Einhorn. **Medical Management of Osteoporosis. Fracture Prevention.** *Clin Orthoped Rel Res.* 348 (1998): 15–21.

Chrischilles, E.A., et. al **A Model of Lifetime Osteoporosis Impact.** *Archives of Intel Medicine,* vol. 151 (1991): 2026–2032.

Consensus Development Conference. **Diagnosis, Prophylaxis and Treatment of Osteoporosis.** *American Journal of Medicine* 94 (1993): 646–650.

Cooper, C., et al. **Secular Trends in Postmenopausal Vertebral Fractures.** *Calcification Tissue International,* vol. 51 (1992): 100–104.

Cooper, C, G. Campion, G., and L. J. Melton. **Hip Fractures in the Elderly: A Worldwide Projection.** *Osteoporosis International* 2 (1992): 285–289.

Cummings, S. R., D. M. Black, and M. C. Nevitt, et al. **Bone Density at Various Sites for Prediction of Hip Fractures. The Study of Osteoporotic Fractures Research Group.** *Lancet* 341 (1993): 72–75.

Cummings, S. R., D. M. Black, and S. M. Rubin. **Lifetime Risks of Hip, Colles' or Vertebral Fracture and Coronary Heart Disease Among White Menopausal Women.** *Achieves of Internal Medicine,* vol. 149 (1989): 2445–2448.

Cummings, S. R., J. L. Kelsey, and M. C. Nevitt. **Epidemiology of Osteoporosis and Osteoporotic Fractures.** *Epidemiology Reviews* 7 (1985): 17–208.

Garnero, P. and P. D. Delmas. **Osteoporosis.** *Endocrinol Metab Clin N. Amer:* 26 (1997): 913–926.

Keene, G. S., J. M. Parker, and G. A. Pryor. **Mortality and Morbidity After Hip Fractures.** *British Medical Journal* 307 (1993): 1248–1250.

Looker, A. C., et al. **Prevalence of Low Femoral Bone Density in Older U.S. Adults From NHANES III.** *J Bone Miner Res* 12, no. 11 (November 1997): 1761–8.

Matthis, C., U. Weber, T. W. O'Neill, et al. **Health Impact Associated With Vertebral Deformities: Results from the European Vertebral Osteoporosis Study (EVOS).** *Osteoporosis Int.* 8 (1998): 364–372.

Melton III, L. J. **The Prevalence of Osteoporosis.** *J Bone Miner Res* 12 (1997): 1769–1771.

Melton III, L. J., E. J. Atkinson, and W. M. O'Fallon, et al. **Long-term Fracture Prediction by Bone Mineral Assessed at Different Skeletal Sites.** *J Bone Min Res.* 8 (1993): 1227–1233.

Melton III, L. J., M. Thamer, N. F. Ray, et al. **Fractures Attributable to Osteoporosis: Report from the National Osteoporosis Foundation** . *J Bone Min Res,* 12 (1997): 16–23

Melton III, L. J. **How Many Women Have Osteoporosis Now?** *J Bone Miner Res* 10, no. 2 (February 1995): 175–7.

Melton III, L. J., W.M. O'Fallon, and B.L. Riggs. **Secular Trends in the Incidence of Hip Fractures.** *Calcification Tissue International,* vol. 41 (1987): 57–64.

Melton III, L. J. **Epidemiology of Age-Related Fractures.** *The Osteoporotic Syndrome.* Edited by L.V. Avioli. New York: Wiley Liss, 1993.

National Osteoporosis Foundation, **Osteoporosis: Review of the Evidence for Prevention, Diagnosis and Treatment and Cost-Effectiveness Analysis.** *Osteoporosis International* 8 (suppl 4) (1998): IS–88S.

Obrant, K. J., et al. **Increasing Age-Adjusted Risk of Fragility Fractures: A Sign of Increasing Osteoporosis in Successive Generations?** *Calcification Tissue International* 44 (1989): 157–167.

Phillips, S., et al. **The Direct Medical Costs of Osteoporosis for American Women Aged 45 and Older, 1986.** *Bone* 9 (1988): 271–279.

Ray, N. F, J. K. Chan, M. Thamer, L. J. Melton III. **Medical Expenditures for the Treatment of Osteoporotic Fractures in the United States in 1995; Report from the National Osteoporosis Foundation.** J *Bone Miner Res* 12 (1997): 24–35.

Riggs, B. L. and L. J. Melton III. **The Prevention and Treatment of Osteoporosis.** *N Engl J Med.* 327 (1992): 620–627.

Rubin, S. M. and S. R. Cummings. **Results of Bone Densitometry Affect Women's Decisions About Taking Measures to Prevent Fractures.** *Ann Int Med.* 116 (1992): 990–995.

Seeman, E. **Osteoporosis: Trials and Tribulations.** *Am J Med.* 103 (1997): 74S–89S.

Silverman, S. L., M. Greenwald, R. A. Klein, and B. L. Drinkwater. **Effect of Bone Density Information on Decisions About Hormone Replacement Therapy: A Randomized Trial.** *Obstet Gynecol.* 89 (1997): 321–325.

US Congress Office of Technology Assessment, **Effectiveness and Costs of Osteoporosis Screening and Hormone Replacement Therapy, Volume II: Evidence on Benefits, Risks and Costs,** OTA-BP-H-144. Washington DC: US Government Printing Office, August 1995.

Wasnich, R. D., P. D. Ross, L. K. Heilbrun, and J. M. Vogel. **Prediction of Postmenopausal Fracture Risk With Use of Bone Mineral Measurements.** *Am J Obstet Gynecol* 153 (1985): 745–751.

The Importance of Healthy Bones Optimal Peak Bone Mass

Borkan, J. M. and M. Quirk. **Expectations and Outcomes After Hip Fracture Among the Elderly.** *Int J Aging Hum Dev* 34, no. 4 (1992): 339–50.

Cooper, C. et al. **Childhood Growth, Physical Activity, and Peak Bone Mass in Women.** *J Bone Miner Res* 10, no. 6 (June 1995): 940–7.

Cooper, C, E. J. Atkinson, S. J. Jacobson, et al. **Population-Based Study of Survival After Osteoporotic Fractures.** *Am J Epidemiol* 173 (1993): 1001–1005.

Harris, S. and B. Dawson-Hughes. **Rates of Change in Bone Mineral Density of the Spine, Heel, Femoral Neck, and Radius in Healthy Postmenopausal Women.** *Bone and Mineral* 17 (1992): 87–95.

Matkovic, V. et al. **Factors That Influence Peak Bone Mass Formation: A Study of Calcium Balance and the Inheritance of Bone Mass in Adolescent Females.** *Am J Clin Nutr* 52, no. 5 (November 1990): 878–88.

Migliara/Kaplan **Health Conditions Study 1997** Owings Mills, Md: Migliara/Kaplan Associates, 1997.

Morris, F. L. et al. **Prospective Ten-Month Exercise Intervention in Premenarcheal Girls: Positive Effects on Bone and Lean Mass.** *J Bone Miner Res* 12, no. 9 (September 1997): 1453–62.

Ray, N. F., J. K. Chan, M. Thamer, L. J. Melton III. **Medical Expenditures for the Treatment of Osteoporotic Fractures in the United States in 1995: Report from The National Osteoporosis Foundation.** *J Bone Miner Res.* 12 (1997): 24–35.

Recker, R. R., et al. **Bone Gain in Young Adult Women.** *JAMA* 268, no. 17 (November 1992): 2403–8.

Teegarden, D. et al. **Peak Bone Mass in Young Women.** *J Bone Miner Res* 10, no. 5 (May 1995): 711–5.

Von der Recke, P, M. A. Hansen, C. Hassager. **The Association Between Low Bone Mass at the Menopause and Cardiovascular Mortality.** *Am J Med.* 106 (1999): 273–278.

Types of Osteoporosis—Primary and Secondary

Hammond, C. B. **Climacteric.** in Scott, J. R., P. J. DiSaia, C. B. Hammond, and W. N. Spellacy, eds. *Danforth's Obstetrics and Gynecology,* Seventh ed. Philadelphia, PA: JB Lippincott Co. 1994.

Horowitz, M. C. and L. G. Raisz. **Cytokines and Prostaglandins in the Aging Skeleton.** in Bilezikian, J. P., J. Glowacki, and C. J. Rosen CJ, eds. *The Aging Skeleton.* New York, NY: Academic Press, 1999: 195–207.

Manolagas, S. C. and R. L. Jilka. **Bone Marrow, Cytokines, and Bone Remodeling: Emerging Insights into the Pathophysiology of Osteoporosis.** *N Engl J Med.* 332 (1995): 305–311.

Pacific, R., C. Brown, E. Pushcheck, et al. **Effect of Surgical Menopause and Estrogen Replacement on Cytokine Release From Human Blood Mononuclear Cells.** *Proc Natl Acad Sci* 88 (1991): 5134–5138.

Prestwood, K. M. and A. M. Kenny. **Osteoporosis: Pathogenesis, Diagnosis, and Treatment in Older Adults.** *Clin Geriatr Med.* 14 (1998): 577–599.

Rosen, C. J. and C. R. Kessenich. **The Pathophysiology and Treatment of Postmenopausal Osteoporosis: an Evidence-Based Approach to Estrogen Replacement Therapy.** *Endocrinol Metab Clin North Am.* 26 (1997): 295–311.

Sato M, Grese TA, Dodge JA, et al. **Emerging Therapies for the Prevention or Treatment of Postmenopausal Osteoporosis.** *J Med Chem.* 42 (1999): 1–24.

Chapter 2   Are You At Risk for Osteoporosis?

Bauer, D. C., et al . **Factors Associated With Appendicular Bone Mass in Older Women. The Study of Osteoporotic Fractures Research Group**. *Ann Intern Med* 118, no. 9 (May 1993): 657–65.

Cummings, S. R., et al. **Risk Factors for Hip Fracture in White Women. Study of Osteoporotic Fractures Research Group**. *N Engl J Med* 332, no. 12 (March 1995): 767–73.

Davis, J. W., Ross, P. D., Vogel, J. M., et al. **Age-Related Changes in Bone Mass Among Japanese-American Men.** *Bone Miner.* 15 (1991): 227–236.

Mazess, R. B., H. S. Barden, P. P. J. Drinka, et al. **Influence of Age and Body Weight on Spine and Femur Bone Mineral Density in US White Men.** *J Bone Miner Res.* 5 (1990): 645–652.

National Osteoporosis Foundation. **Physician's Guide to Prevention and Treatment of Osteoporosis.** Belle Meade, NJ: *Excerpta Medica* 1998.

Riggs, B. L., H. W. Wahner, W. L. Dunn, et al. **Differential Changes in Bone Mineral Density of the Appendicular and Axial Skeleton With Aging.** *J Clin Invest.* 67 (1981): 328–335.

Ross, P. D., J. W. Davis, R. S. Epstein, and R. D. Wasnich. **Pre-existing Fractures and Bone Mass Predict Vertebral Fracture Incidence In Women.** *Ann Int Med.* 1145 (1991): 919–923.

Silman, A. J. **The Patient With Fracture: The Risk of Subsequent Fractures.** *Am J Med.* 98 (1995): 12S–16S.

Slemenda, C. **Prevention of Hip Fractures: Risk Factor Modification.** *Am J Med* 103, no. 2A (August 1997): 65S–71S.

Turner, L. W., J. E. Taylor, and S. Hunt. **Predictors For Osteoporosis Diagnosis Among Postmenopausal Women: Results From a National Survey**. *J Women Aging* 10, no. 3 (1998): 79–96.

Non-Modifiable Risk Factors For Osteoporosis

Afro-American

Abrams, S. A. et al. **Differences in Calcium Absorption and Kinetics Between Black and White Girls Aged 5–16 Years**. *J Bone Miner Res* 10, no. 5 (May 1995): 829–33.

Aloia, J. F. et al. **Risk for Osteoporosis in Black Women**. *Calcif Tissue Int* 59, no. 6 (December 1996): 415–23.

Barondess, D. A., D. A. Nelson, and S. E. Schlaen. **Whole Body Bone, Fat, and Lean Mass in Black and White Men**. *J Bone Miner Res* 12, no. 6 (1997): 967–71.

Bell, N. H. et al. **Evidence for Alteration of the Vitamin D-Endocrine System in Blacks**. *J Clin Invest* 76, no. 2 (August 1985): 470–3.

Bell, N. H. et al. **Demonstration of a Difference in Urinary Calcium, Not Calcium Absorption, in Black and White Adolescents**. *J Bone Miner Res* 8, no. 9 (September 1993): 1111–5.

Cauley, J. A. et al. **Black-White Differences in Serum Sex Hormones and Bone Mineral Density.** *Am J Epidemiol* 139, no. 10 (May 1994): 1035–46.

Cosman, F. et al. **Resistance to Bone Resorbing Effects of PTH in Black Women.** *J Bone Miner Res* 12, no. 6 (1997): 958–66.

Cummings, S. R. et al. **Racial Differences in Hip Axis Lengths Might Explain Racial Differences in Rates of Hip Fracture. Study of Osteoporotic Fractures Research Group.** *Osteoporosis Int* 4, no. 4 (July 1994): 226–9.

Dawson-Hughes, B. et al. **Calcium Retention and Hormone Levels in Black and White Women on High- and Low-Calcium Diets.** *J Bone Miner Res* 8, no. 7 (July 1993): 779–87.

Farmer, M. E. et al. **Race and Sex Differences in Hip Fracture Incidence.** *Am J Public Health* 74, no. 12 (December 1984): 1374–80.

Griffin, M. R. et al. **Black-White Differences in Fracture Rates.** *Am J Epidemiol* 136, no. 11 (December 1992): 1378–85.

Grisso, J. A. et al. **Risk Factors for Hip Fracture in Black Women. The Northeast Hip Fracture Study Group.** *N Engl J Med* 330, no. 22 (June 1994): 1555–9.

Looker, A. C. et al. **Prevalence of Low Femoral Bone Density in Older U.S. Women From NHANES III.** *J Bone Miner Res* 10, no. 5 (May 1995): 796–802.

Looker, A. C. et al. **Calcium Intakes of Mexican Americans, Cubans, Puerto Ricans, Non-Hispanic Whites, and Non-Hispanic Blacks in the United States.** *J Am Diet Assoc* 93, no. 11 (November 1993): 1274–9.

Luckey, M. M. et al. **A Prospective Study of Bone Loss in African-American and White Women—a Clinical Research Center Study.** *J Clin Endocrinol Metab* 81, no. 8 (August 1996): 2948–56.

Meier, D. E. et al. **Calcium, Vitamin D, and Parathyroid Hormone Status in Young White and Black Women: Association With Racial Differences in Bone Mass.** *J Clin Endocrinol Metab* 72, no. 3 (March 1991): 703–10.

Meier, D. E. et al. **Racial Differences in Pre- and Postmenopausal Bone Homeostasis: Association With Bone Density.** *J Bone Miner Res* 7, no. 10 (October 1992): 1181–9.

Parisien, M. et al. **Histomorphometric Assessment of Bone Mass, Structure, and Remodeling: a Comparison Between Healthy Black and White Premenopausal Women.** *J Bone Miner Res* 12, no. 6 (1997): 948–57.

Perry III, H. M. et al. **Aging and Bone Metabolism in African American and Caucasian Women.** *J Clin Endocrinol Metab* 81, no. 3 (March 1996): 1108–17.

Wright, N. M. et al. **Greater Secretion of Growth Hormone in Black Than in White Men: Possible Factor in Greater Bone Mineral Density—a Clinical Research Center Study.** *J Clin Endocrinol Metab* 80, no. 8 (August 1995): 2291–7.

Asian

Bhudhikanok, G. S. et al. **Differences in Bone Mineral in Young Asian and Caucasian Americans May Reflect Differences in Bone Size.** *J Bone Miner Res* 11, no. 10 (October 1996): 1545–56.

Cummings, S. R. et al. **Racial Differences in Hip Axis Lengths Might Explain Racial Differences in Rates of Hip Fracture. Study of Osteoporotic Fractures Research Group.** *Osteoporosis Int* 4, no. 4 (July 1994): 226–9.

Cummings, S. R. et al. **Bone Mass, Rates of Osteoporotic Fractures, and Prevention of Fractures: Are There Differences Between China and Western Countries?** *Chin Med Sci J* 9, no. 3 (September 1994): 197–200.

Davis, J. W. et al. **Estrogen and Calcium Supplement Use Among Japanese-American Women: Effects Upon Bone Loss When Used Singly and in Combination.** *Bone* 17, no. 4 (October 1995): 369–73.

Davis, J. W., P. D. Ross, and R. D. Wasnich. **Relation of Height and Weight to the Regional Variations in Bone Mass Among Japanese-American Men and Women.** *Osteoporosis Int* 5, no. 4 (1995): 234–8.

Han, K. O. et al. **Nonassociation of Estrogen Receptor Genotypes With Bone Mineral Density and Estrogen Responsiveness to Hormone Replacement Therapy in Korean Postmenopausal Women**. *J Clin Endocrinol Metab* 82, no. 4 (April 1997): 991–5.

Hirota, T. et al. **Effect of Diet and Lifestyle on Bone Mass in Asian Young Women.** *Am J Clin Nutr* 55, no. 6 (June 1992): 1168–73.

Ho, S. C. et al. **Hip Fracture Rates in Hong Kong and the United States, 1988 Through 1989.** *Am J Public Health* 83, no. 5 (May 1993): 694–7.

Huang, C. et al. **Contributions of Vertebral Fractures to Stature Loss Among Elderly Japanese-American Women in Hawaii.** *J Bone Miner Res* 11, no. 3 (March 1996): 408–11.

Ito, M. et al. **Spinal Trabecular Bone Loss and Fracture in American and Japanese Women.** *Calcif Tissue Int* 61, no. 2 (August 1997): 123–8.

Kao, P. C. and F. K. P'eng. **How to Reduce the Risk Factors of Osteoporosis in Asia.** *Chung Hua I Hsueh Tsa Chih (Taipei)* 55, no. 3 (March 1995): 209–13.

Lau, E. M. and C. Cooper. **The Epidemiology of Osteoporosis. The Oriental Perspective in a World Context.** *Clin Orthop,* no. 323 (February 1996): 65–74.

Lauderdale, D. S. et al. **Hip Fracture Incidence Among Elderly Asian-American Populations.** *Am J Epidemiol* 146, no. 6 (September 1997): 502–9.

Matsumoto, D. et al. **Cultural Differences in Attitudes, Values, and Beliefs About Osteoporosis in First and Second Generation Japanese-American Women.** *Women Health* 23, no. 4 (1995): 39–56.

Nowack, M. K., S. Brizzolara, and D. A. Lally. **Bone Mineral Content in Hawaiian, Asian, and Filipino Children.** *Hawaii Med J* 54, no. 1 (January 1995): 388–9, 393.

Ross, P. D. et al. **Vertebral Dimension Measurements Improve Prediction of Vertebral Fracture Incidence.** *Bone* 16, no. 4 Suppl (April 1995): 257S–62S.

Sugimoto, T. et al. **Comparison of Bone Mineral Content Among Japanese, Koreans, and Taiwanese Assessed by Dual-Photon Absorptiometry.** *J Bone Miner Res* 7, no. 2 (February 1992): 153–9.

Tobias, J. H. et al. **A Comparison of Bone Mineral Density Between Caucasian, Asian and Afro-Caribbean Women.** *Clin Sci (Colch)* 87, no. 5 (November 1994): 587–91.

Hispanic

Bauer, R. L. **Ethnic Differences in Hip Fracture: a Reduced Incidence in Mexican Americans.** *Am J Epidemiol* 127, no. 1 (January 1988): 145–9.

Bauer, R. L. and R. A. Deyo. **Low Risk of Vertebral Fracture in Mexican American Women.** *Arch Intern Med.* 147. no. 8. (August 1987): 1437–9.

Cooper, C., G. Campion, and L. J. Melton III. **Hip Fractures in the Elderly: a World-Wide Projection.** *Osteoporosis Int* 2, no. 6 (November 1992): 285–9.

Curiel, M. D. et al. **Study of Bone Mineral Density in Lumbar Spine and Femoral Neck in a Spanish Population.** *Osteoporosis Int* 7, no. 1 (1997): 59–64.

Ellis, K. J., S. A. Abrams, and W. W. Wong. **Body Composition of a Young, Multiethnic Female Population.** *Am J Clin Nutr* 65, no. 3 (March 1997): 724–31.

Haddock, L. et al. **The Lumbar and Femoral Bone Mineral Densities in a Normal Female Puerto Rican Population.** *P R Health Sci J* 15, no. 1 (March 1996): 5–11.

Looker, A. C. et al. **Prevalence of Low Femoral Bone Density in Older U.S. Women From NHANES III.** *J Bone Miner Res* 10, no. 5 (May 1995): 796–802.

Looker, A. C. et al. **Calcium Intakes of Mexican Americans, Cubans, Puerto Ricans, Non-Hispanic Whites, and Non-Hispanic Blacks in the United States.** *J Am Diet Assoc* 93, no. 11 (November 1993): 1274–9.

Loria, C. M. et al. **Macronutrient Intakes Among Adult Hispanics: a Comparison of Mexican Americans, Cuban Americans, and Mainland Puerto Ricans.** *Am J Public Health* 85, no. 5 (May 1995): 684–9.

Lubben, J. E., P. G. Weiler, and I. Chi. **Gender and Ethnic Differences in the Health Practices of the Elderly Poor.** *J Clin Epidemiol* 42, no. 8 (1989): 725–33.

Marcus, R. et al. **Correlates of Bone Mineral Density in the Postmenopausal Estrogen/Progestin Interventions Trial.** *J Bone Miner Res* 9, no. 9 (September 1994): 1467–76.

Other Non-Modifiable Risk Factors

Cummings, S. R., D. M. Black, M. C. Nevitt, et al. **Appendicular Bone Density and Age Predict Hip Fracture in Women.** *Journal of the American Medical Association* 263 (1990): 665–668.

Riggs, B. L. et al. **Differential Changes in Bone Mineral Density of the Appendicular and Axial Skeleton with Aging.** *Journal of Clinical Investigation,* (1981) vol. 67, p. 328–335.

Seman, E. et al. **Reduced Bone Mass in Daughters of Women With Osteoporosis.** *New England Journal of Medicine,* 320 (1989): 554–558.

Potentially Modifiable Risk Factors For Osteoporosis

Parathyroid

Bergenfelz, A., S. Valdermarsson, and B. Ahren. **Functional Recovery of the Parathyroid Glands After Surgery for Primary Hyperparathyroidism.** *Surgery* 116, no. 5 (November 1994): 827–36.

Bilezikian, J. P., R. Marcus, and M. A. Levine, editors. **The Parathyroids: Basic and Clinical Concepts.** New York: Raven Press, 1994.

Boechat, M. I. et al. **Decreased Cortical and Increased Cancellous Bone in Two Children With Primary Hyperparathyroidism.** *Metabolism* 45, no. 1 (January 1996): 76–81.

Brockstedt, H. et al. **Reconstruction of Cortical Bone Remodeling in Untreated Primary Hyperparathyroidism and Following Surgery.** *Bone* 16, no. 1 (January 1995): 109–17.

Carling, T. et al. **Vitamin D Receptor Polymorphisms Correlate to Parathyroid Cell Function in Primary Hyperparathyroidism.** *J Clin Endocrinol Metab* 82, no. 6 (June 1997): 1772–5.

Christiansen, P. et al. **Primary Hyperparathyroidism: Biochemical Markers and Bone Mineral Density at Multiple Skeletal Sites in Danish Patients.** *Bone* 21, no. 1 (July 1997): 93–9.

Diamond, T. et al. **Estrogen Replacement May Be an Alternative to Parathyroid Surgery for the Treatment of Osteoporosis in Elderly Postmenopausal Women Presenting With Primary Hyperparathyroidism: a Preliminary Report.** *Osteoporosis Int* 6, no. 4 (1996): 329–33.

Elvius, M. et al. **Seventeen Year Follow-Up Study of Bone Mass in Patients With Mild Asymptomatic Hyperparathyroidism, Some of Whom Were Operated On.** *Eur J Surg* 161, no. 12 (December 1995): 863–9.

Garton, M. et al. **Changes in Bone Mass and Metabolism After Surgery for Primary Hyperparathyroidism.** *Clin Endocrinol (Oxf)* 42, no. 5 (May 1995): 493–500.

Gogusev, J. et al. **Depressed Expression of Calcium Receptor in Parathyroid Gland Tissue of Patients With Hyperparathyroidism.** *Kidney Int* 51, no. 1 (January 1997): 328–36.

Grey, A. et al. **Circulating Levels of Interleukin-6 and Tumor Necrosis Factor-Alpha Are Elevated in Primary Hyperparathyroidism and Correlate With Markers of Bone Resorption—A Clinical Research Center Study** . *J Clin Endocrinol Metab* 81, no. 10 (October 1996): 3450–4.

Grey, A. B. et al. **Accelerated Bone Loss in Postmenopausal Women With Mild Primary Hyperparathyroidism.** *Clin Endocrinol (Oxf)* 44, no. 6 (June 1996): 697–702.

Grey, A. B. et al. **Effect of Hormone Replacement Therapy on Bone Mineral Density in Postmenopausal Women With Mild Primary Hyperparathyroidism. A Randomized, Controlled Trial** *Ann Intern Med.* 125, no. 5 (September 1996): 360–8.

Horowitz, M. et al. **Biochemical Effects of a Calcium Supplement in Postmenopausal Women With Primary Hyperparathyroidism.** *Horm Metab Res* 26, no. 1 (January 1994): 39–42.

Locker, F. G., S. J. Silverberg, and J. P. Bilezikian. **Optimal Dietary Calcium Intake in Primary Hyperparathyroidism.** *Am J Med* 102, no. 6 (June 1997): 543–50.

Parisien, M. et al**. Bone Structure in Postmenopausal Hyperparathyroid, Osteoporotic, and Normal Women**. *J Bone Miner Res* 10, no. 9 (September 1995): 1393–9.

Potts, J. T. Jr. **Primary Hyperparathyroidism.** *In Metabolic Bone Disease.* 3rd ed., editors L. V. Avioli and S. M. Krane. San Diego, CA: Academic Press, 1997.

Silverberg, S. J. et al. **Increased Bone Mineral Density After Parathyroidectomy in Primary Hyperparathyroidism.** *J Clin Endocrinol Metab* 80, no. 3 (March 1995): 729–34.

 Silverberg, S. J. et al. **Longitudinal Measurements of Bone Density and Biochemical Indices in Untreated Primary Hyperparathyroidism**. *J Clin Endocrinol Metab* 80, no. 3 (March 1995): 723–8.

Silverberg, S. J., F. G. Locker, and J. P. Bilezikian. **Vertebral Osteopenia: a New Indication for Surgery in Primary Hyperparathyroidism.** *J Clin Endocrinol Metab* 81, no. 11 (November 1996): 4007–12.

Soreide, J. A. et al. **Characteristics of Patients Surgically Treated for Primary Hyperparathyroidism With and Without Renal Stones.** *Surgery* 120, no. 6 (December 1996): 1033–7; discussion 1037–8.

Vogel, M., M. Hahn, and G. Delling. **Trabecular Bone Structure in Patients With Primary Hyperparathyroidism.** *Virchows Arch* 426, no. 2 (1995): 127–34.

Eating Disorders and Osteoporosis

Abrams, S. A. et al. **Mineral Balance and Bone Turnover in Adolescents With Anorexia Nervosa.** *J Pediatr* 123, no. 2 (August 1993): 326–31.

Andersen, A. E., P. J. Woodward, and N. LaFrance. **Bone Mineral Density of Eating Disorder Subgroups**. *Int J Eat Disord* 18, no. 4 (December 1995): 335–42.

Bachrach, L. K. et al. **Decreased Bone Density in Adolescent Girls With Anorexia Nervosa**. *Pediatrics* 86, no. 3 (September 1990): 440–7.

Bachrach, L. K. et al. **Recovery From Osteopenia in Adolescent Girls With Anorexia Nervosa.** J *Clin Endocrinol Metab* 72, no. 3 (March 1991): 602–6.

Biller, B. M. et al. **Mechanisms of Osteoporosis in Adult and Adolescent Women With Anorexia Nervosa**. *J Clin Endocrinol Metab* 68, no. 3 (March 1989): 548–54.

Brooks, E. R., B. W. Ogden, and D. S. Cavalier. **Compromised Bone Density 11.4 Years After Diagnosis of Anorexia Nervosa**. *J Womens Health* 7, no. 5 (June 1998): 567–74.

Carmichael, K. A. and D. H. Carmichael. **Bone Metabolism and Osteopenia in Eating Disorders**. *Medicine* (Baltimore) 74, no. 5 (September 1995): 254–67.

Davies, K. M. et al. **Reduced Bone Mineral in Patients With Eating Disorders**. *Bone* 11, no. 3 (1990): 143–7.

Fruth, S. J. and T. W. Worrell. **Factors Associated With Menstrual Irregularities and Decreased Bone Mineral Density in Female Athletes**. *J Orthop* Sports Phys Ther 22, no. 1 (July 1995): 26–38.

Garner, D. M., L. W. Rosen, and D. Barry. **Eating Disorders Among Athletes. Research and Recommendations**. *Child Adolesc Psychiatr Clin N Am* 7, no. 4 (October 1998): 839–57.

Gordon, C. M. et al. **Changes in Bone Turnover Markers and Menstrual Function After Short-Term Oral DHEA in Young Women With Anorexia Nervosa**. *J Bone Miner Res* 14, no. 1 (January 1999): 136–45.

Grinspoon, S., D. Herzog, and A. Klibanski. **Mechanisms and Treatment Options for Bone Loss in Anorexia Nervosa**. *Psychopharmacol* Bull 33, no. 3 (1997): 399–404.

Hergenroeder, A. C. **Bone Mineralization, Hypothalamic Amenorrhea, and Sex Steroid Therapy in Female Adolescents and Young Adults**. *J Pediatr* 126, no. 5 Pt 1 (May 1995): 683–9.

Herzog, W. et al. **Outcome of Bone Mineral Density in Anorexia Nervosa Patients 11.7 Years After First Admission**. *J Bone Miner Res* 8, no. 5 (May 1993): 597–605.

Female Athletes and Osteoporosis

Bennell, K. L. et al. **Risk Factors for Stress Fractures in Female Track-and-Field Athletes: a Retrospective Analysis**. *Clin J Sport Med* 5, no. 4 (October 1995): 229–35.

Carbon, R. J. **Exercise, Amenorrhea and the Skeleton**. *Br Med J* 48, no. 3 (July 1992): 546–60.

Claessens, A. L. et al. **Growth and Menarcheal Status of Elite Female Gymnasts.** *Med Sci Sports Exerc* 24, no. 7 (July 1992): 755–63.

Clarkson, P. M. and E. M. Haymes. **Exercise and Mineral Status of Athletes: Calcium, Magnesium, Phosphorus, and Iron**. *Med Sci Sports Exerc* 27, no. 6 (June 1995): 831–43.

Drinkwater, B. L. et al. **Bone Mineral Density After Resumption of Menses in Amenorrheic Athletes**. *JAMA* 256, no. 3 (July 1986): 380–2.

Drinkwater, B. L., B. Bruemner, and C. H. Chesnut 3rd. **Menstrual History As a Determinant of Current Bone Density in Young Adults**. *JAMA* 263, no. 4 (January 1990): 545–8.

Drinkwater, B. L. et al. **Bone Mineral Content of Amenorrheic and Eumenor-rheic Athletes.** *N Engl J Med* 311, no. 5 (August 1984): 277–81.

Etherington, J. et al. **The Effect of Weight-Bearing Exercise on Bone Mineral Density: a Study of Female Ex-Elite Athletes and the General Population.** *J Bone Miner Res* 11, no. 9 (September 1996): 1333–8.

Fehling, P. C. et al. **A Comparison of Bone Mineral Densities Among Female Athletes in Impact Loading and Active Loading Sports.** *Bone* 17, no. 3 (September 1995): 205–10.

Fox, R. P., et al. **Scoliosis and Fractures in Young Ballet Dancers: Relation to Delayed Menarche and Secondary Amenorrhea.** *New England Journal of Medicine* 314 (1986): 1348–1353.

Fruth, S. J. and T. W. Worrell. **Factors Associated With Menstrual Irregularities and Decreased Bone Mineral Density in Female Athletes.** *J Orthop Sports Phys Ther* 22, no. 1 (July 1995): 26–38.

Haberland, C. A.et al. **A Physician Survey of Therapy for Exercise-Associated Amenorrhea: a Brief Report.** *Clin J Sport Med* 5, no. 4 (October 1995): 246–50.

Heinonen, A. et al. **Bone Mineral Density in Female Athletes Representing Sports With Different Loading Characteristics of the Skeleton.** *Bone* 17, no. 3 (September 1995): 197–203.

Heinonen, A. et al. **Bone Mineral Density of Female Athletes in Different Sports.** *Bone Miner* 23, no. 1 (October 1993): 1–14.

Hergenroeder, A. C. **Bone Mineralization, Hypothalamic Amenorrhea, and Sex Steroid Therapy in Female Adolescents and Young Adults.** *J Pediatr* 126, no. 5 Pt 1 (May 1995): 683–9.

Hetland, M. L. et al. **Running Induces Menstrual Disturbances but Bone Mass Is Unaffected, Except in Amenorrheic Women.** *Am J Med* 95, no. 1 (July 1993): 53–60.

Jonnavithula, S. et al. **Bone Density Is Compromised in Amenorrheic Women Despite Return of Menses: a 2–Year Study.** *Obstet Gynecol* 81, no. 5 (Pt 1) (May 1993): 669–74.

Matsumoto, T. et al. **Bone Density and Bone Metabolic Markers in Active Collegiate Athletes: Findings in Long-Distance Runners, Judoists, and Swimmers.** *Int J Sports Med* 18, no. 6 (August 1997): 408–12.

Micklesfield, L. K. et al. **Bone Mineral Density in Mature, Premenopausal Ultramarathon Runners.** *Med Sci Sports Exerc* 27, no. 5 (May 1995): 688–96.

Myburgh, K. H. et al. **Low Bone Mineral Density at Axial and Appendicular Sites in Amenorrheic Athletes.** *Med Sci Sports Exerc* 25, no. 11 (November 1993): 1197–202.

Myerson, M. et al. **Total Body Bone Density in Amenorrheic Runners.** *Obstet Gynecol* 79, no. 6 (June 1992): 973–78.

Okano, H. et al. **Effects of Exercise and Amenorrhea on Bone Mineral Density in Teenage Runners.** *Endocr J* 42, no. 2 (April 1995): 271–6.

Puffer, J. C. **Athletic Amenorrhea and Its Influence on Skeletal Integrity.** *Bull Rheum Dis* 43, no. 5 (August 1994): 5–6.

Putukian, M. **The Female Triad. Eating Disorders, Amenorrhea, and Osteo-porosis**. *Med Clin North Am* 78, no. 2 (March 1994): 345–56.

Rencken, M. L., C. H. Chesnut III, and B. L. Drinkwater. **Bone Density at Multiple Skeletal Sites in Amenorrheic Athletes**. *JAMA* 276, no. 3 (July 1996): 238–40.

Robinson, T. L. et al. **Gymnasts Exhibit Higher Bone Mass Than Runners Despite Similar Prevalence of Amenorrhea and Oligomenorrhea.** *J Bone Miner Res* 10, no. 1 (January 1995): 26–35.

Slemenda, C. W. and C. C. Johnston, Jr. **High Intensity Activities in Young Women: Site-Specific Bone Mass Effects Among Female Figure Skaters.** *Bone Miner* 20, no. 2 (February 1993): 125–32.

Snead, D. B. et al. **Dietary Patterns, Eating Behaviors, and Bone Mineral Density in Women Runners.** *Am J Clin Nutr* 56, no. 4 (October 1992): 705–11.

Snead, D. B. et al. **Reproductive Hormones and Bone Mineral Density in Women Runners.** *J Appl Physiol* 72, no. 6 (June 1992): 2149–56

Snow-Harter, C. et al. **Effects of Resistance and Endurance Exercise on Bone Mineral Status of Young Women: A Randomized Exercise Intervention Trial.** *J Bone Miner Res* 7, no. 7 (July 1992): 761–69.

Snow-Harter, C. M. **Bone Health and Prevention of Osteoporosis in Active and Athletic Women.** *Clin Sports Med* 13, no. 2 (April 1994): 389–404.

Taaffe, D. R. et al. **Differential Effects of Swimming Versus Weight-Bearing Activity on Bone Mineral Status of Eumenorrheic Athletes.** *J Bone Miner Res* 10, no. 4 (April 1995): 586–93.

Warren, M. P. **The Effects of Exercise on Pubertal Progression and Reproductive Function in Girls.** *Journal of Clinical Endocrinology and Metabolism* 51 (1980): 1150–1157, 1980.

White, C. M., A. C. Hergenroeder, and W. J. Klish. **Bone Mineral Density in 15– to 21-Year-Old Eumenorrheic and Amenorrheic Subjects**. *American Journal of Diseases in Children* 146, no. 1 (January 1992): 31–5.

Wolman, R. L.. et al. **Dietary Calcium As a Statistical Determinant of Spinal Trabecular Bone Density in Amenorrhoeic and Estrogen-Replete Athletes.** *Bone Miner* 17, no. 3 (June 1992): 415–23.

Young, N. et al. **Bone Density at Weight-Bearing and Nonweight-Bearing Sites in Ballet Dancers: the Effects of Exercise, Hypogonadism, and Body Weight.** *J Clin Endocrinol Metab* 78, no. 2 (February 1994): 449–54.

Glucocorticoid-Induced Osteoporosis

Adachi, J. D., Benson, W.G., Brown, J., et al. **Etidronate Therapy to Prevent Corticosteroid-Induced Osteoporosis.** *New England Journal of Medicine* 337, no. 6 (1997): 382–387.

Adachi, J. D., W. G. Benson, W.G., Bianchi, F., et al. **Vitamin D and Calcium in the Prevention of Corticosteroid Induced Osteoporosis: A 3 year Follow-up Study**. *Journal of Rheumatology* 23 (1996): 995–1000.

Adinoff, A. D., J. R. Hollister. **Steroid-Induced Fractures and Bone Loss in Patients With Asthma**. *N Engl J Med.* 309 (1983): 265–268.

Adler, R. A., and C. J. Rosen. **Glucocorticoids and Osteoporosis.** *Endocrinology and Metabolism Clinics of North America* 23 (1994): 641–654.

American College of Rheumatology Task Force on Osteoporosis Guidelines**. Recommendations for the Prevention and Treatment of Glucocorticoid-Induced Osteoporosis.** *Arthritis Rheum.* 39 (1996): 1791–1801.

Bernstein, C. N. et al. **Decreased Bone Density in Inflammatory Bowel Disease Is Related to Corticosteroid Use and Not Disease Diagnosis.** *J Bone Miner Res* 10, no. 2 (February 1995): 250–6.

Boot, A. M. et al. **Renal Transplantation and Osteoporosis.** *Arch Dis Child* 72, no. 6 (June 1995): 502–6.

Buckely, L. M., E. S. Leib, K. S. Cartularo, et al. **Calcium and Vitamin D₃ Supplementation Prevents Bone Loss in the Spine Secondary to Low Dose Corticosteroids in Patients with Rheumatoid Arthritis.** *Ann Int Med* 125 (1996): 961–968.

Buckley, L. M. et al. **Effects of Low Dose Corticosteroids on the Bone Mineral Density of Patients With Rheumatoid Arthritis.** *J Rheumatol* 22, no. 6 (June 1995): 1055–9.

Canalis, E. **Mechanism of Glucocorticoid Action in Bone; Implications to Glucocorticoid-Induced Osteoporosis.** *J Cliin Endocrin Metab.* 81 (1996): 3441–3447.

Canalis, E. Clinical Review 83: **Mechanisms of Glucocorticoid Action in Bone: Implications to Glucocorticoid-Induced Osteoporosis.** *J Clin Endocrinol Metab* 81, no. 10 (October 1996): 3441–7.

Cortet, B. et al. **Evaluation of Bone Mineral Density in Patients With Rheumatoid Arthritis. Influence of Disease Activity and Glucocorticoid Therapy.** *Rev Rhum Engl* Ed 64, no. 7–9 (July 1997–September 1997): 451–8.

Dempster, D. W. **Bone Histomorphometry in Glucocorticoid-Induced Osteoporosis.** *J Bone Miner Res* 4, no. 2 (April 1989): 137–41.

Diamond, T. et al. **Cyclical Etidronate Plus Ergocalciferol Prevents Glucocorticoid-Induced Bone Loss in Postmenopausal Women.** *Am J Med* 98, no. 5 (May 1995): 459–63.

Eastell, R**. Management of Corticosteroid-Induced Osteoporosis. UK Consensus Group Meeting on Osteoporosis.** *J Intern Med* 237, no. 5 (May 1995): 439–47.

Eastell, R. et al**. A UK Consensus Group on Management of Glucocorticoid-Induced Osteoporosis: An Update.** *J Intern Med* 244, no. 4 (October 1998): 271–92.

Ebeling, P. R. et al. **Bone Mineral Density and Bone Turnover in Asthmatics Treated With Long-Term Inhaled or Oral Glucocorticoids.** *J Bone Miner Res* 13, no. 8 (August 1998): 1283–9.

Gluck, O. S., Murphy WA, Hahn TJ, Hahn B. **Bone Loss in Adults Receiving Alternate Day Glucocorticoid Therapy.** *Arthritis Rheum* 1981;24: 8929–898.

Gregson RK, R. Rao, A. J. Murrills, et al. **Comparison of Fluticasone Propionate With Beclomethasone Diproprionate.** *Osteoporosis Int.* 8 (1998): 418–422.

Hahn, T. J. **Steroid and Drug-Induced Osteoporosis.** In Favus, M. (ed.): *Primer of Metabolic Bone Diseases and Disorders of Mineral Metabolism.* Philadelphia: Raven Press, 1997, p. 250.

Hall, G. M., M. Daniels, D. V. Doyle, et al**. Effect of Hormone Replacement Therapy on Bone Mass in Rheumatoid Arthritis Patients Treated With and Without Steroids**. *Arthritis and Rheumatism* 37 (19940: 1499–1505.

Hanania, N. A. et al. **Dose-Related Decrease in Bone Density Among Asthmatic Patients Treated With Inhaled Corticosteroids**. *J Allergy Clin Immunol* 96, no. 5 Pt 1 (November 1995): 571–9.

Hopp, R. J. et al. **Longitudinal Assessment of Bone Mineral Density in Children With Chronic Asthma**. *Ann Allergy Asthma Immunol* 75, no. 2 (August 1995): 143–8.

Lane NE, Lukert B. **The Science and Therapy of Glucocorticoid-Induced Bone Loss**. *Endocrinol Metab Clin N Amer.* 27 (1998): 465–483.

Luengo M, del Rio L, Pons F, Picado C. **Bone Mineral Density in Asthmatic Adult Patients Treated With Inhaled Corticosteroids: A Case-Control Study.** *Eur Respir J.* 10 (1997): 2110–2113.

Luengo, M., C. Picado, L. Del Rio, et al**. Treatment of Steroid-Induced Osteopenia With Calcitonin in Corticosteroid-dependentAasthma: A One-year Follow-up Study**. *American Review of Respiratory Disease* 142 (1990): 104–107.

Lukert, B. P., B. E. Johnson, and R. G. Robinson. **Estrogen and Progesterone Replacement Therapy Reduces Glucocorticoid-Induced Bone Loss.** *Journal of Bone and Mineral Research* 7 (1992): 1063–1069.

Reid, I. R., D. J. Wattie, M. C. Evans, et al. **Testosterone Therapy in Glucocorticoid-treated Men**. *Archives of Internal Medicine* 156 (1996): 1173–1177.

Saag, K. G, R. Koehnke, J. R. Caldwell, et al. **Low-dose Long-term Corticosteroid Therapy in Rheumatoid Arthritis: An Analysis of Serious Adverse Events.** *Am J Med.* 96 (1994): 115–123.

Saag, K. G. **Low-dose Corticosteroid Therapy in Rheumatoid Arthritis: Balancing the Evidence.** *Am J Med* 103 (6A)(1997): 31S–39S.

Sambrook, P. N., J. Birmingham, P. Kelly, et al. **Prevention of Corticosteroid Osteoporosis. A Comparison of Calcium, Calcitriol and Calcitonin.** *New England Journal of Medicine* 328 (1993): 1747–1752.

Van Staa, T. P., C. Cooper, L. Abenhaim, et al**. Use of Oral Corticosteroids and Risk of Fractures**. (Abstract 1222*). American Society for Bone and Mineral Research.* December 6, 1998.

Modifiable Risk Factors for Osteoporosis

Bauer, D.C., W. S. Browner, J. A. Cauley, et al. **Factors Associated With Appendicular Bone Mass in Older Women.** *Annals of Internal Medicine* 118 (1993): 657–665.

Corson, S. L. **Oral Contraceptives for the Prevention of Osteoporosis**. *J Reprod Med* 38 (1993): 1015–20.

DeCherney, A. **Bone-Sparing Properties of Oral Contraceptives.** *Am J Obstet Gynecol* 174 (1996): 15–20.

Ettinger, B. **Thyroid Supplements: Effects on Bone Mass.** *Western Journal of Medicine* 136 (1982): 473.

Kleerekoper, M., R. S. Brienza, L. R. Schultz, et al. **Oral Contraceptive Use May Protect Against Low Bone Mass.** *Arch Intern Med* 151 (1991): 1971–6.

Miller, P. D. **Management of Osteoporosis.** *Adv Inter Med.* 44 (1999): 175–207.

National Osteoporosis Foundation. **Physician's Guide to Prevention and Treatment of Osteoporosis.** Washington, DC: *National Osteoporosis Foundation* 1998.

Prestwood, K. M. and A. M. Kenny. **Osteoporosis: Pathogenesis, Diagnosis, and Treatment in Older Adults.** *Clin Geriatr Med.* 14 (1998): 577–599.

United States Preventive Services Task Force. **Guide to Clinical Preventive Services,** 2nd ed. Washington, DC: *US Dept of Health and Human Services.*

Other Risk Factors for Osteoporosis

Cumming, S. R. et.al. **Risk Factors for Hip Fracture in White Women.** *N Engl J Med* 332 (1995): 767–773.

Ross, P. D. D. et al. **Pre-Existing Fractures and Bone Mass Predict Vertebral Fracture Incidence in Women.** *Ann of Int Med* 114 (1992): 919–923.

Men and Osteoporosis

Allain, T., P. Pitt, and C. Moniz. **Osteoporosis in Men.** *British Medical Journal,* 305 (1992): 955–956.

Bendavid, E. J., J. Shan, and E. Barrett-Connor. **Factors Associated With Bone Mineral Density in Middle-Aged Men.** *J Bone Miner Res* 11, no. 8 (August 1996): 1185–90.

Drinka, P. J., J. Olson, S. Bauwens, et al. **Lack of Association Between Free Testosterone and Bone Density from Age in Elderly Males.** *Calcif Tissue Int.* 52 (1993): 67–69.

Drinka, P.J., S.F. Bauwens and A.A. DeSmet. **Atraumatic Vertebral Deformities in Elderly Males.** *Calcification Tissue International* 41 (1987): 299–302.

Elliot, J. R., N. L. Gilchrist, and J. E. Wells. **The Effect of Socioeconomic Status on Bone Density in a Male Caucasian Population.** *Bone* 18, no. 4 (April 1996): 371–3.

Finkelstein, J. S., R. M. Neer, B. M. K. Biller, et al. **Osteopenia in Men With a History of Delayed Puberty.** *N Engl J Med.* 326 (1992): 600–604.

Finkelstein, J. S., A. Klibanski, and R. M. Neer. **A Longitudinal Evaluation of Bone Mineral Density in Adult Men With Histories of Delayed Puberty.** *J Clin Endocrinol Metab* 81, no. 3 (March 1996): 1152–5.

Garn, S. M., T. V. Sullivan, S. A. Decker, et al. **Continuing Bone Expansion and Increasing Bone Loss Over a Two-Decade Period in Men and Women From a Total Community Sample.** *Am J Hun Biol.* 4 (1992): 57–67.

Glynn, N. W. et al. **Determinants of Bone Mineral Density in Older Men.** *J Bone Miner Res* 10, no. 11 (November 1995): 1769–77.

Greenspan, S. L., D. S. Oppenheim, and A. Klibanski. **Importance of Gonadal Steroids to Bone Mass in Men With Hyperprolactinemic Hypogonadism.** *Ann Intern Med.* 110. no. 7. (April 1989): 526–31.

Guo, C. Y, H. Jones, and R. Eastell. **Treatment of Isolated Hypogonadotropic Hypogonadism Effect on Bone Mineral Density and Bone Turnover.** *J Clin Endocrinol Metab.* 82 (1997): 658–665.

Hannan, M. T., D. T. Felson, and J. J. Anderson. **Bone Mineral Density in Elderly Men and Women: Results From the Framingham Osteoporosis Study.** *J Bone Miner Res* 7 (1992): 547–553.

Jackson, J.A. and M. Kleerekoper. **Osteoporosis in Men: Diagnosis, Pathophysiology, and Prevention.** *Medicine,* 69, (1990): 137–152.

Jackson, J.A. **Osteoporosis in Men.** *In Favus, M. (ed.): Primer of Metabolic Bone Diseases and Disorders of Mineral Metabolism,* 2nd ed. Philadelphia: Raven Press, 1993, pp. 255–258.

Johansson, A. G.et al. **Effects of Growth Hormone and Insulin-Like Growth Factor I in Men With Idiopathic Osteoporosis.** *J Clin Endocrinol Metab* 81, no. 1 (January 1996): 44–8.

Jones, G. et al. **Progressive Loss of Bone in the Femoral Neck in Elderly People: Longitudinal Findings From the Dubbo Osteoporosis Epidemiology Study.** *BMJ* 309, no. 6956 (September 1994): 691–5.

Karagas, M. R. et al. **Heterogeneity of Hip Fracture: Age, Race, Sex, and Geographic Patterns of Femoral Neck and Trochanteric Fractures Among the US Elderly.** *Am J Epidemiol* 143, no. 7 (April 1996): 677–82.

Katznelson, L.et al. **Increase in Bone Density and Lean Body Mass During Testosterone Administration in Men With Acquired Hypogonadism.** *J Clin Endocrinol Metab* 81, no. 12 (December 1996): 4358–65.

Kelepouris, N., K. D. Harper, F. Gannon, et al. **Severe Osteoporosis in Men.** *Ann Inter Med.* 123 (1995): 452–460.

Kelly, P. J., N. A. Pocock, P. N. Sambrook, et al. **Dietary Calcium, Sex Hormones and Bone Mineral Density in Men.** *BMJ.* 300 (1990): 1361–1364.

Mann, T., S. K. Oviatt, D. Wilson D, et al. **Vertebral Deformity in Men.** *J Bone Miner Res.* 7 (1992): 1259–1265.

Mazess, R. B., et al. **Influence of Age and Body Weight on Spine and Femur Bone Mineral Density in U.S. White Men.** *Journal of Bone and Mineral Research,* 5 (1990): 645–652.

McElduff, A., M. Wilkinson, P. Ward, et al. **Forearm Mineral Content in Normal Men: Relationship to Weight, Height and Plasma Testosterone Concentrations.** *Bone.* 9 (1998): 281–283.

Meier, D. E., E. S. Orwoll, E. J. Keenan, et al. **Marked Decline in Trabecular Bone Mineral Content in Healthy Men With Age: Lack of Association With Sex Steroid Levels.** *J Am Geriatr Soc.* 35 (1987): 189–197.

Melton III, L. J., W. M. O'Fallon, and B. L. Riggs. **Secular Trends in the Incidence of Hip Fractures.** *Calcif Tissue Int.* 41, no. 2. (August 1987): 57–64.

Murphy, S., K. T. Khaw, A. Cassidy, et al. **Sex Hormones and Bone Mineral Density in Elderly Men.** *Bon Miner.* 20 (1993): 133–140.

Mussolino, M. E., A. C. Looker, J. H. Madans, et al. **Risk Factors for Hip Fracture in White Men: The NHANES 1 Epidemiologic Follow-up Study**. *J Bone Miner Res.* 13 (1998): 918–924.

Need, A. G., et al. **Effects of Nandrolone Decanoate on Forearm Mineral Density and Calcium Metabolism in Osteoporotic Postmenopausal Women**. *Calcification Tissue International,* (1987) vol. 41, p. 7–10.

Nguyen, T. V., J. A. Eisman, P. J. Kelly, et al. **Risk Factors For Osteoporotic Fractures in Elderly Men.** *Am J Epidemiol.* 144(1996): 258–261.

Nguyen, T. V., P. J. Kelly, P. N. Sambrook, et al. **Lifestyle Factors and Bone Density in the Elderly: Implications for Osteoporosis Prevention.** *J Bone Miner Res.* 9 (1994): 1339–1346.

Niewoehner, C**. Osteoporosis in Men: Is It More Common Than We Think?** *Postgrad Med.* 93 (1993): 59–60, 63–70.

Orwoll, E. S., S. K. Oviatt, M. R. McClung MR, et al. **The Rate of Bone Mineral Loss in Normal Men and the Effects of Calcium and Cholecalciferol Supplementation.** *Ann Intern Med* 112 (1990): 29–34.

Orwoll, E. S., S. K. Oviatt, and T. Mann. **The Impact of Osteophytic and Vascular Calcifications on Vertebral Mineral Density Measurements in Men.** *J Clin Endocrinol Metab* 70, no. 4 (April 1990): 1202–7.

Orwoll, E.S., and Klein, R.F. **Osteoporosis in Men.** *Endocrine Reviews* 16 (1995): 87–116.

Poor, G. et al. **Determinants of Reduced Survival Following Hip Fractures in Men.** *Clin Orthop,* no. 319 (October 1995): 260–5.

Poor, G. et al. **Predictors of Hip Fractures in Elderly Men.** *J Bone Miner Res* 10, no. 12 (December 1995): 1900–7.

Poor, G. et al. **Age-Related Hip Fractures in Men: Clinical Spectrum and Short-Term Outcomes.** *Osteoporos Int* 5, no. 6 (1995): 419–26.

Reid, I. R. et al. **Testosterone Therapy in Glucocorticoid-Treated Men.** *Arch Intern Med* 156, no. 11 (June 1996): 1173–7.

Rudman, D., A. G. Feller, S. Hoskote, et al. **Effects of Human Growth Hormone in Men Over 60 Years Old.** *N Engl J Med.* 323 (1990): 1–6.

Scane, A. C., A. M. Sutcliffe, R. M. Francis RM. **Osteoporosis in Men.** *Clin Rheumatol.* 7 (1992): 589–601.

Seaman, E., and L. J. Melton III, **Risk Factors for Spinal Osteoporosis in Men.** *American Journal of Medicine* 75 (1983): 977–983.

Seeman, E. **Osteoporosis in men: Epidemiology, Pathophysiology , and Treatment Possibilities.** *Am J Med.* 95(1993): 22S –28S

Seeman, E. **Osteoporosis in Men.** *Baillieres Clin Rheumatol* 11, no. 3 (August 1997): 613–29.

Seeman, E. **The Dilemma of Osteoporosis in Men.** *Am J Med* 98, no. 2A (February 1995): 76S–88S.

Slemenda, C. W. et al. **Long-Term Bone Loss in Men: Effects of Genetic and Environmental Factors.** *Ann Intern Med.* 117. no. 4. (August 1992): 286–91.

Snyder, P. J., H, Peachey, P. Hannoush, et al. **Effect of Testosterone Treatment on Bone Mineral Density in Men Over 65 years of Age**. *J Clin Endocrinol Metab.* 84 (1999): 1966–1972.

Tenover, J. S. **Effects of Testosterone Supplementation in the Aging Male**. *J Clin Endocrinol Metab.* 75 (1992): 1092–1098.

Tobin, J. D., K. M. Fox, M. L. Cejku. **Bone Density Changes in Normal Men: A 4–19 year Longitudinal Study** . *J Bone Miner Res.* 8 (1993): 102.

Vogel, J. M., J. W. Davis, A. Nomura, et al. **The Effects of Smoking on Bone Mass and the Rates of Bone Loss Among Elderly Japanese-American Men**. *J Bone Miner Res.* 12 (1997): 1495–1501.

Wang, C., D. R. Eyre, D. Clark, et al. **Sublingual Testosterone Replacement Improves Muscle Mass and Strength, Decreases Bone Resorption and Increases Bone Formation Markers in Hypogonadal Men: A Clinical Research Center Study.** *J Clin Endocrinal Metab.* 81 (1996): 3654–3662.

Wishart, J. M., A. G. Need, M. Horowitz, et al. **Effect of Age on Bone Density and Bone Turnover in Men.** *Clin Endocrinol* 42 (1995): 141–146.

Part 2   Diagnosing Osteoporosis

Chapter 3   How To Find Out If You Have Osteoporosis?

Bauer, D. C., W. S. Browner, J. A. Cauley, et al. **Factors Associated With Appendicular Bone Mass In Older Women.** *Ann Intern Med.* 118 (1993): 657–665.

Bauer, D. C. et al. **Quantitative Ultrasound and Vertebral Fracture in Postmenopausal Women. Fracture Intervention Trial Research Group**. *J Bone Miner Res* 10, no. 3 (March 1995): 353–8.

Black, D. M. et al. **Axial and Appendicular Bone Density Predict Fractures in Older Women.** *Journal of Bone and Mineral Research* 7, no. 6 (June 1992): 633–8.

Cummings, S. R., M. C. Nevitt, W. S. Browner, et al. **Risk Factors For Hip Fracture In White Women.** *N Engl J Med.* 332 (1995): 767–773.

Cummings, S. R. et al. **Bone Density at Various Sites for Prediction of Hip Fractures: The Study of Osteoporotic Fractures Research Group.** *Lancet* 341, no. 8850 (April 1993): 962–3.

Cummings, S. R., et al. **Appendicular Bone Density and Age Predict Hip Fracture in Women.** *JAMA* (1990) 263 (1990): 665–707.

Faulkner, K. G., L. A. Roberts, M. R. McClung. **Discrepancies in Normative Data Between Lunar and Hologic DXA Systems**. *Osteoporosis Int.* 6 (1996): 432–436.

Gardsell, P., O. Johnell, B. E. Nilsson, **Predicting Fractures in Women By Using Forearm Bone Densitometry.** *Calcif Tissue Int.* 44 (1989): 235–242

Gardsell, P. et al. **Predicting Various Fragility Fractures in Women by Forearm Bone Densitometry: a Follow-Up Study.** *Calcified Tissue International* 52, no. 5 (May 1993): 348–53.

Gluer, C. C. et al. **Prediction of Hip Fractures From Pelvic Radiographs: the Study of Osteoporotic Fractures. The Study of Osteoporotic Fractures Research Group**. *Journal of Bone and Mineral Research* 9, no. 5 (May 1994): 671–7.

Grampp, S. et al. **Assessment of the Skeletal Status by Peripheral Quantitative Computed Tomography of the Forearm: Short-Term Precision In Vivo and Comparison to Dual X-Ray Absorptiometry.** *J Bone Miner Res* 10, no. 10 (October 1995): 1566–76.

Guglielmi, G. et al. **Osteoporosis: Diagnosis With Lateral and Posteroanterior Dual X-Ray Absorptiometry Compared With Quantitative CT**. *Radiology* 192, no. 3 (September 1994): 845–50.

Hodgson, S. F., C. C. Johnston Jr., for the Osteoporosis Task Force. **AACE Clinical Practice Guidelines For the Prevention and Treatment of Postmenopausal Osteoporosis.** *Endocr Pract.* 2 (1996): 155–171.

Hui, S. L., C. W. Slemenda, and C. C. Johnston. **Baseline Measurement of Bone Mass Predicts Fracture in White Women.** *Ann Intern Med.* 111(1989): 355–361.

Hui, S. L., C. W. Slemenda and C. C. Johnston. **Age and Bone Mass as Predictors of Fracture in a Prospective Study**. *Journal of Clinical Investigation,* 81 (1988): 1804–1809.

Johnston, C. C. and L. J. Melton. **Bone Densitometry.** *Osteoporosis: Etiology, Diagnosis and Management.* Second ed., eds. B. L. Riggs and L. J. Melton, 275–97. Philadelphia: Lippincott-Raven Press, 1995.

Johnston, C. C., C. W. Slemenda and L. J. Melton. **Clinical Use of Bone Densitometry**. *New England Journal of Medicine,* 324 (1991): 1105–1109.

Kanis, J., L. J. Melton, C. Christiansen, C., et al. **The Diagnosis of Osteoporosis**. *Journal of Bone and Mineral Research* 9 (1994): 1137–1141.

Levis, S. and R. Altman. **Bone Densitometry. Clinical Considerations.** *Arthritis Rheum.* 41 (1998): 577–587.

Looker, A. C., E. S. Orwoll, C. C. Johnston, et al. **Prevalence of Low Femoral Bone Bensity in Older US Adults From NHANES III.** *J Bone Min Res.* 12 (1997): 1761–1771.

MeltonIII, L. J. et al. **Long-Term Fracture Prediction by Bone Mineral Assessed at Different Skeletal Sites.** *J Bone Miner Res* 8 (1993): 1227–1233.

Miller PD, Bonnick SL, Rosen CJ, et al. **Clinical Utility of Bone Mass Measurements in Adults; Consensus of an International Panel.** *Sem Arthritis Rheum.* 25 (1996): 361–372.

National Osteoporosis Foundation. **Physician's Guide to Prevention and Treatment of Osteoporosis.** Washington, DC*: National Osteoporosis Foundation*; 1998.

Nevitt, M. C. et al. **Bone Mineral Density Predicts Non-Spine Fractures in Very Elderly Women. Study of Osteoporotic Fractures Research Group.** *Osteoporos Int* 4, no. 6 (November 1994): 325–31.

Nguyen, T. V. et al. **Prediction of Osteoporotic Fractures by Postural Instability and Bone Density**. *British Medical Journal* 307, no. 6912 (October 1993): 1111–5.

Nuti, R. and G. Martini. **Measurements of Bone Mineral Density by DXA Total Body Absorptiometry in Different Skeletal Sites in Postmenopausal Osteoporosis.** *Bone* 13, no. 2 (1992): 173–8.

Osteoporosis Society of Canada Scientific Advisory Board. **Clinical Practice Guidelines For the Diagnosis and Management of Osteoporosis.** *Can Med Assoc J.* 155 (1996): 1113–1133.

Overgaard, K. et al. **Discriminatory Ability of Bone Mass Measurements (SPA and DEXA) for Fractures in Elderly Postmenopausal Women.** *Calcified Tissue International* 50, no. 1 (January 1992): 30–5.

Peck, W.A. **Consensus Development Conference: Diagnosis, Prophylaxis, and Treatment of Osteoporosis.** *American Journal of Medicine.* 94 (1993): 646–650.

Pouilles, J. M. et.al. **Spine and Femur Densitometry at the Menopause: Are Both Sites Necessary in the Assessment of the Risk of Osteoporosis?** *Calcif Tissue Int* 52 (1993): 344–347.

Pouilles, J.M. et al. **Risk Factors of Vertebral Osteoporosis. Results of a Study of 2279 Women Referred to a Menopause Clinic.** *Rev. Rhum. Mal. Osteoarticularie* 58 (1998): 169–177.

Rico, H. et al. **Comparison Between Metacarpal Bone Measurements by Computerized Radiogrammetry and Total Body DEXA in Normal and Osteoporotic Women.** *Clin Rheumatol* 13, no. 4 (December 1994): 593–7.

Ross, P. D., J. W. Davis, R. S. Epstein, and R. D. Wasnich RD. **Pre-existing Fractures and Bone Mass Predict Vertebral Fracture Incidence In Women.** *Ann Int Med.* 114 (1991): 919–923.

Ross, P. et al. **Predicting Vertebral Deformity Using Bone Densitometry at Various Skeletal Sites and Calcaneus Ultrasound.** *Bone* 16, no. 3 (March 1995): 325–32.

Ross, P.D. et al. **Definition of a Spine Fracture Threshold Based Upon Prospective Fracture Risk.** *Bone*, 1987: 271–278.

Rubin, S. M. and S. R. Cummings. **Results of Bone Densitometry Affect Women's Decisions About Taking Measures to Prevent Fractures.** *Annals of Internal Medicine,* 116 (1992): 990–995.

Ryan, P. J. et al. **The Effect of Vertebral Collapse on Spinal Bone Mineral Density Measurements in Osteoporosis.** *Bone Miner* 18, no. 3 (September 1992): 267–72.

Schott, A. M. et al. **Ultrasound Discriminates Patients With Hip Fracture Equally Well As Dual Energy X-Ray Absorptiometry and Independently of Bone Mineral Density.** *J Bone Miner Res* 10, no. 2 (February 1995): 243–9.

Silman, A. J. **The Patient With Fracture: The Risk of Subsequent Fractures.** *Am J Med.* 98 (suppl 2A)1995: 12S–16S.

Sowers, M. F. **Clinical Epidemiology and Osteoporosis. Measures and Their Interpretation.** *Endocrinol Metab Clin N Amer.* 26 (1997): 219–231.

Wasnich, R.D., et al. **A Comparison of Single and Multi-site BMC Measurements for Assessment of Spine Fracture Probability.** *Journal of Nuclear Medicine,* 30 (1989): 1166–1171.

Wasnich, R. D., et.al. **Prediction of Postmenopausal Fracture Risk with Use of Bone Mineral Measurements**. *American Journal of Obstetrics and Gynecology,* 153 (1985: 745–751.

World Health Organization (WHO) Study Group**. Assessment of Fracture Risk and Its Application To Screening For Postmenopausal Osteoporosis**. *WHO Technical Report Series* 843. Geneva: WHO, 1994.

Bone Mineral Density Testing Guidelines

Aarlot, M. E., et al. **Apparent Pre- and Postmenopausal Bone Loss Evaluated by DXA at Different Skeletal Sites in Women**: **The OFELY Cohort**. *J Bolne MinerRes* 12 (1997): 683–690.

American College of Radiology. **ACR Standard for Performance of Adult Dual or Single X-Ray Absorptiometry.** (DXA/pDXA/SXA) 1998.

Avioli, L. V. **Clinician's Manual on Osteoporosis**, 2nd ed. London, UK: *Science Press;* 1997.

Baran, D. T. **Quantitative Ultrasound: A Technique To Target Women With Low Bone Mass For Preventative Therapy.** *Am J Med* 98 (1995): 488–51S.

Bauer, D. C., C. C. Gluer, J.A. Cauley, et al. **Broadband Ultrasound Attenuation Predicts Fractures Strongly and Independently of Densitometry in Older Women. A Prospective Study of Osteoporotic Fractures Group**. *Arch Int Med.* 157 (1997): 629–634.

Black, D. M., D. C. Bauer, Y. Lu. **Should BMD Be Measured At Multiple Sites to Predict Fracture Risk inElderly Women**? *J Bone Min Res.* 10 (1995): S140.

Blake GM, Fogelman I**. Applications of Bone Densitometry For Osteoporosis**. *Endocrinol Metab Clin N Amer.* 27 (1998): 267–285.

Bonnick, S. L. **Clinical Indications for Bone Densitometry.** In Bonnick, S.L.: Bone Densitometry in Clinical Practice. Humana Press, 1998, pp. 197–212.

Bracker, M. D. and N. B. Watts. **How To Get the Most Out of Bone Densitometry. Results Can Help Assess Fracture Risk and Guide Therapy.** *Postgraduate medicine.* 104 (1998): 77–86.

Cummings, S. R. and D. Black. **Bone Mass Measurements and Risk of Fracture in Caucasian Women: A Review of Findings From Prospective Studies**. *Am J Med.* 98 (1995): 24S–28S.

Cummings, S.R., D. M. Black, and M. C. Nevitt. **Bone Density At Various Sites and Prediction of Hip Fracture In Women**. *Lancet* 341 (1993): 72–75.

Davis, J., P. Ross, R. Wasnich. **Evidence for Both Generalized and Regional Low Bone Mass Among Elderly Women.** *J Bone Min Res.* 9 (1994): 305–309.

Faulkner, K. G., et al. **Discrepancies in Normative Data Between Lunar and Hologic DXA Systems.** *Osteoporosis Int* 6 (1996): 432–436.

Faulkner, K.G., M. R. McClung, D. J. Ravn, et al. **Monitoring Skeletal Response To Therapy In Early Postmenopausal Women: Which Bone to Measure.** *J Bone Min Res.* 11 (1996): S96.

Genant, H. K., et.al. **Noninvasive Assessment of Bone Mineral and Structure: State of the Art.** *J Bone Miner Res* 11 (1996): 707–730.

Genant, H. K., et al. **Universal Standardization for Dual X-Ray Absorptiometry: Patient and Phantom Cross-Calibration Results**. *J Bone Miner Res* 9 (1991): 1503–1514.

Gluer, C. C., Cummings Sr, D. C. Bauer, et al. **Osteoporosis: Association of Recent Fractures With Quantitative U.S. Findings**. *Radiology* 199 (1996): 725–732.

Gluer, C. C. **Quantitative Ultrasound Techniques For the Assessment of Osteoporosis: Expect Agreement on Current Status. The International Quantitative Ultrasound Consensus Group**. *J Bone Min Res.* 12 (1997): 1280–1288.

Grampp, S., et al. **Comparisons of Noninvasive Bone Mineral Measurements in Assessing Age-Related Loss, Fracture Discrimination and Diagnostic Classification**. *J Bone MinerRes* 12 (1997): 697–710.

Greenspan, S. L., et al. **Classification of Osteoporosis in the Elderly is Dependent on Site-Specific Analysis**. *Calcif Tissue Int* 58 (1996): 409–414.

Huang, C., P. D. Ross, A. J. Yates, et al. **Prediction of Fracture Risk by Radiographic Absorptiometry and Quantitative Ultrasound: A Prospective Sudy.** *Calcif Tissue Int.* 63 (1998): 380–384.

Johnston, Jr., C. C. et al. **Clinical Use of Bone Densitometry**. *NEJM* 324 (1991): 1105–1109.

Kanis, J.A. et.al. **Perspective: The Diagnosis of Osteoporosis**. *J Bone Mineral Res* 9 (1994: 1137–1141.

Kanis, J. A., J. Devogelaer, and C. Gennari. **Practical Guide for the Use of Bone Mineral Measurements in the Assessment of Treatment of Osteoporosis: A Position Paper of the European Foundation for Osteoporosis and Bone Disease.** *Osteoporosis Int.* 6 (1996): 256–261.

Kanis, J. **Assessment of Bone Mass and Osteoporosis**. In Kanis, J. (ed.): Osteoporosis. Oxford: Blackwell Science, 1994, pp. 114–147.

Kleerekoper, M., et al. **Comparison of Radiographic Absorptiometry with Dual Energy X-Ray Absorptiometry and Quantitative Computed Tomography in Normal Older White and Black Women**. *J Bone Mine Res* 9 (1994): 1745–1749.

Lane, N. E., M. Jergus, and H. K. Genant. **Osteoporosis and Bone Mineral Density Assessment**. In Koopman, W. (ed.): Arthritis and Allied Diseases: *A Textbook of Rheumatology,* 13th ed. Baltimore: Williams & Wilkins, 1996, pp 153–171.

Levis, S. and R. Altman. **Bone Densitometry. Clinical Considerations**. *Arthritis Rheum.* 41 (1998): 577–587.

Lufkin, E. G. and M. Zilkowski. **Diagnosis and Management of Osteoporosis.** *American Family Physician Monograph* No. 1, 1996.

Michaeli, D. A., A. Mirshahi, J. Singer, et al. **A New X-Ray Based on Osteoporosis Screening Tool Provides Accurate and Precise Assessment of Phalanx Bone Mineral Content.** *J Clin Densitometry 2 (*1999): 23–30.

Miller, P. D., et al. **Guidelines for the Clinical Utilization of Bone Mass Measurement in the Adult Population**. *Calcif Tissue Int* 57 (1995): 251–252.

Miller, P. D., S. L. Bonnick, C. C. Johnston, et al. **The Challenges of Peripheral Bone Density Testing. Which Patients Need Additional Central Density Skeletal Measurements**? *J Clin Densitometry* 1 (1998): 211–217.

Miller, P. D., et al. **Prediction of Fracture Risk I: Bone Density.** *Am J Med* 312 (1996): 257–259.

Miller, P. D. **Diagnostic Prediction of Increased Risk of Hip Fracture: A Clinician's Perspective.** *Prediction of Hip Fracture* Johannes Ringe (ed), 1996, 52–61.

Miller, P. D. **The Interpretation of Bone Mineral Density: Clues to Misdiagnosis.** *Osteoporosis Index* 2 Rev. (1996): 8–9.

Nevitt, M. C., B. Ettinger, D. M. Black, et al. **The Association of Radiographically Detected Vertebral Fractures Wth Back Pain and Function: A Prospective Study.** *Ann Intern Med.* 128 (1998): 793–800.

Osteoporosis Society of Canada Scientific Advisory Board. **Clinical Practice Guidelines for the Diagnosis and Management of Osteoporosis.** *Can Med Assoc J* 155 (1996): 1113–1133.

Parfitt, M. A. **Interpretation of Bone Density Measurements: Disadvantages of a Percentage Scale and a Discussion of Some Alternatives.** *J Bone Min Res* 5 (1990): 537–540.

Rizzoli, R., D. Slosman and J. Bonjour. **The Role of Dual Energy X-Ray Absorptiometry of Lumbar Spine and Proximal Femur in the Diagnosis and Follow-Up of Osteoporosis.** *Am J Med.* 98 (1995): 33S–36S.

United States Preventive Services Task Force. **Guide to Clinical Preventive Services,** 2nd ed. Washington, DC: *US Dept of Health and Human Services.*

Van Daele, P. L. A, H. Burger, C. E. D. H. De Laep and H. A. P. Pols. **Ultrasound Measurement of the Bone.** *Clin Endocrinol.* 44 (1996): 363–369.

WHO Study Group. **Assessment of Fracture Risk and Its Application To Screening For Postmenopausal Osteoporosis: Report of a WHO Study Group.** *WHO Technical Report Series* 843, Geneva, Switzerland: World Health Organization, 1994.

Yates, A. J. et al. **Radiographic Absorptiometry in the Diagnosis of Osteoporosis.** *Am J Med* 98 (1995)(S1): 41S–47S.

Medicare and Insurance Coverage

Medicare Coverage of and Payment for Bone Mass Measurements. Federal Register Vol.63, no. 131 (June 24, *1998) Rules and Regulations.*

Other Medical Testing for Osteoporosis

Bauer, D. C., D. M. Black, S M. Ott, et al. **Biochemical Markers Predict Spine But Not Hip BMD Response to Bisphosphonates: The Fracture Intervention Trial (FTT).** *J Bone Min Res.* 12 (1997): S150.

Boen, H., R. W. Downs, J. R. Tucci JR, et al. **Dose-Response Relationships for Bisphosphonates Treatment in Osteoporotic Elderly Women.** *J Clin Endocrinol Metab* 82 (1997): 265–274.

Delmas, P. D. **Biochemical Markers of Bone Turnover for the Clinical Assessment of Metabolic Bone Disease.** *Endo Metabolism Clinics of North American* 19 (1990): 1–18.

Garnero, P., E. Hausher, M. C. Chapuy, et al. **Bone Resorption Markers Predict Hip Fracture Risk in Elderly Women. The EPIDOS Prospective Study**. *J Bone Miner Res*. 11 (1996): 1531–1538.

Garnero, P., E. Sornay-Rendu, M. C. Chapuy, and P. D. Delmas. **Increased Bone Turnover in Late Postmenopausal Women is a Major Determinant of Osteoporosis**. *J Bnoe Min Res*11 (1996): 337–339.

Garnero, P. et al. **Comparison of New Biochemical Markers of Bone Turnover in Late Postmenopausal Osteoporotic Women in Response to Alendronate Treatment.** *J Clin Endocrinol Metab* 79, no. 6 (December 1994): 1693–700.

Garnero, P., and Delmas, P.D. **New Developments in Biochemical Markers of Osteoporosis.** *Calcified Tissue International* 59 (1996): S2–S9.

Gertz, B.J. **Monitoring Bone Resorption in Early Postmenopausal Women by an Immunoassay for Cross-Linked Collagen Peptides in Urine**. *Journal of Bone and Mineral Research* 9 (1994): 135–142.

Kleerekoper, M., and G. W. Edelson. **Biochemical Sudies in the Evaluation and Management of Osteoporosis: Current Status and Future Prospects**. *Endocrinology Practice* 2 (1996): 13–19.

Marcus, R., L. Holloway, and B. Wells. **Turnover Markers Only Weakly Predict Bone Response to Estrogen: The Postmenopausal Estrogen/Progestin Interventions Trial (PEPI)**. *J Bone Min Res* 12 (1997): S103.

Melton III, L. J., D. Khosla, E. J. Atkinson, et.al. **Relationship of Bone Turnover to Bone Density and Fractures**. *J Bone Min Res* 12 (1997): 1083–1091.

Pedrazzoni, M. et al. **Acute Effects of Bisphosphonates on New and Traditional Markers of Bone Resorption**. *Calcif Tissue Int* 57, no. 1 (July 1995).

Pedrazzoni, M.,et al. **Clinical Observations With a New Specific Assay for Bone Alkaline Phosphatase: A Cross-Sectional Study in Osteoporotic and Pagetic Subjects and a Longitudinal Evaluation of the Response to Ovariectomy, Estrogens, and Bisphosphonates.** *Calcif Tissue Int* 59, no. 5 (November 1996): 334–8.

Part 3   The Prevention and Treatment of Osteoporosis

Universal Recommendations

Chapter 4   **Eliminating The Risks**

Tobacco and Osteoporosis

Cummings, S. R., et al. **Risk Factors for Hip Fracture in White Women. Study of Osteoporotic Fractures Research Group**. *N Engl J Med* 332, no. 12 (March 1995): 767–73.

Everson, R. B., et al. **Effect of Passive Exposure to Smoking on Age at Natural Menopause**. *BMJ* 293 (1986): 792.

Forsen, L., et al. **Interaction Between Current Smoking, Leanness, and Physical Inactivity in the Prediction of Hip Fracture**. *J Bone Miner Res 9*, no. 11 (November 1994): 1671–8.

Hansen, M. A., et al. **Potential Risk Factors for Development of Postmeno-pausal Osteoporosis—Examined Over a 12–Year Period.** *Osteoporosis International 1*, no. 2 (February 1991): 95–102.

Hollenbach, K. A., E. Barrett-Connor, S. L. Edelstein, and T. Holbrook. **Cigarette Smoking and Bone Mineral Density in Older Men and Women.** *Am J Public Health* 83 (1993): 1265–70.

Hopper. J. L. and E. Seeman. **The Bone Density of Female Twins Discordant for Tobacco Use.** *New England Journal of Medicine* 330, no. 6 (February 1994): 387–92.

Jensen, J., C. Christiansen, and P. Rodbro. **Cigarette Smoking, Serum Estrogens, and Bone Loss During Hormone-Replacement Therapy Early After Menopause.** *New England Journal of Medicine 313*, no. 16 (October 1985): 973–5.

Johnston, J. D. **Smokers Have Less Dense Bones and Fewer Teeth.** *J R Soc Health* 114 (1994): 265–9.

Kiel, D. P., et al. **The Effect of Smoking at Different Life Stages on Bone Mineral Density in Elderly Men and Women.** *Osteoporos Int* 6, no. 3 (1996): 240–8.

Kiel, D. P., et al. **Smoking Eliminates the Protective Effect of Oral Estrogens on the Risk for Hip Fracture Among Women.** *Annals of Internal Medicine* 116 (1992): 716–721.

Krall, E. A. and B. Dawson-Hughes. **Smoking and Bone Loss Among Post-menopausal Women.** *Journal of Bone and Mineral Research* 6, no. 4 (April 1991): 331–8..

MacMahon, B., et al. **Cigarette Smoking and Urinary Estrogens.** *New England Journal of Medicine* 307 (1982): 1062–1065.

McKinlay, S. M., N. L. Bifano, and J. B. McKinlay. **Smoking and Age at Meno-pause in Women.** *Annals of Internal Medicine* 102 (1985): 350–356.

Michnovicz, J. J., et al. **Increased 2–Hydroxylation of Estradiol as a Possible Mechanism for the Anti-Estrogenic Effect of Cigarette Smoking.** *New England Journal of Medicine,* (1986): 1305–1309.

Valimaki, M. J. ,et al. **Exercise, Smoking, and Calcium Intake During Adolescence and Early Adulthood As Determinants of Peak Bone Mass. Cardiovascular Risk in Young Finns Study Group.** *British Medical Journal* 309, no. 6949 (July 1994): 230–5.

Alcohol and Osteoporosis

Bikle, D. D., et al. **Alcohol-Induced Bone Disease: Relationship to Age and Parathyroid Hormone Levels.** *Alcohol Clin Exp Res* 17, no. 3 (June 1993): 690–5.

Bikle, D. D., et al. **Bone Disease in Alcohol Abuse.** *Annals of Internal Medicine* 103 (1985): 42–48.

Chon, K. S., et al. **Alcoholism-Associated Spinal and Femoral Bone Loss in Abstinent Male Alcoholics, As Measured by Dual X-Ray Absorptiometry.** *Skeletal Radiology* 21, no. 7 (1992): 431–6.

Crilly, R. G., et al. **Bone Histomorphometry, Bone Mass, and Related Parameters in Alcoholic Males.** *Calcif Tissue Int* 43, no. 5 (November 1988): 269–76.

Diamond, T., et al. **Ethanol Reduces Bone Formation and May Cause Osteoporosis.** *American Journal of Medicine* 86, no. 3 (March 1989): 282–8.

Diez, A., et al. **Alcohol-Induced Bone Disease in the Absence of Severe Chronic Liver Damage.** *J Bone Miner Res* 9, no. 6 (June 1994): 825–31.

Felson, D. T. et al **Alcohol Consumption and Hip Fractures: The Framingham Study.** *American Journal of Epidemiology* 128, no. 5 (November 1988): 1102–10.

Felson, D. T., et al. **Alcohol Intake and Bone Mineral Density in Elderly Men and Women. The Framingham Study.** *Am J Epidemiol* **142, no. 5 (September 1995): 485–92.**

Gonzalez-Calvin, J. L. et al. **Mineral Metabolism, Osteoblastic Function and Bone Mass in Chronic Alcoholism**. *Alcohol and Alcoholism* 28, no. 5 (September 1993): 571–9.

Hemenway, D. et al. **Fractures and Lifestyle: Effect of Cigarette Smoking, Alcohol Intake, and Relative Weight on the Risk of Hip and Forearm Fractures in Middle-Aged Women**. *American Journal of Public Health* 78, no. 12 (December 1988): 1554–8.

Holbrook, T. L. and E. Barrett-Connor. **A Prospective Study of Alcohol Consumption and Bone Mineral Density.** *BMJ* 306, no. 6891 (June 1993): 1506–9.

Klein, R. F. **Alcohol-Induced Bone Disease: Impact of Ethanol on Osteoblast Proliferation.** *Alcohol Clin Exp Res* 21, no. 3 (May 1997): 392–9.

Laitinen, K., et al. **Bone Mineral Density and Abstention-Induced Changes in Bone and Mineral Metabolism in Noncirrhotic Male Alcoholics**. *American Journal of Medicine* 93, no. 6 (December 1992): 642–50**.**

Laitinen, K., et al. **Effects of Three Weeks' Moderate Alcohol Intake on Bone and Mineral Metabolism in Normal Men.** *Bone Miner* 13, no. 2 (May 1991): 139–51.

Laitinen, K., et al. **Is Alcohol an Osteoporosis-Inducing Agent for Young and Middle-Aged Women**? *Metabolism* 42, no. 7 (July 1993): 875–81.

May, H., S. Murphy, and K. T. Khaw. **Alcohol Consumption and Bone Mineral Density in Older Men.** Gerontology 41, no. 3 (1995): 152–8.

Naves Diaz, M., T. W. O'Neill, and A. J. Silman. **The Influence of Alcohol Consumption on the Risk of Vertebral Deformity. European Vertebral Osteoporosis Study Group.** *Osteoporos Int* 7, no. 1 (1997): 65–71.

Odvina, C. V., et al. **Effect of Heavy Alcohol Intake in the Absence of Liver Disease on Bone Mass in Black and White Men.** *J Clin Endocrinol Metab* 80, no. 8 (August 1995): 2499–503.

Peris, P . et al. **Reduced Spinal and Femoral Bone Mass and Deranged Bone Mineral Metabolism in Chronic Alcoholics.** *Alcohol and Alcoholism* 27, no. 6 (November 1992): 619–25.

Peris, P. et al. **Bone Mass Improves in Alcoholics After Two Years of Abstinence.** *J Bone Miner Res* 9, no. 10 (October 1994): 1607–12.

Peris, P., et al. **Vertebral Fractures and Osteopenia in Chronic Alcoholic Patients.** *Calcif Tissue* Int 57, no. 2 (August 1995): 111–4

Tuppurainen, M., et al. **Risks of Perimenopausal Fractures—a Prospective Population-Based Study.** *Acta Obstet Gynecol Scand* 74, no. 8 (September 1995): 624–8.

Caffeine ond Osteoporosis

Barger-Lux, M. J. and R. P. Heaney. **Caffeine and the Calcium Economy Revisited.** *Osteoporos Int* 5, no. 2 (March 1995): 97–102.

Barger-Lux, M. J., R. P. Heaney, and M. R. Stegman. **Effects of Moderate Caffeine Intake on the Calcium Economy of Premenopausal Women.** *American Journal of Clinical Nutrition,* (1990) vol. 52, p.722–725.

Gringe, M. J., C. A. C. Cloupland, S. J. Cliffe, et al. **Cigarette Smoking, Alcohol and Caffeine Consumption, and Bone Mineral Density in Postmenopausal Women.** *Osteoporosis Int.* 8 (1998): 355–363.

Heaney, R. P. and R. R. Recker. **Effects on Nitrogen, Phosphorus, and Caffeine on Calcium Balance in Women.** *Journal of Laboratory and Clinical Medicine.*

Lloyd, T., et al. **Dietary Caffeine Intake and Bone Status of Postmenopausal Women.** *Am J Clin Nutr* 65, no. 6 (June 1997): 1826–30.

Massey, L. K. and K. J. Wise. **The Effect of Dietary Caffeine on Urinary Excretion of Calcium, Magnesium, Phosphorus, Sodium and Potassium in Healthy Young Females.** *Nutrition Research* 4 (1984): 43–50.

Massey, L. K. and T. A.Berg. **The Effect of Dietary Caffeine on Urinary Excretion Calcium, Magnesium, Phosphorus, Sodium, Potassium, Chloride and Zinc in Healthy Males.** *Nutrition Research* 5 (1985): 1281–1284.

Massey, L. K., D. J. Sherrard, and E. A. Bergman. **Dietary Caffeine Lowers Ultrafiltrable Calcium Levels in Women Consuming Low Dietary Calcium.** *Journal of Bone Mineral Research* 4 (1989): S1–249.

Scientific Status **Summary of the Institute of Food Technologists' Expert Panel on Food Safety and Nutrition: Caffeine.** *Institute of Food Technologies,* Chicago, Illinois.

Falls and Fall Prevention

Cummings, S. R. and M. C. Nevitt. **Non-Skeletal Determinants of Fractures: The Potential Importance of the Mechanics of Falls.** *Osteoporos Int Suppl,* no. 1 (1994): S67–70.

Cummings, S. R., and Nevitt, M.C. **Epidemiology of Hip Fractures and Falls.** In Kleerekoper, M., and S. M. Krane, (eds.) *Clinical Disorders of Bone and Mineral Metabolism.* New York: Mary Ann Liebert, Inc., 1989, pp. 231–236.

Dargent-Molina, P., et al. **Fall-Related Factors and Risk of Hip Fracture: The EPIDOS Prospective Study. Epidemiologie De L'Osteoporose.** *Lancet* 348, no. 9021 (July 1996): 145–9.

Ensrud, K. E., et al. **Postural Hypotension and Postural Dizziness in Elderly Women.** *Archives of Internal Medicine,* 152 (1992): 1057–1064.

Felson, D. T. **Prevention of Hip Fractures.** *Hospital Practice,* (1988) p. 23–38.

Graafmans, W. C., et al. **Falls in the Elderly: A Prospective Study of Risk Factors and Risk Profiles.** *Am J Epidemiol* 143, no. 11 (June 1996): 1129–36.

Greenspan, S. L., et al. **Fall Severity and Bone Mineral Density As Risk Factors for Hip Fracture in Ambulatory Elderly.** *JAMA* 271, no. 2 (January 1994): 128–33.

Hayes, W. C., et al. **Etiology and Prevention of Age-Related Hip Fractures.** *Bone* 18, no. 1 Suppl (January 1996): 77S–86S.

Hindmarsh, J. J. and E. H. Estes. **Falls in Older Persons.** *Archives of Internal Medicine* 149 (1989): 2217–2222.

Lauritzen, J. B. **Hip Fractures: Incidence, Risk Factors, Energy Absorption, and Prevention.** *Bone* 18, no. 1 Suppl (January 1996): 65S–75S.

Luukinen, H., et al. **Risk Factors for Recurrent Falls in the Elderly in Long-Term Institutional Care.** *Public Health* 109, no. 1 (January 1995): 57–65.

Luukinen, H. et al. **Social Status, Life Changes, Housing Conditions, Health, Functional Abilities and Life-Style As Risk Factors for Recurrent Falls Among the Home-Dwelling Elderly.** *Public Health* 110, no. 2 (March 1996): 115–8.

Maki, B. E., P. J. Holliday, and A. K. Topper. **A Prospective Study of Postural Balance and Risk of Falling in an Ambulatory and Independent Elderly Population.** J Gerontol 49, no. 2 (March 1994): 72–84.

Melton III, L.J., and B. L. Riggs. **Risk Factors for Injury After a Fall.** *Clinics in Geriatric Medicine* 1 (1985): 525–539.

Myers, A. H., et al. **Risk Factors Associated With Falls and Injuries Among Elderly Institutionalized Persons.** *Am J Epidemiol* 133, no. 11 (June 1991): 1179–90.

Nevitt, M.C., and S. R. Cummings. **Type of Fall and Risk of Hip and Wrist Fractures: The Study of Osteoporotic Fractures.** *Journal of the American Geriatric Society* 41: 1226–1234.

Nevitt, M.C., and S. R. Cummings, S.R. **Falls and Fractures in Older Women.** In Vellas, B., M. Troupet, L. Rubenstein, et al. (eds.) *Falls, Balance and Gait; Disorders in the Elderly.* Paris: Elsevier, 1992, pp. 69–80.

Peck, W.A. **Falls and Hip Fracture in the Elderly.** *Hospital Practice* (1986): 72A–72K.

Pinilla, T. P., et al. **Impact Direction From a Fall Influences the Failure Load of the Proximal Femur As Much As Age-Related Bone Loss.** *Calcif Tissue Int* 58, no. 4 (April 1996): 231–5.

Ray, W. A., et al. **Psychotropic Drug Use and the Risk of Hip Fracture.** *New England Journal of Medicine* 316 (1987): 363–369.

Rubenstein, L. Z., K. R. Josephson, and D. Osterweil. **Falls and Fall Prevention in the Nursing Home.** *Clin Geriatr Med* 12, no. 4 (November 1996): 881–902.

Rubenstine, L. Z., et al. The Value of Assessing Falls in Elderly Population. *Annals of Internal Medicine* 113 (1990): 308–316.

Speechley, M. and M. E. Tinetti. **Falls and Injuries in Vigorous Community Elderly Persons.** *J Am Geriatr Soc* 39, no. 1 (January 1991): 46–52.

Tinetti, M. E., M. Speechley, and S. F. Ginter. **Risk Factors for Falls Among Elderly Persons Living in the Community.** *N Engl J Med* 319, no. 26 (December 1988): 1701–7.

Tinetti, M. E., W. Lin, and E. B. Claus. **Predictors and Prognosis of Inability to Get Up After Falls Among Elderly Persons.** *JAMA* 269 (1993): 65–70.

Tinetti, M. E. and M. Speechley. **Prevention of Falls Among the Elderly.** *New England Journal of Medicine* 320 (1989): 1055–1059.

Chapter 5   Vitamins and Minerals

Calcium

Allender, P. S. et al. **Dietary Calcium and Blood Pressure: A Meta-Analysis of Randomized Clinical Trials.** *Ann Intern Med* 124, no. 9 (May 1996): 825–31.

Aloia, J. F., A. Vaswani, J. K. Yeh, et al. **Calcium Supplementation With and Without Hormone Replacement Therapy to Prevent Postmenopausal Bone Loss.** *Annals of Internal Medicine* 120 (1994): 97–103.

Barrett-Connor, E. **The RDA for Calcium in the Elderly: Too Little, Too Late.** *Calcification Tissue International* 44 (1989): 303–307.

Bronner, F. **Calcium and Osteoporosis.** *Am J Clin Nutr* 60, no. 6 (December 1994): 831–6.

Bucher, H. C., et al. **Effects of Dietary Calcium Supplementation on Blood Pressure. A Meta-Analysis of Randomized Controlled Trials.** *JAMA* 275, no. 13 (April 1996): 1016–22.

Bullamore, J. R., J. C. Gallagher, R. Wilson, et al. **Effect of Age on Calcium Absorption.** *Lancet* 1 (1977): 535–537.

Cappuccio, F. P., et al. **Epidemiologic Association Between Dietary Calcium Intake and Blood Pressure: A Meta-Analysis of Published Data.** *Am J Epidemiol* 142, no. 9 (November 1995): 935–45.

Chan, E. L. et al. **Age-Related Changes in Bone Density, Serum Parathyroid Hormone, Calcium Absorption and Other Indices of Bone Metabolism in Chinese Women.** *Clinical Endocrinology* (Oxford) 36, no. 4 (April 1992): 375–81.

Chan, G. M. **Dietary Calcium and Bone Mineral Status of Children and Adolescence.** *American Journal of Diseases in Children* 145 (1991): P 631–634.

Chapuy, M. C., M. E. Aarlot, F. Duboeuf, et al. **Vitamin D$_3$ and Calcium Prevent Hip Fractures in Elderly Women.** *New England Journal of Medicine* 327 (1992): 1637–1642.

Chapuy, M. C., P. Chapuy, and P. J. Meunier. **Calcium and Vitamin D Supplements: Effects on Calcium Metabolism in Elderly People.** *American Journal of Clinical Nutrition* 46 (1987): 324–328.

Dawson-Hughes, B. et al. **Calcium Retention and Hormone Levels in Black and White Women on High- and Low-Calcium Diets.** *Journal of Bone and Mineral Research* 8, no. 7 (July 1993): 779–87.

Dawson-Hughes, B. et al. **A controlled Trial of the Effect of Calcium Supplementation on Bone Density in Postmenopausal Women.** *New England Journal of Medicine*, 323 (1990): 878–883.

Dawson-Hughes, D., G. E. Dallal, E. A. Krall., et al. **A Controlled Trial of the Effect of Calcium Supplementation on Bone Density in Postmenopausal Women.** *New England Journal of Medicine* 328 (1993): 460.

Elders, P. J. M., J. C. Netelenbos, P. Lips, et al. **Calcium Supplementation Reduces Vertebral Bone Loss in Perimenopausal Women: A Controlled Trial in 248 Women Between 46 and 55 Years of Age.** *Journal of Clinical Endocrinology and Metabolism* 73 (1991): 533–540.

Hansen, M. A .et al. **Potential Risk Factors for Development of Postmenopausal Osteoporosis—Examined Over a 12-Year Period.** *Osteoporosis International* 1, no. 2 (February 1991): 95–102.

Harris, S. and B. Dawson-Hughes. **Rates of Change in Bone Mineral Density of the Spine, Heel, Femoral Neck and Radius in Healthy Postmenopausal Women.** *Bone Miner* 17, no. 1 (April 1992): 87–95.

Heaney, R. P. **Nutritional Factors in Osteoporosis.** *Annu Rev Nutr* 13 (1993): 287–316.

Heaney, R. P. **Skeletal Development and Maintenance: The Role of Calcium and Vitamin D.** *Adv Endocrinol Metab* 6 (1995): 17–38.

Heaney, R. P. **Thinking Straight About Calcium.** *New England Journal of Medicine* 328 (1993): 503.

Heaney, R. P., et al. **Calcium Nutrition and Bone Health in the Elderly.** *American Journal of Clinical Nutrition* 36 (1982): 986–1013.

Heaney, R. P., R. R. Recker, and P. D. Savill. **Calcium Balance and Calcium Requirements in Middle-Aged Women.** *American Journal of Clinical Nutrition* 30 (1977): 1603–1611.

Holbrook, T. L. and E. Barrett-Connor. **An 18–Year Prospective Study of Dietary Calcium and Bone Mineral Density in the Hip.** *Calcif Tissue Int* 56, no. 5 (May 1995): 364–7.

Holbrook, T. L., E. Barrett-Connor, and D. L. Wingard. **Dietary Calcium and Risk of Hip Fracture: 14–Year Prospective Population Study.** *Lancet* 2, no. 8619 (November 1988): 1046–9.

Horowitz, M., et al. **Effect of Calcium Supplementation on Urinary Hydroxyproline in Osteoporotic Postmenopausal Women.** *American Journal of Clinical Nutrition*, vol 39, (1984): 857–859.

Johnson Jr., C.C., J. Z. Miller, C. W. Slemenda, et al. **Calcium Supplementation and Increases in Bone Mineral Density in Children.** *New England Journal of Medicine* 327 (1992): 82–87.

Johnston, C. C., et al. **Calcium Supplementation and Increases in Bone Mineral Density in Children.** *New England Journal of Medicine* 327 (1992): 82–87.

Kanis, J. **Calcium Requirements for Optimal Skeletal Health.** *Calcified Tissue International* 49 (supplement) (1991): S33–S41.

Komar, L. et al. **Calcium Homeostasis of an Elderly Population Upon Admission to a Nursing Home.** *J Am Geriatr Soc* 41, no. 10 (October 1993): 1057–64.

Lau, E. M. C. and J. Woo. **Nutrition and Osteoporosis.** *Curr Opin Rheumatol* 10 (1998): 368–372.

Lee, C. J., G. S. Lawler, and G. H. Johnson. **Effects of Calcium Supplementation of the Diets with Calcium and Calcium-rich Foods on Bone Density of Elderly Females With Osteoporosis.** *American Journal of Clinical Nutrition* 34 (1981): 819–823.

Looker, A. C. et al. **Prevalence of Low Femoral Bone Density in Older U.S. Women From NHANES III.** *J Bone Mine Res* 10, no. 5 (May 1995): 796–802.

Looker, A. C., et al. **Calcium Intakes of Mexican Americans, Cubans, Puerto Ricans, Non-Hispanic Whites, and Non-Hispanic Blacks in the United States.** *J Am Diet Assoc* 93, no. 11 (November 1993): 1274–9.

Matkovic, V. and R. P. Heaney. **Calcium Balance During Human Growth: Evidence for Threshold Behavior.** *American Journal of Clinical Nutrition* 55, no. 5 (May 1992): 992–6.

National Institutes of Health **(NIH) Consensus Development Panel on Optimal Calcium Intake. Optimal Calcium Intake**. *Journal of the American Medical Association.* 272(1994): 1942–1948.

Nordin, B. E. C. and R. P. Heaney. **Calcium Supplementation of the Diet: Justified by the Present Evidence.** *BMJ* 300 (1990): 1056–1060.

Pak, C. Y. C. and L. V. Avioli. **Factors Affecting Absorbability of Calcium From Calcium Salts and Food.** *Calcification Tissue International* 43 (1988): 55–60.

Palmieri, G. M. **Calcium, Why and How Much**? *Miner Electrolyte Metab* 21, no. 1–3 (1995): 236–41.

Recker, R. R. **Prevention of Osteoporosis: Calcium Nutrition.** *Osteoporosis International* 3 Suppl 1 (1993): 163–5.

Recker, R. R., **Calcium Absorption and Achlorhydria.** *New England Journal of Medicine* 313 (1985): 70–73.

Recker, R. R., S. Hinders, K. M. Davies, et al. **Correcting Calcium Nutritional Deficiency Prevents Spine Fractures in Elderly Women.** *Journal of Bone Mineral Research* 11 (1996): 1961–1966.

Recker, R. R., K. M. Davies, S. M. Hinders, et al. **Bone Gain in Young Adult Women**. *Journal of the American Medical Association* 268 (1992): 2403–2408.

Reid, I. R., R. W. Ames, M. C. Evans, et al. **Effect of Calcium Supplementation on Bone Loss in Postmenopausal Women**. *New England Journal of Medicine* 323 (1990): 878–881.

Reid, I. R., et al. **Effect on Calcium Supplementation on Bone Loss in Postmenopausal Woman.** *New England Journal of Medicine* 328 (1993): 460–464.

Renner, E. **Dairy Calcium, Bone Metabolism, and Prevention of Osteoporosis.** *Journal of Dairy Science* 77, no. 12 (December 1994): 3498–505.

Riis, B., K. Thomsen, and C. Christiansen. **Does Calcium Supplementation Prevent Postmenopausal Bone Loss**? *New England Journal of Medicine* 316 (1987): 173–177.

Soroko, S. et al. **Lifetime Milk Consumption and Bone Mineral Density in Older Women.** *Am J Public Health* 84, no. 8 (August 1994): 1319–22.

Sowers, M. R. **Epidemiology of Calcium and Vtamin D in Bone Loss.** *Journal of Nutrition* 123 (1993): 413–417.

Spencer, H., and Lender, M. **Adverse Effects of Aluminum-Containing Antacids on Mineral Metabolism**. *Gastroenterology* 76 (1979): 603.

Stracke, H. et al. **Osteoporosis and Bone Metabolic Parameters in Dependence Upon Calcium Intake Through Milk and Milk Products.** *European Journal of Clinical Nutrition* 47, no. 9 (September 1993): 617–22.

Tilyard, M. W., G. F. S. Spears, J. Thompson, et al. **Treatment of Postmenopausal Osteoporosis with Calcitriol and Calcium**. *New England Journal of Medicine* 326 (1992): 357–362.

Ulrich, C. M. et al. **Bone Mineral Density in Mother-Daughter Pairs: Relations to Lifetime Exercise, Lifetime Milk Consumption, and Calcium Supplements**. *Am J Clin Nutr* 63, no. 1 (January 1996): 72–9.

Wolman, R. L. et al. **Dietary Calcium As a Statistical Determinant of Spinal Trabecular Bone Density in Amenorrhoeic and Oestrogen-Replete Athletes**. *Bone Miner* 17, no. 3 (June 1992): 415–23.

Vitamin D

Aloia, J. **The Role of Calcitriol in the Treatment of Postmenopausal Osteoporosis**. *Metabolism* 39 (1990): S35–38.

Chapuy, M. C., M. E. Arlot, F. Duboeu, et al. **Vitamin D$_3$ and Calcium to Prevent Hip Fractures in Elderly Women**. *N Engl J Med* 327 (1992): 1637–1642.

Dawson-Hughes, B., S. S. Harris, E. A. Krall, et al. **Effect of Calcium and Vitamin D Supplementation on Bone Density in Men and Women 65 Years of Age or Older**. *N Engl J Med* 337 (1997): 670–676.

Dawson-Hughes, B. **Calcium and Vitamin D Nutritional Needs of Elderly Women**. *J Nutr* 126, no. 4 Suppl (April 1996): 1165S–7S.

Dawson-Hughes, B., G. E. Dallal, E. A. Krall, et al. **Effect of Vitamin D Supplementation on Wintertime and Overall Bone Loss in Healthy Postmenopausal Women**. *Annals of Internal Medicine* 115 (1991): 502–512.

Gallagher, J.C. and B.L. Riggs. **Action of 1,25 Dihydroxyvitamin D$_3$ on Calcium Balance and Bone Turnover and its Effect on Vertebral Fracture Rate**. *Metabolism* 39 (1990): S30–34.

Komar L., J. Nives, F. Cosman, et al. **Calcium Homeostasis of an Elderly Population Upon Admission to a Nursing Home**. *J Am Geriatr Soc* 41 (1993): 1057–1064.

LeBoff, MS, Hurwitz S, Franklin J, et al. **Occult Vitamin D Deficiency in Postmenopausal US Women With Hip Fracture**. *JAMA* 281 (1999): 1505–1511.

Riggs, B. L. and K. I. Nelson. **Effect of Long-Term Treatment with Calcitriol on Calcium Absorption and Mineral Metabolism in Postmenopausal Osteoporosis**. *Journal of Clinical Endocrinology and Metabolism* 61 (1985): 457–461.

Slovik, D.M., et al. **Deficient Production of 1,25 Dihydroxyvitamin D in Elderly Osteoporotic Patients**. *New England Journal of Medicine* 305 (1981): 372–374.

Tilyard, J. **Low-Dose Calcitriol Versus Calcium in Established Postmenopausal Osteoporosis**. *Metabolism* 39(1990): S50–52.

Vandevyver, C., T. Wyliin, J. J. Cassiman et al. **Influence of the Vitamin D Receptor Alleles on Bone Mineral Density in Postmenopausal and Osteoporotic Women**. *Journal of Bone and Mineral Research* 12 (1997): 241–247.

Other Vitamins and Minerals

Beasttie, J. H. and A. Avenell. **Trace-Element Nutrition and Bone Metabolism**. *Nutrition Research Reviews* 5 (1992): 167–188.

Bowes and Church's Food Values of Portions Commonly Used. Ed. By Pennington, J. A. T. and H. N. Church, Philadelphia: J.B. Lippincott Co., 1985.

Chandra, R. K., **Effect of Vitamin and Trace-Element Supplementation on Immune Response and Infection in Elderly Subjects.** *Lancet* 340 (1992): 1124–1127.

Heaney, R. P. **Nutritional Factors in Bone Health.** Osteoporosis, Etiology, Diagnosis and Management. Ed. By Riggs, B. L. and L. J. Melton. New York: Raven Press, 1988.

Rico, H. **Minerals and Osteoporosis.** *Osteoporosis International* 2 (1991): 20–25.

Walser, M., et.al., eds. **Nutrition Management.** *The Johns Hopkins Handbook.* Philadelphia: W.B.Saunders Co., 1984.

Chapter 6

Exercise and Osteoporosis

Aloia, J. F., et al. **Premenopausal Bone Mass is Related to Physical Activity.** *Archives of Internal Medicine* 148 (1988): 121–123.

Bloomfield, S. A., et al. **Non-Weight-Bearing Exercise May Increase Lumbar Spine Bone Mineral Density in Healthy Postmenopausal Women.** *American Journal of Physical Medicine and Rehabilitation* 72, no. 4 (August 1993): 204–9.

Bouxsein, M. L., and R. Marcus. **Overview of Exercise and Bone Mass.** In Lane, N.E. (ed): Osteoporosis. *Rheumatic Disease Clinics of North America.* Philadelphia: W.B. Saunders, 1994, pp. 787–802.

Bravo, G., et al. **Impact of a 12–Month Exercise Program on the Physical and Psychological Health of Osteopenic Women.** *J Am Geriatr Soc* 44, no. 7 (July 1996): 756–62.

Brown, A. B., N. McCartner, and D. G. Sale. **Positive Adaptations to Weight-Lifting Training in the Elderly.** *Journal of Applied Physiology* 69 (1990): 1725–1733.

Caplan, G. A., J. A. Ward, and S. R. Lord. **The Benefits of Exercise in Postmenopausal Women.** *Australian Journal of Public Health* 17, no. 1 (March 1993): 23–6.

Chow, R., J. E. Harrison, and J. Dornn. **Prevention and Rehabilitation of Osteoporosis: Exercise and Osteoporosis.** *Internal Journal of Rehabilitation* Research 12 (1989): 49–56.

Chow, R., J. E. Harrison, and C. Notarius. **Effect of Two Randomised Exercise Programs on Bone Mass of Healthy Postmenopausal Women.** *British Journal of Medicine* 295 (1987): 1441–1444.

Colletti, L. A., et al. **The Effects of Muscle-Building Exercise on Bone Mineral Density of the Radius, Spine and Hip in Young Men.** *Calcification Tissue International* (1989).

Dallky, G. P., K. S. Stocke, A. A. Ehsani, et al. **Weight-Bearing Exercise Training and Lumbar Bone Mineral Content in Postmenopausal Women.** *Annals of Internal Medicine* 108 (1988): 824–828.

Dalsky, G. P. **The Role of Exercise in the Prevention of Osteoporosis**. *Comprehensive Therapy*, (1989) vol. 15, p. 30–37.

Dawson-Hughes, B., et al. **Bone Density of the Radius, Spine and Hip in Relation to Ideal Body Weight in Postmenopausal Women**. *Calcification Tissue International* 40 (1987): 310–314.

Etherington, J., et al. **The Effect of Weight-Bearing Exercise on Bone Mineral Density: A Study of Female Ex-Elite Athletes and the General Population**. *J Bone Miner Res* 11, no. 9 (September 1996): 1333–8.

Fiatarone, M. A., et al. **High-Intensity Strength Training in Nonagenarians**. *JAMA* 263 (1990): 3029–3034.

Fleck, S. J. and J. Kraemer. **Designing Resistance Exercise Programs**. *Campaign, IL: Human Kinetics Books*, 1987.

Granhead, H., R. Jonson, and T. Hansson. **The Loads on the Lumbar Spine During Extreme Weight Lifting**. *Spine* 12 (1987): 146–149.

Grove, K. A. and B. R. Londeree. **Bone Density in Postmenopausal Women: High Impact Vs Low Impact Exercise.** *Med Sci Sports Exerc* 24, no. 11 (November 1992): 1190–4.

Gutin, B., and M. J. Kasper. **Can Vigorous Exercise Play a Role in Osteoporosis Prevention?** *Osteoporosis International,* 2 (1992): 55–69.

Hatori, M., et al. **The Effects of Walking at the Anaerobic Threshold Level on Vertebral Bone Loss in Postmenopausal Women.** *Calcified Tissue International* 52, no. 6 (June 1993): 411–4.

Heinonen, A., et al. **Randomised Controlled Trial of Effect of High-Impact Exercise on Selected Risk Factors for Osteoporotic Fractures**. *Lancet* 348, no. 9038 (November 1996): 1343–7.

Jaglal, S. B., N. Kreiger, G. Darlington. **Past and Recent Physical Activity and Risk of Hip Fracture**. *Am j Epidemiol* 138 (1993): 107–118.

Kanders, B., D. Dempster, and R. Lindsay. **Interaction of Calcium Nutrition and Physical Activity on Bone Mass in Young Women**. *Journal of Bone Mineral Research* 3 (1988): 145–149.

Krall, E. A. and B. Dawson-Hughes. **Walking Is Related to Bone Density and Rates of Bone Loss**. *American Journal of Medicine* 96, no. 1 (January 1994): 20–6.

Kritz-Silverstein, D. and E. Barrett-Connor. **Grip Strength and Bone Mineral Density in Older Women.** *Journal of Bone and Mineral Research* 9, no. 1 (January 1994): 45–51.

Lane, N. E., D. Bloch, H. H. Jones, et al. **Long-Distance Running, Bone Density and Osteoarthritis**. *JAMA* 255L (1986): 1147–1151.

Lane, N. E., D. Bloch, H. H. Jones, et.al. **Running, Osteoarthritis and Bone Density: Initial Longitudinal Study.** *American Journal of Medicine* 88 (1989): 452–459.

Lau, E. M. et al. **The Effects of Calcium Supplementation and Exercise on Bone Density in Elderly Chinese Women.** *Osteoporosis International* 2, no. 4 (July 1992): 168–73.

LeBlanc, A., et al. **Spinal Bone Mineral After Five Weeks of Bed Rest.** *Calcification Tissue International*, (1987) vol. 41, p. 259–261.

Leiheter, I., A. Simkin, J. Y. Margulies, et al. **Gain in Mass Density of Bone Following Strenuous Physical Activity**. *Journal of Orthopedic Research* 7 (1984): 86–90.

Michel, B. A., et al. **Impact of Running on Lumbar Bone Density: a 5–Year Longitudinal Study.** *Journal of Rheumatology* 19, no. 11 (November 1992): 1759–63.

National Osteoporosis Foundation **Boning Up on Osteoporosis**. Washington, D.C. *National Osteoporosis Foundation* 1998.

National Osteoporosis Foundation **Handbook on Exercises for Women with Osteoporosis**. Washington , D.C.: *National Osteoporosis Foundation*.

Nelson, M. E., M. A. Fiatarone, C. M. Morganti, et al**. Effects of High-Intensity Strength-Training on Multiple Risk Factors for Osteoporotic Fractures. A Randomized Controlled Trial.** *JAMA* 272 (1994): 1909–1914.

Nelson, M. E., C. N. Meredith, B. Dawsoln-Hughes, et al**. Hormone and Bone Mineral Status in Endurance-Trained and Sedentary Postmenopausal Women**. *Journal of Clinical Endocrinology and Metabolism* 66 (1988): 927–933.

Notelovitz, M., Martin, D., Tesar, R., et al. **Estrogen Therapy and Variable-Resistance Weight-Training Increase Bone Mineral Density in Surgically Menopausal Women**. *Journal of Bone and Mineral Research* 6 (1991): 583–590.

Osteoporosis Society of Canada Scientific Advisory Board. **Clinical Practice Guidelines For the Diagnosis and Management of Osteoporosis.** *Can Med Assoc J* 155 (1996): 1113–1133.

Paganini-Hill, A., A. Chao, R. K. Ross, et al**. Exercise and Other Factors in the Prevention of Hip Fractures: The Leisure World Study.** *Epidemiology* 2 (1991): 16–25, 1991.

Prince, R. L. et al. **Prevention of Postmenopausal Osteoporosis: A Comparative Study of Exercise, Calcium Supplementation, and Hormone-Replacement Therapy.** *New England Journal of Medicine* 325, no. 17 (October 1991): 1189–95.

Probart, C. K., et al**. The Effect of Modern Aerobic Exercise on Physical Fitness Among Women 70 Years or Older.** *Maturitus*14 (1991): 49–56.

Pruitt, L. A., et al. **Weight-Training Effects on Bone Mineral Density in Early Postmenopausal Women**. *Journal of Bone and Mineral Research* 7, no. 2 (February 1992): 179–85.

Puntila, E., H. Kroger, I. Lakka, et al. **Physical Activity in Adolescence and Bone Density in Peri- and Postmenopausal Women: A Population Based Study.** *Bone* 21 (1997): 363–367.

Rutherford, O. M. and D. A. Jones. **The Relationship of Muscle and Bone Loss and Activity Levels With Age in Women**. *Age and Aging* 21, no. 4 (July 1992): 286–93.

Shangold, M.M. **Exercise in the Menopausal Woman**. *Obstetrics and Gynecology* 75(1990): 535–585.

Simkin, A., J. Ayalon, and I. Leichter. **Increased Trabecular Bone Density Due to Bone-Loading Exercises in Postmenopausal Osteoporotic Women.** *Calcification Tissue International* 4 (1987): 59–63.

Sinaki, M**. Postmenopausal Spinal Osteoporosis: Physical Therapy and Rehabilitative Principles.** *Mayo Clinic Proceedings* 57 (1992): 699–675.

Sinaki, M. **The Role of Exercise in Preventing Osteoporosis.** *Journal of Musculoskeletal Medicine* (1992): 67–83.

Sinaki, M. and B. A. Mikkelsen. **Postmenopausal Spinal Osteoporosis: Flexion Versus Extension Exercises**. *Archives of Physical Medicine and Rehabilitation* 65 (1984): 593–596.

Sinaki, M. **Musculoskeletal Rehabilitation**. In Riggs, B. L., and J. L. Melton III, J.L., eds. *Osteoporosis: Etiology, Diagnosis and Management, 2nd ed.* Philadelphia: Lippincott-Raven, 1995, pp. 435–471.

Sinaki, M., E. Itoi, J. W. Rogers., et al. **Correlation of Back Extensor Strength With Thoracic Kyphosis and Lumbar Lordosis in Estrogen-Deficient Women**. *American Journal of Physical Medicine and Rehabilitation* 75 (1996): 370–374.

Sinaki, M., D. A. Dale, and D. L. Hurley**. Living with Osteoporosis: Guidelines for Women Before and After Diagnosis.** Toronto*: B.C. Decker,* 1988.

Slemenda, C. W., et al. **Role of Physical Activity in the Development of Skeletal Mass in Children.** *Journal of Bone Mineral Research* 6 (1991): 1227–1233.

Smith, E. L., et al. **Deterring Bone Loss by Exercise Intervention in Premenopausal and Postmenopausal Women**. *Calcification Tissue International* 44 (1989): 312–321.

Smith, L. **Bone Concerns**. *Women and Exercise: Physiology and Sports Medicine*. Shangold, M. M. and G. Mirkin, eds. Philadelphia: F.A. Davis Co., 1988.

Tsukahara, N., et al. **Cross-Sectional and Longitudinal Studies on the Effect of Water Exercise in Controlling Bone Loss in Japanese Postmenopausal Women**. *J Nutr Sci Vitaminol* (Tokyo) 40, no. 1 (February 1994): 37–47.

Welten, D. C., et al. **Weight-Bearing Activity During Youth is a More Important Factor for Peak Bone Mass Than Calcium Intake**. *Journal of Bone and Mineral Research* 9: 1089–1096, 1994.

Zhang, J. P., J. Feldblum, and S. A. Fortney. **Moderate Physical Activity and Bone Density Among Perimenopausal Women**. *American Journal of Public Health.* 82: 736–738, 1992.

Pharmacological Recommendations

Chapter 7

Estrogen

Aitken, J.M. and D. M. Hart. **Osteoporosis After Oophorectomy.** *BMJ* 3 (1973)515–518.

Albright, F., P. H. Smith, and A.M. Richarson. **Postmenopausal Osteoporosis: Its Clinical Features**. *JAMA* 116 (1941): 2465–2474

American College of Physicians Clinical Guidelines. **Guidelines for Counseling Postmenopausal Women About Preventative Hormone Therapy**. *Annals of Internal Medicine* 117 (1992): 1038–1041.

Andrews, W. B. **What's New in Preventing and Treating Osteoporosis?** *Postgrad Med* 104 (1998): 89–97.

Archer, D. F., J. H. Pickar, and F. Bottiglioni. **Bleeding Patterns in Postmenopausal Women Taking Continuous, Combined, or Sequential Regimens of Conjugated Estrogen with Medroxyprogesterone Acetate**. *Obstetrics and Gynecology* 83 (1994): 686–692.

Armamento-Villareal, R. C., et al. **Estrogen Status and Heredity Are Major Determinants of Premenopausal Bone Mass.** *J Clin Invest* 90, no. 6 (December 1992): 2464–71.

Bush, T. I., M. K. Whiteman. Editorial. **Hormone Replacement Therapy and Risk of Breast Cancer.** *JAMA* 281 (1992): 2140–2141.

Bush, T.L., E. Barrett-Connor, L. D. Cowan, et al. **Cardiovascular Mortality and Noncontraceptive Use of Estrogen in Women: Results From the Lipid Research Clinics Program Follow-Up Study**. *Circulation* 75 (1987): 112–119.

Calle, E. E. **Hormone Replacement Therapy and Colorectal Cancer: Interpreting the Evidence.** *Cancer Causes Control* 8 (1997): 127–129.

Cann, C. E., et al. **Decreased Spinal Mineral Content in Amenorrheic Women.** *JAMA* 251 (1984): 626–629.

Cantatore, F. P. et al. **Effect of Estrogen Replacement on Bone Metabolism and Cytokines in Surgical Menopause.** *Clin Rheumatol* 14, no. 2 (March 1995): 157–60.

Capstur, S. M., M. Morrow, T. A. Sellers. **Hormone Replacement Therapy and Risk of Breast Cancer with a Favorable Histology. Results of the Iowa Women's Health Study.** *JAMA* 281 (1999): 2091–2097.

Cauley, J. A., D. G. Seeley, K. Ensrud, et al. **For the Study of Osteoporotic Fractures Research Group. Estrogen Replacement Therapy and Fractures in Older Women.** *Ann Int Med* 129 (1995): 9–16.

Cauley JA, Seeley DG, Ensrud K, et al. **Estrogen Replacement Therapy and Fractures in Older Women.** *Ann Intern Med* 122 (1995): 9–16..

Christiansen, C. **What Should Be Done at the Time of Menopause?** *Am J Med* 98 (1995): 56S–59S.

Colditz, G. A. **Relationship Between Estrogen Levels, Use of Hormone Replacement Therapy and Breast Cancer.** *J Nat Cancer Inst* 90 (1998): 814–823.

Colditz, G.A., et al. **Prospective Study of Estrogen Replacement Therapy and Risk of Breast Cancer in Postmenopausal Women.** *JAMA* 262 (1990): 2648–2653.

Colditz, G.A., S. E. Hankinson, D. J. Hunter, et al. **The Use of Estrogens and Progestins and the Risk of Breast Cancer in Postmenopausal Women.** *New England Journal of Medicine* 332 (1995): 1589–1593.

Collaborative Group on Hormonal Factors in Breast Cancer. **Breast Cancer and Hormone Replacement Therapy: Collaborative Reanalysis of Data From 51 Epidemiological Studies Involving 52,705 Women With Breast Cancer and 108,411 Women Without Breast Cancer.** *Lancet* 350 (1997): 1047–1059.

Daly, E., M. P. Vessey, M. M. Hawkins, et al. **Risk of Venous Thromboembolism In Users of Hormone Replacement Therapy.** *Lancet* 348 (1996): 977–980.

Dupont, W. D. and D. L. Page. **Menopausal Estrogen Replacement Therapy and Breast Cancer.** *Archives of Internal Medicine* 151 (1991): 67–72.

Eriksen, E. F., et al. **Evidence of Estrogen Receptors in Normal Human Osteoblast-Like Cells.** *Science* 241, no. 4861 (July 1988): 84–6.

Ettinger, B., H. K. Genant, C E. Cann. **Long-Term Managed Estrogen Therapy Prevents Bone Loss and Fracture.** *Ann Intern Med* 102 (1985): 319–324.

Ettinger, B., A. Pressman, P. Sklarin, et al. **Associations Between Low Levels of Serum Estradiol, Bone Density, and Fractures Among Elderly Women: The Study of Osteoporotic Fractures.** J *Clin Endocrinol Metab* 83 (1998): 2239–2243.

Ettinger, B., et al. **Low-Dosage Micronized 17-B-Estradiol Prevents Bone Loss in Postmenopausal Women.** *American Journal of Obstetrics and Gynecology* 166 (1992): 479–488.

Eye Disease Case-Control Study Group. **Risk Factors for Neovascular Age-Related Macular Degeneration.** *Arch Ophthalmol* 110 (1992): 1701–1708.

Felson, D. T., Y. Zhang, M. T. Hannon, et al. **The Effect of Postmenopausal Estrogen Therapy on Bone Density in Elderly Women.** *N Engl J Med* 329 (1993): 1141–1146.

Grady, D., S. M. Rubin, D. B. Petiti, et al. **Hormone Therapy to Prevent Disease and Prolong Life in Postmenopausal Women.** *Ann Intern Med* 117 (1992): 1016–1017.

Grodstein, F., M. J. Stampfer, J. E. Manson, et al. **Postmenopausal Estrogen and Progestin Use and the Risk of Cardiovascular Disease.** *N Engl J Med* 335 (1996): 453–461.

Hall, G. M., M. Daniels, D. V. Doyle, T. D. Spector. **Effect of Hormone Replacement Therapy on Bone Mass in Rheumatoid Arthritis Patients Treated With and Without Steroids.** *Arthritis Rheum* 37 (1994): 1499–1505.

Harris, S. T., et al. **The Effects of Estrogen (Ogen) on Spinal Bone Density of Postmenopausal Women.** *Archives of Internal Medicine* 151 (1991): 1980–1984.

Henrich, J. B. **The Postmenopausal Estrogen/Breast Cancer Controversy.** *JAMA* 268 (1992): 1985–1990.

Horowitz, M. C. **Cytokines and Estrogen in Bone: Anti-Osteoporotic Effects.** *Science* 260, no. 5108 (April 1993): 626–7.

Horsman, A., M. Jones, R. Francis, C. Nordin. **The Effect of Estrogen Dose on Postmenopausal Bone Loss.** *N Engl J Med* 309 (1983): 1405–7.

Horsman, A., et al. **The Effect of Estrogen Dose on Postmenopausal Bone Loss.** *New England Journal of Medicine* 309 (1993): 1405–1407.

Hulley, S., D. Grady, T. Bush, et al. **Randomized Trial of Estrogen Plus Progestin for Secondary Prevention of Coronary Heart Disease in Postmenopausal Women. Heart and Estrogen/Progestin Replacement Study. (HERS) Research Group.** *JAMA* 280 (1998): 605–613.

Ingram, D., K. Sander, M. Kolybaba, et al. **Case-Control Study of Phytoestrogens and Breast Cancer.** *Lancet* 350 (1997): 990–994.

Jick, H., L. E. Derby, M. W. Myers, et al. **Risk of Hospital Admission For Idiopathic Venous Thromboembolism Among Users of Postmenopausal Estrogens.** *Lancet* 348 (1996): 981–983

Johnson, S. R. **The Clinical Decision Regarding Hormone Replacement Therapy**. Endocrin Metab Clin N Amer 26 (1997): 4113–435.

Kanis, J. A. **Estrogens, Menopause, and Osteoporosis.** *Bone* 19, no. 5 Suppl (November 1996): 185S–90S.

Kiel, D. P., D. T. Felson, J. J. Anderson, et al. **Hip Fracture and the Use of Estrogen in Postmenopausal Women. The Framingham Study**. *New England Journal of Medicine* 317 (1987): 1169–1174.

Krall, E. D., B. Dawsoln-Hughes, M. T. Hannan, et al. **Postmenopausal Estrogen Replacement and Tooth Retention.** *Am J Med* 102 (1997): 536–542.

Lim, S. K et al. **Altered Hydroxylation of Estrogen in Patients With Postmenopausal Osteopenia.** *J Clin Endocrinol Metab* 82, no. 4 (April 1997): 1001–6.

Lindsay, R. **Prevention and Treatment of Osteoporosis**. *Lancet* 341 (1993): 801–805.

Lindsay, R., J. M. Aitken, J. B. Anderson, et al. **Long-Term Prevention of Postmenopausal Osteoporosis By Estrogen.** *Lancet* 1 (1976): 1038–1041.

Lindsay, R., and J. F. Tohme. **Estrogen Treatment of Patients With Established Postmenopausal Osteoporosis.** *Obstetrics and Gynecology* 76 (1990): 290–295.

Lindsay, R., et al. **Prevention of Spinal Osteoporosis in Oophorectomized Woman**. *Lancet* (1980): 1151–1153.

Lufkin, E. G., et al**. Treatment of Postmenopausal Osteoporosis with Transdermal Estrogen**. *Ann Internal Med* 117 (1992): 1–9.

Marslew, J. U., et al. **Bleeding Pattern and Climacteric Symptoms During Different Sequential Combined HRT Regimens in Current Use.** *Maturitas* 19 (1994): 225–237.

Maxim, P., B. Ettinger, G. M. Spitalny. **Fracture Protection Provided by Long-Term Estrogen Treatment**. *Osteoporosis Int* 5 (1995: 23–29.

Notelovitz, M. **Adjutive Estrogen Therapy: A Rational Approach to HRT**. *Contemporary* Obstetrics/Gynecology 44 (1999): 54–64.

Pacifici, R. **Estrogen, Cytokines, and Pathogenesis of Postmenopausal Osteoporosis.** *J Bone Miner Res* 11, no. 8 (August 1996): 1043–51.

Paganini-Hill, A., and V. W. Henderson. **Estrogen Deficiency and Risk of Alzheimer's Disease in Women.** *American Journal of Epidemiology* 140 (1994): 256–261.

Postmenopausal Estrogen/: Progestin Interventions (PEPI) Trial. **Effects of Hormone Replacement Therapy on Endometrial Histology in Postmenopausal Women.** JAMA 25 (1996): 370–375.

Prince, R. L. et al. **The Effects of Menopause and Age on Calcitropic Hormones: A Cross-Sectional Study of 655 Healthy Women Aged 35 to 90.** *J Bone Miner Res* 10, no. 6 (June 1995): 835–42.

Prince, R. L., M. Smith, and I. M. Dick. **Prevention of Postmenopausal Osteoporosis: A Comparative Study of Exercise, Calcium Supplementation, and Hormone-Replacement Therapy.** *New England Journal of Medicine* 325 (1991): 1189–1195.

Rebar, R. W. and I. B. Spitzer. **The Physiology and Measurement of Hot Flushes.** *American Journal of Obstetrics and Gynecology* 156 (1987).12184–1288.

Rosen, C. J., C. R. Kessenich. **The Pathophysiology and Treatment of Postmenopausal Osteoporosis: An Evidence-Based Approach to Estrogen Replacement Therapy.** *Endocrinol Metab Clin North Am* 26 (1997): 295–311.

Ryan, P. J., R. Harrison, G. M. Blake, et al. **Compliance with Hormone Replacement Therapy (HRT) After Screening For Postmenopausal Osteoporosis.** *British Journal of Obstetrics and Gynecology* 99 (1992): 325–328.

Salamone, L. M., A. R. Pressman, D. G. Seeley, J. A. Cauley. **Estrogen Replacement Therapy.** *Arch Intern Med* 156 (1996): 1293–1297.

Santoro, N., V. T. Miller. **Menopause and the Postmenopausal State.** *Curr Pract Med* 1 (1998): 423–428.

Sato, M., T. A. Grese, J. A. Dodge, et al. **Emerging Therapies For the Prevention or Treatment of Postmenopausal Osteoporosis.** *J Med Chem* 42 (1999): 1–24.

Schneider, D. L., E. L. Barrett-Connor, and D. J. Morton. **Timing of Postmenopausal Estrogen for Optimal Bone Mineral Density. The Rancho Bernardo Study.** *JAMA* 277, no. 7 (February 1997): 543–7.

Slemenda, C. W. et al. **Sex Steroids, Bone Mass, and Bone Loss. A Prospective Study of Pre-, Peri-, and Postmenopausal Women.** *J Clin Invest* 97, no. 1 (January 1996): 14–21.

Sowers, M. R. and D. A. Galuska. **Epidemiology of Bone Mass in Premenopausal Women.** *Epidemiol Rev* 15, no. 2 (1993): 374–98.

Stanford, J. L., N. S. Weiss, L. F. Voigt, et al. **The Use of Estrogens and Progestins and the Risk of Breast Cancer in Postmenopausal Women.** *JAMA* 274 (1995): 137–142.

Steinberg, K. K., et al. **A Meta-Analysis of the Effect of Estrogen Replacement Therapy on the Risk of Breast Cancer.** *JAMA* 268 (1991): 1900–1902.

Steiniche, T. **A Randomized Study on the Effects of Estrogen/Gestagen or High Dose Oral Calcium on Trabecular Bone Remodeling in Postmenopausal Osteoporosis.** *Bone* 10, no. 5 (1989): 313–20.

Tang, M. X., D. Jacobs, Y. Stern, et al. **Effects of Estrogen During Menopause On Risk and Age at Onset of Alzheimer's Disease.** *Lancet* 348 (1996): 429–432.

Taylor, M. **Alternatives to Conventional Hormone Replacement Therapy.** *Comprehensive Therapy* 23(1997): 514–532.

Turner, R. T., B. L. Riggs, and T. C. Spelsberg. **Skeletal Effects of Estrogen.** *Endocr Rev* 15, no. 3 (June 1994): 275–300.

Van Hoof, H. J., et al. **Hormone Replacement Therapy Increases Serum 1,25–Dihydroxyvitamin D: A Two–Year Prospective Study.** *Calcif Tissue Int* 55, no. 6 (December 1994): 417–9.

Vedi, S. and J. E. Compston. **The Effects of Long-Term Hormone Replacement Therapy on Bone Remodeling in Postmenopausal Women.** *Bone* 19, no. 5 (November 1996): 535–9.

Wingo, P.A., et al. **The Risk of Breast Cancer in Postmenopausal Women Who Have Used Estrogen Replacement Therapy.** *JAMA* 257 (1987): 209–215.

Women's Health Initiative Study Group. **Design of the Women's Health Initiative Clinical Trial and Observational Study.** *Control Clin Trials* 19 (1998): 61–109.

Woodruff, J. D., and J. H. Pickar. **Incidence of Endometrial Hyperplasia in Postmenopausal Women Taking Conjugated Estrogens (Premarin) with Medroxyprogesterone Acetate or Conjugated Estrogens Alone.** *American Journal of Obstetrics and Gynecology* 1709 (1994): 1213–1223.

Writing Group for the PEPI Trial. **Effects of Hormone Therapy on Bone Mineral Density: Results From the Postmenopausal Estrogen/Progestin Interventions (PEPI) Trial.** *JAMA* 276 (1996): 1389–1396.

Natural Estrogens

Brandi, M. L. **Flavanoids: Biochemical Effects and Therapeutic Applications.** *Bone and Mineral* 19(1992): S3–S14.

Knight, D. C., and J. A. Eden. **A Review of the Clinical Effects of Phytoestrogens.** *Obstetrics and Gynecology* 87 (1996): 897–904.

Lien, L. L., and E. J. Lien. **Hormone Therapy and Phytoestrogens.** *Journal of Clinical Pharmacy and Therapeutics* 21(1996): 101–111.

Passeri, M., et al. **Effect of Ipriflavone on Bone Mass in Elderly Osteoporotic Women.** *Bone and Mineral* 19 (1992): S57–S62.

Chapter 8

Medications Used to Treat Osteoporosis

Fosamax® alendronate

Adami, S., et al. **Treatment of Postmenopausal Osteoporosis with Continuous Daily Oral Alendronate in Comparison with Either Placebo or Intranasal Salmon Calcitonin.** *Osteoporosis International.* (1993) supp. 3: S21–7.

Black, D. M., S. R. Cummings, D. B. Karpt, et al. **Randomized Trial of Effect of Alendronate on Risk of Fracture in Women With Existing Vertebral Fractures. Fracture Intervention Trial Research Group.** *Lancet* 348 (1996): 1535–1541.

Bone, H. G., et al. **Dose-Response Relationships for Alendronate Treatment in Osteoporotic Elderly Women. Alendronate Elderly Osteoporosis Study Centers.** *J Clin Endocrinol Metab* 82, no. 1 (January 1997): 265–74.

Chesnut III, C. H., et al. **Alendronate Treatment of the Postmenopausal Osteoporotic Woman: Effect of Multiple Dosages on Bone Mass and Bone Remodeling.** *Am J Med* 99, no. 2 (August 1995): 144–52.

Cummings, S. R., D M. Black, D. E. Thompson, et al. **Effect of Alendronate on Risk of Fracture in Women With Low Bone Density But Without Vertebral Fractures: Results From the Fracture Intervention Trial.** *JAMA* 280 (1998): 2077–2082.

DeGroen, P. C., D. F. Lubbe, L. J. Hirsch, et al. **Esophagitis Associated with the Use of Alendronate**. *N. Engl J Med*. 1335 (1996): 1016–1021.

Devogelaer, J. P. **Clinical Use of Bisphosphonates.** *Curr Opin Rheumatol* 8, no. 4 (July 1996): 384–91.

Eastell, R. **Treatment of Postmenopausal Osteoporosis.** *N Engl J Med* 338 (1998): 736–746.

Ensrud, K. E., D. M. Black, L. Palermo, et al. **Treatment with Alendronate Prevents Fractures in Women at Highest Risk**. *Arch Intern Med* 157 (1997): 2617–2624.

Ettinger, B., A. Pressman, J. Schein. **Clinic Visits and Hospital Admissions For Care of Acid-Related Upper Gastrointestinal Disorders in Women Using Alendronate for Osteoporosis.** *Am J Managed Care* 4 (1998): 1377–1382.

Gertz, B. J. et al. **Studies of the Oral Bioavailability of Alendronate.** *Clin Pharmacol Ther* 58, no. 3 (September 1995): 288–98.

Greenspan, S. L. et al. **Alendronate Stimulation of Nocturnal Parathyroid Hormone Secretion: A Mechanism to Explain the Continued Improvement in Bone Mineral Density Accompanying Alendronate Therapy.** *Proc Assoc Am Physicians* 108, no. 3 (May 1996): 230–8.

Harris, S. T. et al. **The Effect of Short Term Treatment with Alendronate on Vertebral Density and Biochemical Markers of Bone Remodeling in Early Postmenopausal Women**. *J Clin Endocrinol Metab* 76, no. 6 (June 1993): 1399–406.

Hosking, D., C. E. D. Chilvers, C. Christiansen, et al. **The Early Postmenopausal Intervention Cohort Study Group. Prevention of Bone Loss With Alendronate in Postmenopausal Women Under Sixty Years of Age**. *N Engl J Med* 33 (1998): 485–492.

Hosking, D., E. D. Clair , D. Chilvers, et al. **Prevention of Bone Loss With Alendronate in Postmenopausal Women Under Sixty Years of Age**. *N Engl J Med* 338 (1998): 485–492.

Karpf, D. B. et al. **Prevention of Nonvertebral Fractures by Alendronate.** *JAMA* 277, no. 14 (April 1997): 1159–64.

Liberman, U. A. et al. **Effect of Oral Alendronate on Bone Mineral Density and the Incidence of Fractures in Postmenopausal Osteoporosis. The Alendronate Phase III Osteoporosis Treatment Study Group** . *N Engl J Med* 333, no. 22 (November 1995): 1437–43.

Licata, A. A. **Bisphosphonate Therapy**. *Am J Med Sci* 313, no. 1 (January 1997): 17–22.

Lindsay, R., F. Cosman, R. A. Lobo RA, et al. **Addition of Alendronate to Ongoing Hormone Replacement Therapy in the Treatment of Osteoporosis: A Randomized, Controlled Clinical Trial**. *J Clin Endocrinol Metab* 84 (1998): 3076–3081.

McClung, M. R. **Current Bone Mineral Density Data on Bisphosphonates in Postmenopausal Osteoporosis.** *Bone* 19, no. 5 Suppl (November 1996): 195S–8S.

Orr-Walker, B. et al. **Effects of Prolonged Bisphosphonate Therapy and Its Discontinuation on Bone Mineral Density in Postmenopausal Osteoporosis.** *Clin Endocrinol (Oxf)* 46, no. 1 (January 1997): 87–92.

Papaloulos, S. E., et al. **The Use of Bisphosphonates in the Treatment of Osteoporosis.** *Bone* 13 (1992): S41–9

Patel, S. **Current and Potential Future Drug Treatments for Osteoporosis.** *Ann Rheum Dis* 55, no. 10 (October 1996): 700–14.

Paterson, A. H., et al. **Role of Bisphosphonates in Prevention and Treatment of Bone Metastases From Breast Cancer.** *Can J Oncol* 5 Suppl 1 (December 1995): 54–7.

Reid, I. R., et al. **Biochemical and Radiologic Improvement in Paget's Disease of Bone Treated With Alendronate: A Randomized, Placebo-Controlled Trial.** *Am J Med* 101, no. 4 (October 1996): 341–8.

Rosen, C. J. and C. R. Kessenich. **Comparative Clinical Pharmacology and Therapeutic Use of Bisphosphonates in Metabolic Bone Diseases.** *Drugs* 51, no. 4 (April 1996): 537–51.

Ruml, L. A., et al . **Prevention of Hypercalciuria and Stone-Forming Propensity During Prolonged Bed Rest by Alendronate.** *J Bone Miner Res* 10, no. 4 (April 1995): 655–62.

Saag, K. G., R. Emkey, T. J. Schnitzer, et al. **Alendronate For the Prevention and Treatment of Corticosteroid-Induced Osteoporosis.** *N Eng J Med* 339 (1998): 292–299.

Tucci, J. R . F., R. P. Tonino, R. D. Emkey, et al. **Effects of Three Years of Oral Alendronate Treatment in Postmenopausal Women with Osteoporosis.** *Am J Med* 101 (1996): 488–501.

Vasikaran, S. D., et al **The Effect of Alendronate on Renal Tubular Reabsorption of Phosphate.** *Bone Miner* 27, no. 1 (October 1994): 51–6.

Vitte, C., H. Fleisch, and H. L. Guenther. **Bisphosphonates Induce Osteoblasts to Secrete an Inhibitor of Osteoclast-Mediated Resorption.** *Endocrinology* 137, no. 6 (June 1996): 2324–33.

Watts, N. B. **Treatment of Osteoporosis With Biphosphonates.** *Endocrinol Metab Clin N. Amer* 27 (1998): 419–439.

Miacalcin® Salmon calcitonin

Adachi, J. D., W. B. Bensen, M. J. Bell, et al. **Salmon Calcitonin Nasal Spray in the Prevention of Corticosteroid-Induced Osteoporosis.** *Br J Rheumatol* 36 (1997): 255–259.

Adami, S., et al. **Treatment of Postmenopausal Osteoporosis with Continuous Daily Oral Alendronate in Comparison with Either Placebo or Intranasal Salmon Calcitonin.** *Osteoporosis International* (1993) supp. 3, S21–7.

Avioli, L. V. **The Role of Calcitonin in the Prevention of Osteoporosis.** *Endocrinol Metab Clin North Am* 27, no. 2 (June 1998): 411–8.

Burckhardt, P., et al. **The Effect of Treatment with Calcitonin on Vertebral Fracture Rate in Osteoporosis.** *Osteoporosis Int* 1993, 3: 24–30.

Campodarve, I., B. L. Drinkwater, K. L. Insogna, et al. **Intranasal Salmon Calcitonin (INSC) 50–200 IU Does Not Prevent Bone Loss in Early Postmenopausal Women** (abstract). *J Bone Miner Res* 9 (suppl 1) (1994): S391.

Cardona, J. M. and E. Pastor. **Calcitonin Versus Etidronate for the Treatment of Postmenopausal Osteoporosis: A Meta-Analysis of Published Clinical Trials.** *Osteoporos Int* 7, no. 3 (1997): 165–74.

Christiansen, C. **Use of Nasally Administered Salmon Calcitonin in Preventing Bone Loss.** *Calcif Tissue Int* 49 (S1) (1991): S14–S15

Civitelli, R., et al. **Bone Turnover in Postmenopausal Osteoporosis: Effect of Calcitonin Treatment.** *Journal of Clinical Investigation* 82 (1988): 1268–1274.

Ellerington, M. C. et al. **Intranasal Salmon Calcitonin for the Prevention and Treatment of Postmenopausal Osteoporosis.** *Calcif Tissue Int* 59, no. 1 (July 1996): 6–11.

Erlacher, L., et al. **Salmon Calcitonin and Calcium in the Treatment of Male Osteoporosis: The Effect on Bone Mineral Density.** *Wien Klin Wochenschr* 109, no. 8 (April 1997): 270–4.

Flicker, L. et al. **Nandrolone Decanoate and Intranasal Calcitonin As Therapy in Established Osteoporosis.** *Osteoporos Int* 7, no. 1 (1997): 29–35.

Gennari, C., D. Agnusdei, A. Camporeale. **Use of Calcitonin in the Treatment of Bone Pain Associated With Osteoporosis.** *Calcif Tissue Int* 49 (suppl 2) (1991): S9–S13.

Gennari, C. **Comparative Effects on Bone Mineral Content of Calcium Plus Salmon Calcitonin Given in Two Different Regimens in Postmenopausal Osteoporosis.** *Current Therapeutics and Research* 28 (1985): 455–464.

Gonnelli, S., et al. **Treatment of Postmenopausal Osteoporosis With Recombinant Human Growth Hormone and Salmon Calcitonin: A Placebo Controlled Study.** *Clin Endocrinol* (Oxf) 46, no. 1 (January 1997): 55–61.

Grigoriou, O., et al. **Effects of Nasal Administration of Calcitonin in Oophorectomized Women: Two–Year Controlled Double-Blind Study.** *Maturitas* 28, no. 2 (December 1997): 147–51.

Gruber, H. E., et al. **Long-Term Calcitonin Therapy in Postmenopausal Osteoporosis.** *Metabolism* 33 (1984): 295–303.

Healey, J. H., S. A. Paget, P. Williams-Russo, et al. **A Randomized Controlled Trial of Salmon Calcitonin to Prevent Bone Loss in Corticosteroid-Treated Temporal Arteritis and Polymyalgia Rheumatica.** *Calcif Tissue Int* 58 (1996): 73–80.

Holloway, L., et al. **Skeletal Effects of Cyclic Recombinant Human Growth Hormone and Salmon Calcitonin in Osteopenic Postmenopausal Women.** *J Clin Endocrinol Metab* 82, no. 4 (April 1997): 1111–7.

Kanis, J. A.. et al. **Evidence for Efficacy of Drugs Affecting Bone Metabolism in Preventing Hip Fracture.** *BMJ* 305, no. 6862 (November 1992): 1124–8.

Kapetanos, G. et al. **A Double-Blind Study of Intranasal Calcitonin for Established Postmenopausal Osteoporosis.** *Acta Orthop Scand* 275, no. Suppl (October 1997): 108–11.

Levernieux, J., D. Julien and F. Caulin. **A Double-Blind Study on the Effect of Calcitonin on Pain and Acute Resorption Related to Recent Osteoporotic Crush Fractures**. Calcitonin 1984: Selected Short Communications, International Symposium Calcitonin 1984 Milan. Ed. By Doepfner, W. Amsterdam: *Excerpta Medica*, 1986.

Luengo, M., F. Pons, M. J. Martinez de Osaba, et al. **Prevention of Further Bone Mass Loss By Nasal Calcitonin in Patients on Long-term Glucocorticoid Therapy for Asthma: A Two-year-Followup Study**. *Thorax* 49 (11) (1994): 1099–1102.

Lyritis, G. P., N. Tsakalakos, B. Magiasis, et al. **Analgesic Effect of Salmon Calcitonin in Osteoporotic Vertebral Fractures: A Double-Blind Placebo Controlled Clinical Study**. *Calcif Tissue Int* 49 (1991): 360–372.

MacIntyre, I., et al. **Calcitonin for Prevention of Postmenopausal Bone Loss**. *Lance* 1 (1988): 900–901.

Mazzuoli, G. F., et al. **Effects of Salmon Calcitonin on the Bone Loss Induced by Ovariectomy**. *Calcification Tissue International* 47 (1990): 209–214.

Mazzuoli, G. F., et al. **Effects of Salmon Calcitonin in Postmenopausal Osteoporosis: A Controlled Double-Blind Clinical Study**. *Calcification Tissue International* 38 (1986): 3–8.

McDermott, M.T. and G.S. Kidd. **The Role of Calcitonin in the Development and Treatment of Osteoporosis**. *Endocrine Reviews* 8 (1987): 377–390.

Montemurro, L., et al. **Prevention of Corticosteroid-Induced Osteoporosis with Salmon Calcitonin in Sacroid Patients**. *Calcified Tissue International* 49 (1991): 71–76.

Overgaard, K., J. Riss, C. Christiansen, et al. **Effect of Calcitonin Given Intranasally in Early Postmenopausal Bone Loss**. *BMJ* 299 (1989): 477–479.

Overgaard, K. **Effect of Intranasal Salmon Calcitonin Therapy on Bone Mass and Bone Turnover in Early Postmenopausal Women: A Dose-Response Study**. *Calcif Tissue Int* 55 (1994): 82–86.

Overgaard, K., et al. **Effect of Calcitonin Given Intranasally on Bone Mass and Fracture Rates in Established Osteoporosis: A Dose-Response Study**. *BMJ* 305 (1992): 556–561.

Overgaard, K., R. Lindsay, and C. Christiansen. **Patient Responsiveness to Calcitonin Salmon Nasal Spray: A Subanalysis of a Two–Year Study**. *Clin Ther* 17, no. 4 (July 1995–August 1995): 680–5.

Reginster, J. Y., et al. **One Year Controlled Randomized Trial of Prevention of Early Postmenopausal Bone Loss by Intranasal Calcitonin**. *Lancet* 2 (1987): 1481–1483.

Reginster, J. Y. **Management of High Turnover Osteoporosis with Calcitonin**. *Bone* 13 (1992): S37–S40.

Rico, H., E. R. Hernandez, M. Revilla, et al. **Salmon Calcitonin Reduces Vertebral Fracture Rate in Postmenopausal Crush Fracture Syndrome**. *Bone Miner* 16 (1992): 131–138.

Rico, H., M. Revilla, E. R. Hernandez, et al. **Total and Regional Bone Mineral Content and Fracture Rate in Postmenopausal Osteoporosis Treated**

With Salmon Calcitonin: A Prospective Study. *Calcif Tissue Int* 56 (1995): 181–185.

Rico, H., et al. Salmon Calcitonin Reduces Vertebral Fracture Rate in Postmenopausal Crush Fracture Syndrome. *Bone and Mineral* 16 (1992): 113–128.

Ringe, J. D. and D. Welzel. Salmon Calcitonin in the Therapy of Corticoid-Induced Osteoporosis. *European Journal of Clinical Pharmacology* 33 (1987): 35–39.

Silverman, S. L., C. Chesnut, K. Andriano, et al. The PROOF Study Group. Salmon Calcitonin Nasal Spray (NS-CT) Reduces Risk of Vertebral Fracture(s) (VF) in Established Osteoporosis and Has Continuous Efficacy with Prolonged Treatment: Accrued Five-Year Worldwide Data of the PROOF Study. *Bone* 23 (suppl) (1998): Abstract 1108.

Thamsborg, G., et al. Effect of Different Doses of Nasal Salmon Calcitonin on Bone Mass. *Calcitonin Tissue International* 48 (1991): 302–307.

Wallach, S. Calcitonin Treatment in Osteoporosis. *Drug Therapy* (April 1993): 61–74.

Evista® Raloxifene

Balfour, J. A. and K. L. Goa . Raloxifene. *Drugs Aging* 12 (1998): 335–341.

Cummings, S. R., D. Black, E. Barrett-Conner, et al. The Effect of Raloxifene on Risk of Breast Cancer in Postmenopausal Women: Results From the MORE Randomized Trial. Multiple Outcomes of Raloxifene Evaluation. *JAMA* 281 (1999): 2189–2197.

Cummings, S. R., L. Norton, S. Eckert, et al. Raloxifene Reduces the Risk of Breast Cancer and May Decrease the Risk of Endometrial Cancer in Postmenopausal Women. Two-Year Findings from the Multiple Outcomes of Raloxifene Evaluation (MORE) Trial. *Proc ASCO* 17 (1998): 2a.

Delmas, P. D., N. H. Bjarnason, B. H. Mitlak, et al. Effects of Raloxifene on Bone Mineral Density, Serum Cholesterol Concentrations, and Uterine Endometrium in Postmenopausal Women. *N Engl J Med* 337 (1997): 1641–1647.

Ensrud, K., D. Black, R. Recker, et al. The Effect of Two and Three Years of Raloxifene on Vertebral and Nonvertebral Fractures in Postmenopausal Women with Osteoporosis. *ASBMR-IBMS* 23 (1998): S174.

Ettinger, B., D. Black, B. Mitlak, et al. Reduction of Vertebral Fracture Risk in Postmenopausal Women with Osteoporosis Treated With Raloxifene. *JAMA* 282 (1999): 637–645.

Johnell, Olef. Alendonate Plus Raloxifene Found to Increase BMD More Than Either Agent Alone. M.D., *New Dimensions in Osteoporosis* 1, no. 5, Fall 1999.

Lukfin, E. G., M. D. Whitaker, R. Argueta, et al. Raloxifene Treatment of Postmenopausal Osteoporosis. *Journal of Bone and Mineral Research* 12 (Supplement 1) (1997): S150.

Miller, P. D. Management of Osteoporosis. *Adv Intern Med* 44 (1999): 175–207.

Spencer, C. P., E. P. Morris, J. M. Rymer. Selective Estrogen Receptor Modulators: Women's Panacea for the Next Millennium? *Am J Obstet Gynecol* 180 (1999): 763–770.

Walsh, B. W., L. H. Kuller, R. A. Wild, et al. **Effects of Raloxifene on Serum Lipids and Coagulation Factors in Healthy Postmenopausal Women**. JAMA 279 (1998): 1445–1451.

Actonel® Risedronate

Eastell, R., H. Minne, O. Sorensen, et al. **Risedronate Reduces Fracture Risk in Women With Established Postmenopausal Osteoporosis**. *Calcif Tissue Int* 64 (suppl 1 (1999), Abstract 0–25; in press, Osteoporosis Int.

Fleisch, H. A. **Bisphosphonates: Preclinical Aspects and Use in Osteoporosis**. *Ann Intern Med*. 29 (1997): 55–62.

Fogelman, I., C. Ribot, R. Smith, et al. **Risedronate Produces Dose-Dependent Increases in Bone Mineral Density in Postmenopausal Women with Low Bone Mass**. *Calcif Tissue Int* 64 (suppl 1) (1999)Abstract P-79.

Harris, S. T., N. B. Watts, H. K. Genant, et al. **Effects of Risedronate Treatment on Vertebral and Nonvertebral Fractures in Women With Postmenopausal steoporosis**. *JAMA* 282 (1999): 1344–1352.

Harris, S. **Risedronate Plus Estrogen Found More Effective Than Estrogen Alone in Increasing BMD at Cortical Sites**. *New Dimensions in Osteoporosis* 1, no. 5, Fall 1999.

Hooper, M., P. Ebeling, A. Roberts, et al. **Risedronate Prevents Bone Loss in Early Postmenopausal Women**. *Calcif Tissue Int*. 64 (suppl 1) (1999): P-80.

McClung, M., et al. **Risedronate Treatment of Postmenopausal Women with Low Bone Mass: Preliminary Data**. (Abstract.) *World Congress on Osteoporosis*, May 1996. Amsterdam.

Mortense, L., P. Charles, P. J. Bekker, et al. **Risedronate Increases Bone Mass in an Early Postmenopausal Population: Two Years of Treatment Plus One Year of Follow-Up**. *J Clin Endocrinol Metab* 83 (1998): 396–402.

Reasner, C. A., M. D. Stone, D. J. Hosking, et al. **Acute Changes in Calcium Homeostasis During Treatment of Primary Hyperparathyroidism With Risedronate**. *J Clin Endocrinol Metab* 77 (1993): 1067–1071.

Reid, D., S. Cohen, S. Pack, et al. **Risedronate Reduces the Incidence of Vertebral Fractures in Patients on Chronic Corticosteroid Therapy** (abstract). *American College of Rheumatology* November 9, 1998.

Roux, C., P. Ravaul, M. C. Cohen-Solal, et al. **Biologic, Histologic, and Densitometric Effects of Oral Risedronate on Bone in Patients With Multiple Myeloma**. *Bone* 15 (1994): 41–49.

Russell, R. G., P. I. Crocher, M. J. Rogers. **Bisphosphonates: Pharmacology, Mechanisms of Action and Clinical Uses**. *Osteoporosis Int* Suppl 2 (1999): S66–S80.

Sahni, M., H. L. Guenther, H. Fleisch, et al. **Bisphosphonates Act on Rat Bone Resorption Through the Mediation of Osteoblasts**. *J Clin Invest* 91 (1993): 2004–2011.

Sorensen, H. A. and K. Johansen. **A Meta-Analysis on the Effectiveness of Bisphosphonates in Preventing Vertebral Fractures**. *Bone* 23(suppl), Abstract F297,1998.

Watts, Nelson, M.D. **One Year Data Show Risedronate Rapidly Reduces Vertebral Fracture Risk in Postmenopausal Women With Osteoporosis**. *New Dimensions in Osteoporosis* 1, no. 5 (1999).

Other Pharmacologic Agents

Etidronate

Adachi, J., et al. **Intermittent Cyclic Therapy With Etidronate in the Prevention of Corticosteroid-Induced Bone Loss**. *J Rheumatol* 21, no. 10 (October 1994): 1922–6.

Adachi, J. D., W. G. Bensen, J. Brown, et al. **Intermittent Etidronate Therapy to Prevent Corticosteroid-Induced Osteoporosis**. *N Engl J Med* 337 (1997): 382–387.

Adachi, J., et al**. Intermittent Cyclical Etidronate Therapy Prevents Corticosteroid-Induced Bone Loss**. *Arthritis and Rheumatism* 36 (1993): S51.

Diamond, T., et al. **Cyclical Etidronate Plus Ergocalciferol Prevents Glucocorticoid-Induced Bone Loss in Postmenopausal Women.** *Am J Med* 98, no. 5 (May 1995): 459–63.

Harris, S. T., Watts, N. B., Jackson, R. D., et al**. Four-Year Study of Intermittent Cyclic Etidronate Treatment of Postmenopausal Osteoporosis: Three years of Blinded Therapy**. *American Journal of Medicine* 95 (1992): 285.

Harris, S. T., et al. **Four-Year Study of Intermittent Cyclic Etidronate Treatment of Postmenopausal Osteoporosis: Three Years of Blinded Therapy Followed by One Year of Open Therapy.** *American Journal of Medicine* 95, no. 6 (December 1993): 557–67.

Jackson, R. D., et al. **Cyclical Etidronate Treatment of Postmenopausal Osteoporosis: Four-Year Experience**. *Eleventh International Conference on Calcium Regulating Hormones*. Florence, Italy, April 24–29, 1992.

Miller, P. D., N. B. Watts, A. A. Licata, et al. **Cyclical Etidronate in the Treatment of Postmenopausal Osteoporosis: Efficacy and Safety After Seven Years of Treatment.** *Am J Med* 103 (1997): 468–476.

Miller, P. D. **Critical Drug Appraisal: Etidronate Intermittent Cyclic Therapy for Postmenopausal Osteoporosis.** *Br J Clin Pract* 50, no. 1 (January 1996–February 1996): 23–31.

Papapoulos, S. E., et al. **The Use of Biophosphonates in the Treatment of Osteoporosis.** *Bone* 13 (1992): S41–S49.

Roux, C., P. Oriente, R. Laan, et al. **Randomized Trial of Effect of Cyclical Etidronate in the Prevention of Corticosteroid-Induced Bone Loss**. *J Clin Endocrin Metab*. 83 1998): 1128–1133.

Sebaldt, R. J. et al. **Intermittent Cyclic Therapy With Etidronate Prevents Corticosteroid-Induced Bone Loss: Two Years of Follow-Up.** *Scand J Rheumatol* Suppl 103 (1996): 91–3.

Smith, M. L., et al. **Effect of Etidronate Disodium on Bone Turnover Following Surgical Menopause.** *Calcification Tissue International* 44 (1989): 74–79.

Storm, T., et al. **Effect of Intermittent Cyclical Etidronate Therapy of Bone Mass and Fracture Rate in Women with Postmenopausal Osteoporosis.** *New England Journal of Medicine* 322 (1990): 1265–1271.

Storm, T., et al. **Five Years of Clinical Experience With Intermittent Cyclical Etidronate for Postmenopausal Osteoporosis.** *J Rheumatol* 23, no. 9 (September 1996): 1560–4.

Struys, A., A. A. Snelder, and H. Mulder. **Cyclical Etidronate Reverses Bone Loss of the Spine and Proximal Femur in Patients With Established Corticosteroid-Induced Osteoporosis.** *Am J Med* 99, no. 3 (September 1995): 235–42.

Watts, N. B., S. T. Harris, H. K. Genant, et al. **Intermittent Cyclical Etidronate Treatment of Postmenopausal Osteoporosis.** *N Engl J Med* 323 (1990): 73–79.

Watts, N. B. **Treatment of Osteoporosis With Bisphosphonates.** *Endocrinol Metab Clin North Am* 27 (1998): 419–439.

Watts, N.B., et al. **Intermittent Cyclical Etidronate Treatment of Postmenopausal Osteoporosis.** *New England Journal of Medicine* 323 (1990): 73–79.

Wimalawansa, S. J. **Combined Therapy With Estrogen and Etidronate Has an Additive Effect on Bone Mineral Density in the Hip and Vertebrae: Four-Year Randomized Study.** *Am J Med* 99, no. 1 (July 1995): 36–42.

Sodium Fluoride

Battman, A., et al. **Serum Fluoride and Serum Osteocalcin Levels in Response to a Novel Sustained-Release Monofluorophosphate Preparation: Comparison With Plain Monofluorophosphate.** *Osteoporos Int* 7, no. 1 (1997): 48–51.

Cauley, J. A., et al. **Effects of Fluoridated Drinking Water on Bone Mass and Fractures: The Study of Osteoporotic Fractures.** *J Bone Miner Res* 10, no. 7 (July 1995): 1076–86.

Fratzl, P., et al. **Abnormal Bone Mineralization After Fluoride Treatment in Osteoporosis: A Small-Angle X-Ray-Scattering Study.** *J Bone Miner Res* 9, no. 10 (October 1994): 1541–9.

Guaydier-Souquieres, G. et al. **In Corticosteroid-Treated Respiratory Diseases, Monofluorophosphate Increases Lumbar Bone Density: A Double-Masked Randomized Study.** *Osteoporos Int* 6, no. 2 (1996): 171–177.

Heaney, R.P., et al. **Fluoride Therapy for the Vertebral Crush Fracture Syndrome: A Status Report.** *Annals of Internal Medicine,* (1989) vol. 111, p. 678–680.

Hedlund, L. R. and J. C. Gallagher. **Increased Incidence of Hip Fracture in Osteoporotic Women Treated with Sodium Fluoride.** *Journal of Bone and Mineral Research* 4 (1989): 223–225

Hillier, S. et al. **Water Fluoridation and Osteoporotic Fracture.** *Community Dent Health* 13 Suppl 2 (September 1996): 63–68.

Kleerekoper, M. **Fluoride and the Skeleton.** *Crit Rev Clin Lab Sci* 33, no. 2 (April 1996): 139–161.

Kleerekoper, M., and D. B. Medlovic. **Sodium Fluoride Therapy of Postmenopausal Osteoporosis.** *Endocrine Reviews* 14 (1993): 312–323, 1993.

Lens, W. E., W. G. Jacobs, J. W. Biljsma, et al. **Effects of Sodium Fluoride on the Prevention of Corticosteroid Induced-Osteoporosis.** *Osteoporosis Int* 7 (1997): 575–582.

Lundy, M. W. et al. **Histomorphometric Analysis of Iliac Crest Bone Biopsies in Placebo-Treated Versus Fluoride-Treated Subjects.** Osteoporos Int 5, no. 2 (March 1995): 115–29.

O'Duffey, J. D., et al. **Mechanism of Acute Lower Extremity Pain Syndrome in Fluoride-Treated Osteoporotic Patients.** *American Journal of Medicine* 80 (1986: 561–566.

Pak, C. Y. C., et al. **Controlled Comparison of a Nonrandomized Trial with Slow-Release Sodium Fluoride: Final Update of a Randomized Controlled Trial in Postmenopausal Osteoporosis.** *Journal of Bone and Mineral Research* 11 (1996): 160–168.

Pak, C.Y.C., et al. **Safe and Effective Treatment of Osteoporosis with Intermittent Slow Release Sodium fluoride: Augmentation of Vertebral Bone Mass and Inhibition of Fractures.** *Journal of Clinical Endocrinology and Metabolism,* (1989) vol. 68, p. 150–159.

Pak, C. Y. C., K. Saghaeek, B. Adams-Huet, et al. **Treatment of Postmenopausal Osteoporosis with Slow-Release Sodium Fluoride: Final Update of a Randomized Controlled Trial.** *Annals of Internal Medicine* 123 (1995): 401–408.

Pak, C. Y. C., et al. **Perspective: Slow-Release Sodium Fluoride in Osteoporosis.** *Journal of Bone and Mineral Research* 11 (1996): 561–564.

Riggs, B. L., et al. **Clinical Trial of Fluoride Therapy in Postmenopausal Osteoporotic Women: Extended Observations and Additional Analysis.** *Journal of Bone and Mineral Research* 9 (1994): 265–275.

Riggs, B. L., S. F. Hodgson, W. M. O'Fallon, et al. **Effect of Fluoride Treatment on the Fracture Rate in Postmenopausal Women with Osteoporosis.** *New England Journal of Medicine* 322 (1990): 802–809.

Rizzoli, R. et al. **Sodium Monofluorophosphate Increases Vertebral Bone Mineral Density in Patients With Corticosteroid-Induced Osteoporosis.** *Osteoporos Int* 5, no. 1 (January 1995): 39–46.

Sebert, J. L. et al. **Monofluorophosphate Increases Lumbar Bone Density in Osteopenic Patients: A Double-Masked Randomized Study.** *Osteoporos Int* 5, no. 2 (March 1995): 108–14.

Sogaard, C. H. et al. **Marked Decrease in Trabecular Bone Quality After Five Years of Sodium Fluoride Therapy—Assessed by Biomechanical Testing of Iliac Crest Bone Biopsies in Osteoporotic Patients.** Bone 15, no. 4 (July 1994–August 1994): 393–9.

Other Pharmacological Medications Under Evaluation

Cauey, J. A., et al. **Effects of Thiazide Diuretic Therapy on Bone Mass, Fractures and Falls.** *Annals of Internal Medicine,* 118 (1993): 666–673.

Felson, D.T., et al. **Thiazide Diuretics and the Risk of Hip Fracture.** *JAMA* 265(1991): 370–373.

Fuleihan, G. E. **Tissue-Specific Estrogen—The Promise For the Future.** *N Engl J Med* 337 (1997): 1686–1687.

Heidrich, F. E., A. Stergachis and K. M. Gross. **Diuretic Drug Use and the Risk of Hip Fracture.** *Annals of Internal Medicine,* 115 (1991): 1–6.

Lindsay, R., J. Nieves, C. Formica, et al. **Randomized Controlled Clinical Trial of the Effect of Parathyroid Hormone on Vertebral Bone Mass and Fracture Incidence Among Postmenopausal Women on Estrogen With Osteoporosis.** *Lancet* 350 (1997): 550–556.

Love, R. R., H. S. Barden, R. B. Mazess, et al. **Effect of Tamoxifen on Lumbar Spine Bone Mineral Density in Postmenopausal Women After Five Years**. *Archives of Internal Medicine* 154 (1994): 2585–2588.

McDonald, C. C. and J. H. Stewart. The Scottish Breast Cancer Committee. **Fatal Myocardial Infarction in the Scottish Adjuvant Tamoxifen Trial.** *J Natl Cancer Inst.* 85 (1993): 1398–1406.

Peretz, A., J. J. Body, J. C. Dumon, et al**. Cyclical Pamidronate Infusions in Postmenopausal Osteoporosis.** *Maturitass* 25 (1996): 69–75.

Powles, T. J., et al. . **Effect of Tamoxifen on Bone Mineral Density Measured by Dual-Energy X-Ray Absorptiometry in Healthy Premenopausal and Post-menopausal Women**. *J Clin Oncol* 14, no. 1 (January 1996): 78–84.

Rifkind, B. M., J. E. Rossouw. **Of Designed Drugs, Magic Bullets and Gold Standards**. *JAMA* 279 (1998): 1482–1484.

Rutqvst, L. E, A. Mattson, for the Stockholm Breast Cancer Study Group**. Cardiac and Thromboembolic Morbidity Among Postmenopausal Women With Early Stage Breast Cancer in a Randomized Trial of Adjuvant Tamoxifen.** *J. Natl Cancer Inst.* 85 (1993): 1398–1406.

Thiazides, I., A. Z. LaCroix, et al**. Thiazide Diuretic Agents and the Incidence of Hip Fracture.** *New England Journal of Medicine* 322 (1990): 286–290.

Thiebaud, D., P. Burckhardt, J. Melchior, et al. **Two Years' Effectiveness of Intravenous Pamidronate (APD) Versus Oral Fluoride for Osteoporosis Occurring in Postmenopause.** *Osteoporosis Int.* 4 (1994): 76–83.

Van Leewen, F. E., J. Bernraadt, J. W. W. Coebergh, et al**. Risk of Endometrial Cancer After Tamoxifen Treatment of Breast Cancer.** *Lancet* 343 (1994): 448–452.

Wasnich, R., J. Davis, P. Ross, et al. **Effects of Thiazides on Rates of Bone Loss: A Longitudinal Study.** *British Medical Journal* 301 (1990): 1303–1305.

Wasnich, R. D., et al. **Thiazide Effect on the Mineral Content of Bone.** *New England Journal of Medicine* 309 (1983): 344–347.

Index

T

Tamoxifen, 196–197
Tea and caffeine, 69
Teeth, 172
Testosterone, 32, 181
Thyroid, 15
Tobacco, *see* smoking, 55–60
Trabecular bone, 9
Treatment of osteoporosis, 55–197
Types of osteoporosis, 14–15

U

Uterine cancer, 174

V

Vitamin B6, 28
Vitamin C, 99
Vitamin D, 28, 32, 96–98
Vitamin D3, 91, 96–98
Vitamin K, 99

W

Walking, 118–123
Wedge fracture, 2–3
Weight-bearing exercise, 118–123
Weight lifting, 123–141
Weight training, 123–141
Women and osteoporosis, 23–24

X

X-rays, 42

Y

Youth and osteoporosis, 87, 90
Yogurt, 85

Z

Zinc, 99

Ordering Information and Order Form for Osteoporosis: Unmasking A Silent Thief

If *Osteoporosis: Unmasking a Silent Thief ISBN 0-917073-03-7* is currently unavailable at your local bookstore, make a copy of the form below and order direct.

Address Information

Name _____

Organization Name _____

Address _____

_____

City_____ State _____ Zip _____

Phone Number _____

Payment Information

❏ Check (Make Checks payable to: *Osteoporosis Testing Center of Michigan*)

❏ VISA   ❏ Mastercard   ❏ Discover

Card Number _____ Exp. Date _____

Signature _____

Name of Cardholder (please print)_____

Order Information

Osteoporosis: Unmasking a Silent Thief ____copies @ $24.95 ea. = $ _____

20% Discount for two or more books (above line x.20) = $ _____

Subtotal (subtract line 2 from line 1) = $ _____

Michigan Residents add 6% sales tax (above subtotal x.06) = $ _____

Shipping & Handling ($ 5.00 for first book) = $ _____

Shipping & Handling ($2.00 for each additional book) = $ _____

TOTAL (add subtotal to above 3 lines—pay this amount) = $ _____

Phone orders call:	1 517-592-WELL (9355)
Fax orders:	1 517-592-2544
Mail orders:	*Osteoporosis Testing Center of Michigan*
	107 Chicago Street
	Brooklyn, MI 49230
Website orders:	www.osteotestcenter.com

Overnight or two day Federal Express shipping available. Please call for rates.

Discounts on this book are available for bulk purchases. Please write or call for information on our discount program.